3 ASSASSINATIONS:

The Deaths of John & Robert Kennedy and Martin Luther King

INTERIM
HISTORY

3 ASSASSINATIONS:
The Deaths of
John & Robert Kennedy
and Martin Luther King

Edited by Janet M. Knight

FACTS ON FILE, INC.   NEW YORK

3 ASSASSINATIONS:

The Deaths of
John & Robert Kennedy
and Martin Luther King

Library of Congress Catalog Card Number: 77-154630

ISBN 0-87196-189-X

9 8 7 6 5 4 3 2 1

PRINTED IN THE UNITED STATES OF AMERICA

CONTENTS

i

INTRODUCTION

Among the many murders of the violence-filled 1960s there were 3 assassinations that battered the emotions of millions of Americans—and of non-Americans as well—with exceptional force. For what many consider good reasons, these 3 deaths appear to be linked in the public mind. The first of the 3 victims was an American President, John F. Kennedy. The 2d was a civil rights leader and the nation's most prominent Negro, the Rev. Dr. Martin Luther King Jr. And the 3d was a brother of the slain President and himself a leading candidate for election to the Presidency, Robert F. Kennedy.

Assassination is a crime as old as the violent history of mankind. Myths of our forebears tell of gods and human heroes who stealthily slew or were slain in struggles for power, prestige or profit. The literature of the world is filled with the names of actual or fictional Caesars and Macbeths, Lincolns and Trujillos, all struck down by assassins. The bible narrates the story of the creation of the first man and woman, the birth of their 2 sons and then the assassination of one son by the other. Throughout history the murders of men and women, of high station and low, have been commonplace occurrences, yet homicide still has the ability to horrify.

The English word *assassin* is derived from the Arabic *hashshashin,* a drinker of the drug hashish. The term originated in Persia in the 11th century when a secret organization founded among the Ismailis (a Muslim sect) by Hasan ibn-al-Sabbah terrorized Christian Crusaders and other enemies through secret murder by assassins under the influence of hashish. The group spread terror over Persia, Syria and other parts of Asia Minor for nearly 2 centuries. In modern times the word *assassin* is generally defined as a hired or appointed murderer who kills by surprise or by secret or treacherous assault, usually for political reasons.

In the U.S. up to the early 1960s the act of the assassin, an *assassination,* did not figure prominently in contemporary American life. For although it was true that the nation had had its share of this type of murder—3 American Presidents

1

assassinated in office, attempts made on the lives of 3 other Presidents, the murders of many other prominent people— Americans generally viewed these acts as part of their historical past. Recent assassinations were, for the most part, associated with poorer, politically unstable nations or dictatorial regimes in Latin America, Asia and Africa. But in the course of 5 short years, from 1963 to 1968, the horrors of assassination were brought home to America with great clarity.

The 1960s began on an optimistic note: After 8 years a new party had taken office; the country was not engaged in any major world conflict, and the electorate had overcome old prejudices to choose John F. Kennedy, a young, Roman Catholic Senator from Massachusetts as President. 3 years later Pres. Kennedy was assassinated in Dallas, Tex. and it seemed as though shortly thereafter the country became gradually overrun with violence: urban ghettos erupted in waves of burning, looting and sniper-fire; college campuses were taken over by student militants; anti-Vietnamese war demonstrators fought with police, and crime in the street was rampant.

Civil rights leader Martin Luther King Jr., an advocate of non-violence, was assassinated on a motel balcony in Memphis, Tenn. Apr. 4, 1968. This act precipitated even more violence as areas in 125 U.S. cities erupted in racial disorders that caused 46 deaths and more than $67 million in property damage. 2 months later Robert F. Kennedy, junior U.S. Senator from New York and younger brother of the slain President, was shot in a Los Angeles hotel kitchen. He died the next day.

These 3 men—John Kennedy, Martin King and Robert Kennedy—had many common characteristics. They were all young (John Kennedy, the oldest, was 46 when he died), all family men (they had 17 children among them), all political liberals. And all were charismatic, a trait that brought them large groups of devoted followers. All 3 were also painfully aware that death might overtake them at any time, and each spoke of this possibility at various times during his career. These similarities helped foster a belief, both in the U.S. and abroad, that the assassinations were part of a great conspiracy by right-wing plotters.

After the murder of Pres. Kennedy's alleged assassin, Lee Harvey Oswald, Pres. Lyndon B. Johnson sought to quell conspiracy rumors by appointing a commission, headed by

JFK

Warren Commission

Chief Justice Earl Warren, to investigate both killings. The Warren Commission report, issued Sept. 24, 1964, asserted that there had been no conspiracy and that Lee Oswald and his slayer, Jack Ruby, had each acted alone. The report received a mixed reception: it was generally accepted by government officials and large segments of the American public and strongly rejected by several writers and scholars. Perhaps the most adverse reaction to the report came from New Orleans District Atty. Jim Garrison, who, early in 1967, undertook his own flamboyant investigation of the assassination of John F. Kennedy.

MLK reaction

The death of the Rev. Dr. King was viewed by the Negro community at large as a white plot to rid the civil rights movement of one of its foremost black leaders. This was one of the major reasons for the angry, violent reaction in the nation's urban ghettos. Added to this anger was the disappointment at the fact that King's assassin, James Earl Ray, never went to trial; instead, he pleaded guilty and was directly sentenced to a 99-year prison term. Suspicions that he was a hired killer were, therefore, never quieted.

1968 Nat Com on Causes & Prevent Vio

After Robert Kennedy's assassination Pres. Johnson announced that he was creating yet another investigative commission—the National Commission on the Causes & Prevention of Violence, headed by Milton S. Eisenhower. Its mission, Johnson explained, was to probe the continuing violence in the U.S. and submit recommendations as to "how we can stop it." He also urged Congress to "pass laws to bring the insane traffic in guns to a halt."

In a preliminary report, issued June 5, 1969, a task force appointed by the commission acknowledged that while there had been 19th-Century periods of "greater relative turbulence" in the U.S., the 1960s "rank as one of our most violent eras" and that the scope and magnitude of recent protests, violence, unrest and assassinations were "essentially unprecedented in our history." The commission then issued 9 reports dealing with various aspects of violence in America: on campus unrest, firearms, TV violence, justice system reform, urban crime, youth reform, group violence, civil disobedience and political assassination. In the latter study, the panel traced the patterns of assassinations and the similarities in backgrounds of the assassins. It concluded that conditions that might lead to an increased risk of conspiratorial assassinations appeared to be developing in the U.S.

This book is a factual account of the assassinations of John and Robert Kennedy and Martin Luther King, of subsequent developments and of the effects these events had on the country. The data and other material used came principally from FACTS ON FILE, the press and U.S. government studies.

THE ASSASSINATION
OF
JOHN F. KENNEDY

John Fitzgerald Kennedy

Wide World

JOHN FITZGERALD KENNEDY (1917-63)

John Fitzgerald Kennedy, born May 29, 1917 in Brookline, Mass. (a Boston suburb), was the 2d son of 9 children of Joseph Patrick and Rose Fitzgerald Kennedy. His father was a bank president, investment banker, realtor, chairman of both the Securities & Exchange Commission and Maritime Commission, and ambassador to Britain (1937-40). His mother was the daughter of Boston Mayor John F. (Honey Fitz) Fitzgerald. His grandfather was Patrick J. Kennedy, a Boston saloon-keeper and state senator. As minority Irish-Catholics (in predominantly English-Protestant Boston), the Kennedys were a close-knit family in which religious obligations, competition and family loyalty were stressed.

John Kennedy was educated in Boston private and New York public schools and at the Choate Preparatory School (Wallingford, Conn.). He tried to enroll in Princeton in 1935 but had to leave after a few months when he suffered severe jaundice attacks. He then attended economics courses taught by Harold Laski at the London School of Economics 1935-6. Later he entered Harvard, where he graduated BS cum laude *in 1940 with a major in economics. 6 months of his junior year at Harvard (in 1938) were spent working as his father's secretary in the U.S. embassy in London. He wrote his senior honor thesis (1940) on the description and explanation of Britain's unpreparedness for war. Later he expanded the thesis into a book,* Why England Slept, *which sold 85,000 copies. Profits from the book were largely donated to help rebuild bombed Plymouth, England.*

Rejected for enlistment by the Army because of a back injury suffered while playing college football, Kennedy was accepted later in 1941 by the Navy and commissioned a junior-grade lieutenant. He became a combat hero in the Solomon Islands in 1943 when a Japanese destroyer split his PT boat (PT-109) and he towed an injured crewman to a nearby island; he received Navy and Marine Corps medals for heroism. Kennedy was hospitalized in 1943-4 with a recurrence of his back injury and malaria; surgeons replaced one of his injured vertebrae with a metal disc. He was released from the Navy in 1945. For awhile he worked for the International News Service covering the UN conference in San Francisco and the Potsdam Conference. The U.S. Junior Chamber of Commerce chose him as one of the "10 outstanding young men of 1946."

Kennedy was elected to the U.S. House of Representatives from Massachusetts' 11th District in 1946 for the first of 3 terms. In 1952 he was elected to the U.S. Senate by defeating Republican incumbent Henry Cabot Lodge Jr. by 70,000 votes. During his first Senate term he attacked the Eisenhower Administration's role in Indochina and demanded that the U.S. back Vietnam independence in 1954. He was absent from the Senate from the fall of 1954 to May 1955 because of 2 more spinal operations. The hospitalization prevented him from voting for or against the censure of Sen. Joseph R. McCarthy (R., Wis.). During his long convalescence he wrote Profiles in Courage. *Published in 1956, it became a best-seller and won the 1957 Pulitzer Prize for biography.*

Kennedy made the Presidential nominating speech for Adlai Stevenson at the 1956 Democratic National Convention but was defeated by Sen. Estes Kefauver (Tenn.) in balloting for the Vice Presidential nomination. In 1957 he proposed independence for Algeria. He was reelected to the Senate in 1958 by an 875,000-vote majority, the largest ever won in a Massachusetts election. He had a liberal voting record during his Senate tenure. 2 collections of his speeches and statements, dealing primarily with foreign policy, were published —The Strategy of Peace *(1960) and* To Turn the Tide *(1961).*

In Jan. 1960 Kennedy announced his candidacy for President, then entered and won 9 primaries. He was nominated for President at the Los Angeles Democratic Convention on the first ballot and chose Sen. Lyndon B. Johnson (D., Tex.) as his running mate. Defeating Republican ex-Vice Pres. Richard M. Nixon by only 119,450 votes, Kennedy became the youngest elected and first Roman Catholic President. He was inaugurated as 35th U.S. President Jan. 20, 1961. Excerpts from his inaugural address:

"Let the word go forth from this time and place, to friend and foe alike, that the torch has been passed to a new generation of Americans ... unwilling to witness or permit the slow undoing of those human rights to which this nation has always been committed.... So let us begin anew—remembering on both sides that civility is not a sign of weakness and

sincerity is always subject to proof. Let us never negotiate out of fear. But let us never fear to negotiate.... In the long history of the world, only a few generations have been granted the role of defending freedom in its hour of maximum danger. I do not shrink from this responsibility—I welcome it.... The energy, the faith, the devotion which we bring to this endeavor will light our country and all who serve it—and the glow from that fire can truly light the world. And so, my fellow Americans: ask not what your country can do for you—ask what you can do for your country. My fellow citizens of the world: ask not what America will do for you, but what together we can do for the freedom of man."

Principal domestic proposals of the Kennedy Administration's "New Frontier" program included increased federal aid to education, medical care for the aged, aid to economically depressed areas, broader civil rights, an accelerated space program and tax reforms. Many of the domestic proposals were blocked in Congress. He was more successful in foreign affairs: his principal accomplishments included the establishment of the Peace Corps, the Latin American Alliance for Progress and the nuclear test-ban treaty. An unsuccessful attempt in 1961 by anti-Castro Cubans to invade Cuba's Bay of Pigs embarrassed the Kennedy Administration. But in 1962 Kennedy's firm stand forced the Soviet Union to dismantle its missile bases in Cuba.

A patron of the arts, Kennedy strove to encourage public interest in American culture and the arts. During his Administration, the White House played host to many distinguished scientists, writers, artists and musicians, including cellist Pablo Casals, who had not played in the U.S. since the Theodore Roosevelt era.

Kennedy married Jacqueline Lee Bouvier, daughter of New York financier John V. Bouvier 3d and stepdaughter of Hugh D. Auchincloss, Sept. 12, 1953 in Newport, R.I. They had 3 children: Caroline Bouvier, born in 1957, John Fitzgerald Jr., born in 1960, and Patrick Bouvier, who died shortly after his birth in 1963. A 4th child, an unnamed girl, had been stillborn Aug. 23, 1956.

ASSASSINATION & AFTERMATH

President Slain in Dallas Motorcade

Pres. John F. Kennedy, 46, was assassinated in Dallas, Tex. Nov. 22, 1963.

The President, accompanied by his wife, Jacqueline (who was touring with him for the first time since the 1960 election), had flown to San Antonio, Tex. Nov. 21, 1963 to begin a 2-day, 5-speech "nonpolitical" tour of politically divided Texas. Many observers expected that he would use the trip to try to heal the widening breach between liberal Texas Democrats supporting Sen. Ralph Yarborough and conservative Democrats who backed Gov. John B. Connally Jr.

While the political division in Texas was in part responsible for Kennedy's trip, political tensions there almost led to a cancellation of his visit. White House aides and the Secret Service, advised of an unusually radical mood in the state, became increasingly concerned for the President's safety. Most of their apprehension focused on Dallas, a city with a high homicide rate, whose citizens were mainly white collar workers who had been greatly influenced by right-wing extremists. The concern was based on 2 recent incidents: (1) Vice Pres. Lyndon B. Johnson, then a Texas Senator and Democratic Vice Presidential nominee, had been hissed and spat on by a mob of about 1,000 persons in Dallas' Adolphus Hotel Nov. 4, 1960 after he had attended a Democratic rally. (2) U.S. Amb.-to-UN Adlai E. Stevenson had been abused by anti-UN demonstrators Oct. 24, 1963 after having received a standing ovation from about 1,750 persons when he addressed a UN Day celebration in Dallas' Memorial Auditorium Theater. Leaving the celebration, Stevenson was jeered by anti-UN pickets, spat on and struck on the head with a picket sign that read: "Get the UN out of the U.S." 70-100 persons participated in the protest. Stevenson, unhurt, refused to press charges. (A telegram of apology, signed by 100 Dallas civic and business leaders, including Mayor Earle Cabell and Chamber of Commerce Pres. Robert Cullum, was sent to Stevenson Oct. 25, and a copy of it was sent to Pres. Kennedy. Texas Gov.

Connally Oct. 25 assailed the attack on Stevenson as an "affront to ... decency.")

For weeks before Kennedy's visit Dallas newspaper editorials and local police had pleaded with citizens to avoid any demonstrations or disturbances that might harm the Chief Executive. The day before the President's arrival in Dallas, a handbill appearing on the city's streets Nov. 21 showed 2 photos of Kennedy; beneath them were the caption "Wanted for Treason" and a list of "alleged" charges against the President. On the morning of Kennedy's arrival, Nov. 22, the *Dallas Morning News* contained a full-page black-bordered advertisement headed "Welcome Mr. Kennedy to Dallas." The ad, sponsored by "the American Factfinding Committee," consisted of questions and statements critical of the President and his Administration.

While still in Ft. Worth the morning of Nov. 22 the Presidential party discussed the risks involved in Presidential public appearances. Kennedy was reported to have remarked that "if anybody really wanted to shoot the President of the United States, it was not a very difficult job—all one had to do was get [on] a high building some day with a telescopic rifle, and there was nothing anybody could do to defend against such an attempt."

Kennedy addressed the Chamber of Commerce in Ft. Worth the morning of Nov. 22 and then flew to Dallas with his wife and Gov. and Mrs. John B. Connally. Vice Pres. Johnson, as was customary, made the trip from Ft. Worth to Dallas in a separate plane.

Landing at Love Field, the Kennedys and Connallys entered a special Presidential limousine, its protective clear plastic bubble-top removed, to ride in a motorcade past cheering crowds in Dallas to the Trade Mart, where Kennedy was scheduled to speak. Kennedy was reported pleased at the enthusiastically friendly reception he was receiving in Dallas. The Presidential limousine was followed by a sedan occupied by 8 Secret Service men, and the Secret Service car was followed by an open convertible carrying Mr. and Mrs. Johnson and Sen. Ralph W. Yarborough.

3 shots were fired at 12:30 p.m. CST as the President's car approached the Triple Underpass leading to Stemmons Freeway near the end of the 10-mile journey through Dallas.

The shots came from a 6th-floor window of the Texas School Book Depository Building, a warehouse overlooking part of the motorcade's route. 2 bullets hit the President; the first passed through his neck, and the 2d shattered the right side of his skull. Kennedy, who was sitting with his wife in the rear of the car, fell face down on the seat. One of the bullets passed through the President's body and hit Gov. Connally, who was sharing the "jump" seats with his wife. The bullet tore through Connally's back, smashed 3 ribs, punctured his lung, broke his right wrist and penetrated his left thigh. The 2 wives immediately aided their stricken husbands, and the car was driven at high speed to Parkland Memorial Hospital about 4 miles away. Johnson's car followed.

Kennedy lost consciousness immediately on being hit. He died without regaining consciousness, despite resuscitative efforts by 15 physicians* rushed to his side in the hospital emergency room. The cause of death was given as "a gunshot wound in the brain." He was the 4th U.S. President to be assassinated in office.

Dr. Tom Shires, chief surgeon at the hospital and professor of surgery at the University of Texas Southwest Medical School, said after questioning the attending physicians that he was "absolutely sure" Kennedy "never knew what hit him." Although the time of the President's death was listed officially at 1 p.m., the doctors admitted that they could not say exactly when he had died. According to Shires: "Medically, it was apparent the President was not alive when he was brought in [to the hospital]. There was no spontaneous respiration.... Technically, however, by using vigorous resuscitation, intravenous tubes and all the usual supportive measures, we were able to raise a semblance of a heartbeat."

A Roman Catholic priest, the Very Rev. Oscar L. Huber, assisted by the Rev. James Thompson, administered his church's last rites to the dead President at the hospital.

---

* The 15 physicians were Drs. Charles James Carrico, Malcolm O. Perry, Charles R. Baxter, William Kemp Clark, Robert N. McClelland, Marion T. Jenkins, Fouad A. Bashour, Adolph H. Giesecke, Paul C. Peters, Ronald C. Jones, Charles Crenshaw, Gene C. Akin, Jackie H. Hunt, Don T. Curtis, Kenneth Salyer.

The body, in a bronze casket, was taken from the hospital about 2 p.m. in an ambulance and put aboard the Presidential plane at Love Field. Mrs. Kennedy, the widow, rode with the casket.

(An earlier attempt on Pres. Kennedy's life had been thwarted Dec. 15, 1960, when Secret Service agents arrested Richard Paul Pavlick, 73, of Belmont, N.H., in West Palm Beach, Fla. on charges of planning to assassinate Kennedy, then President-elect, at his Palm Beach house. Pavlick, an ex-mental patient, told the agents he had planned to kill Kennedy and himself by rigging himself as a "human bomb" because he resented "the underhanded way" Kennedy had been elected. Equipment for making the bomb was found in Pavlick's car and room.)

Johnson Becomes President

Shortly after Pres. Kennedy was pronounced dead, emergency security arrangements were made for Vice Pres. and Mrs. Lyndon B. Johnson to leave Parkland Hospital and return to Love Field. It was decided that the Johnsons would board the Presidential jet, *Air Force One,* rather than the Vice President's aircraft, because the former had better communications equipment. From the plane Johnson telephoned Atty. Gen. Robert F. Kennedy, the late President's brother, who advised the Vice President to take the Presidential oath of office before the plane left Dallas.

Johnson, 55, was sworn in as 36th President of the U.S. at 2:38 p.m. CST Nov. 22, 1963 in the private Presidential cabin in the central compartment of *Air Force One* while the plane was still on the runway at Dallas' Love Field. Mrs. Claudia Alta (Lady Bird) Johnson stood at her husband's right. Mrs. Jacqueline Kennedy, for whose arrival the ceremony was delayed for about 5 minutes, stood at Johnson's left, her clothes still splattered with her husband's blood.*

The oath of office was administered by Federal Judge Sarah T. Hughes of the Northern District of Texas. About 30 persons were present as Johnson placed his left hand on a small,

---

* Mrs. Kennedy reportedly rejected all suggestions that she change her clothes. She said she wanted to "let them see what they've done."

black, leather-covered bible, raised his right hand and repeated after Judge Hughes:

"I do solemnly swear that I will perform the duties of the President of the United States to the best of my ability and defend, protect and preserve the Constitution of the United States. So help me God."

9 minutes after the ceremony the Presidential plane left Love Field to fly Pres. Johnson, Mrs. Johnson, Mrs. Kennedy and the body of the late Pres. Kennedy back to Washington. It arrived at Andrews Air Force Base at about 6 p.m. EST.

In a brief speech to the nation at Andrews Base, Johnson said: "We have suffered a loss that cannot be weighed.... I will do my best. That is all I can do. I ask for your help and God's."

The new President then began a series of conferences with Congressional leaders, Cabinet members and advisers that started at Andrews Base, continued aboard the helicopter that took him and Mrs. Johnson to the White House and was resumed Nov. 23, when he conferred with ex-Presidents Dwight D. Eisenhower and Harry S. Truman.

Johnson held his first Cabinet meeting the afternoon of Nov. 23. White House Press Secy. Pierre Salinger said that Johnson "asked the Cabinet members to continue in service" because "he needed their help in the time ahead." In response, Salinger said, State Secy. Dean Rusk and Amb.-to-UN Adlai E. Stevenson "pledged the support of the Cabinet and said the Cabinet was prepared to serve the President as long as he wanted them to serve." Johnson also asked the members of the White House staff to remain, and he asked all U.S. ambassadors abroad to stay on duty and not to submit the letters of resignation customary when a new President took office.

(Rusk and 5 other Cabinet members had been in a plane over the Pacific Nov. 22 when news of the assassination was radioed to them. En route to a U.S.-Japanese meeting in Tokyo Nov. 25-27, they immediately ordered the plane to return to Washington. The other Cabinet members in the plane were Treasury Secy. Douglas Dillon, Interior Secy. Stewart L. Udall, Agriculture Secy. Orville L. Freeman, Labor Secy. W. Willard Wirtz and Commerce Secy. Luther H. Hodges. The Japanese talks were postponed.)

Suspect Captured in Dallas Theater

Lee Harvey Oswald, 24, a pro-Communist ex-Marine employed at the Texas School Book Depository Building, from which the assassination shots were fired, was captured in the Texas Theater in Dallas at 2:15 p.m. CST Nov. 22, 1963 after a 1¾-hour manhunt that started seconds after Pres. Kennedy was shot.

Dallas Police Chief Jesse E. Curry, who had been riding in the motorcade ahead of the President's car, said he had realized from the sound of the shots that they had come from the depository building and had immediately ordered the building searched.

Oswald was in a lunchroom with other workers when the first officer reached the depository; he was identified by the building manager as one of the people employed there. But by the time other police officers arrived, Oswald had left.

Policemen searching the building found an Italian-made 6.5-mm. Mannlicher-Carcano rifle, fitted with a Japanese 4-power telescopic sight near the 6th-floor window. This rifle was later proven to be the assassination weapon.

An elevator operator then told the officers that he had taken Oswald to the building's top floor before the Presidential motorcade arrived; Oswald, however, remained behind while the other employes went down later to see the motorcade. A description of Oswald was immediately broadcast.

Shortly thereafter Patrolman J. D. Tippit, 38, who was patrolling the Oak Cliff area of Dallas in a radio car, saw a man answering the broadcast description and got out of his car to question him. According to witnesses, the suspect drew a revolver, fired 4 shots into Officer Tippit, killing him instantly, and fled. One of the witnesses then used the police car radio to report the killing, and police quickly spread through the area, where they unsuccessfully searched nearby buildings for the killer.

While the search was going on, police headquarters received a call from the cashier of the Texas Theater, 6 blocks from the scene of the patrolman's murder, to report that a man acting suspiciously had entered. Police Chief Curry and 6 officers sped to the theater and found Oswald at 2:15 p.m. in the 3d row from the back. As they approached him, he leaped

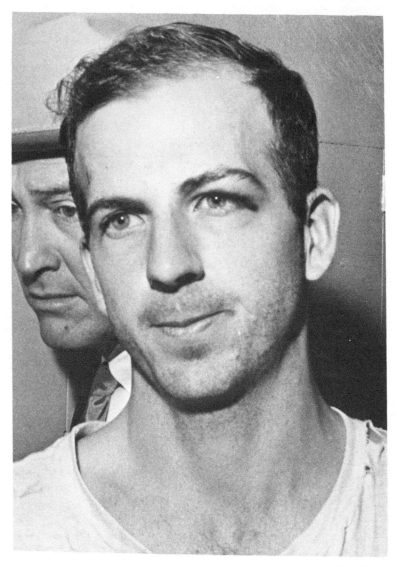

Wide World

Lee Harvey Oswald in Dallas police station Nov. 22, 1963
after his arrest for John F. Kennedy's murder

up, reached for a .38-caliber revolver in his shirt and shouted, "This is it!" The police disarmed him after he had pulled the trigger at least once without the revolver firing. The weapon was later identified as the one used to kill Tippit.

Brought to police headquarters, where he was subjected to almost continuous interrogation, Oswald denied shooting anybody. Paraffin tests proved, however, that he had recently discharged a firearm.

At 7:10 p.m. Nov. 22 Oswald was formally charged with murdering Tippit, and at 1:30 a.m. Nov. 23 he was arraigned on charges of murdering Kennedy. Dallas police officials expressed certainty Nov. 23 that the evidence they had gathered was sufficient to convict Oswald of both crimes.

(The Communist Party of the U.S.A. in New York Nov. 23, 1963 denounced the assassination "as a monstrous crime against the country" and denied that Oswald "has any association with the Communist Party.")

Oswald's Background

Lee Harvey Oswald was an embittered man, reared in poverty, who had described himself as a Marxist and as the secretary of the New Orleans chapter of the pro-Castro Fair Play for Cuba Committee.*

Oswald was born in New Orleans Oct. 18, 1939, 2 months after the death of his father. His mother, Marguerite Claverie Oswald, had 2 older sons, one from an earlier marriage. When Oswald was 3 he was placed in an orphanage with his brothers for a year so that his mother could work. In Ft. Worth, Tex. and New Orleans, where he spent most of his youth, Oswald was considered "a loner," "bookish" (although his school grades were often below average) and opposed to discipline.

When Oswald was 12 the family moved to New York for 1½ years. In New York, where he refused to attend school, he was placed under psychiatric study at an institution for truants.

---

* Vincent Theodore Lee, national director of the Fair Play for Cuba Committee, said in Buffalo, N.Y. Nov. 23, 1963 that "we have never issued a charter in that area [New Orleans]" and that he did not know whether Oswald was a member of his committee. Supporters of the Fair Play for Cuba Committee disclosed in New York Dec. 27, 1963 that the committee was disbanding. They said its demise had been hastened by Oswald's assertion that he had been an official of the group.

He was described by the chief psychiatrist as "an emotionally, quite disturbed youngster" who had a "personality pattern disturbance with schizoid features and passive-aggressive tendencies"; the psychiatrist recommended psychiatric treatment.

Thwarted at 16 (because of his age) in an attempt to join the Marines, Oswald quit school to work. During this period he began to read Communist literature and expressed a desire to join the Communist Party. He reentered high school when the family returned to Ft. Worth but dropped out at 17 to join the Marines, where his military performance was regarded as mediocre. Trained in aviation electronics, he served in Japan, achieved no rank higher than PFC and was convicted twice in summary courts-martial (for failing to register a weapon and for using profanity to a noncommissioned officer). As a trainee, he qualified for the rifle rating of "sharpshooter" (the 2d highest of 3 possible ratings), but he later slipped to the lowest qualifying rating of "marksman."

Oswald was released from active duty Sept. 11, 1959 on his plea that he had to help support his mother, and he was put in the inactive Reserve. But he was discharged later as an undesirable after he appeared Oct. 31, 1959 at the U.S. embassy in Moscow and announced his desire to renounce his U.S. citizenship. (While in the Soviet Union, Oswald wrote to Texas Gov. John B. Connally Jr., then Secretary of the Navy, to demand a reversal of his undesirable discharge. The reversal was refused.) Oswald turned in his U.S. passport at the U.S. embassy Nov. 2, 1959 and signed an affidavit "affirm[ing] that my allegiance is to the Soviet Socialist Republic."

Although he never actually became a Soviet citizen, Oswald lived and worked in Minsk for about 2½ years and married Marina Nicholaevna Prusakova, a Minsk pharmacist.

Apparently disillusioned with the USSR, Oswald wrote to Sen. John G. Tower (R., Tex.) in Jan. 1962 to complain that he had been trying to quit the Soviet Union since July 20, 1960 but that "the Soviets refuse to permit me and my Soviet wife to leave." Tower turned the letter over to the U.S. State Department. With the aid of the State Department, which also lent him $435.71 for travel expenses (Oswald repaid the loan by Jan. 1963), Oswald was permitted to leave the USSR in June 1962 with his wife and infant daughter.

(Soviet Amb.-to-U.S. Anatoly F. Dobrynin turned over to U.S. State Secy. Dean Rusk Nov. 30, 1963 a sheaf of documents from the USSR's consular files on Oswald. The papers reportedly dealt with Oswald's visit to the Soviet Union and his attempts to get visas to go there again. The USSR's action, taken on Soviet initiative, was described as unprecedented.)

After living in Ft. Worth, Tex. for about 4 months, the Oswalds moved to Dallas, where Oswald attempted Apr. 10, 1963 to kill retired U.S. Army Maj. Gen. Edwin A. Walker, known for extreme rightist views, with a mail-order rifle. 2 weeks later Oswald went to New Orleans.

In July 1963 Oswald attempted to join the anti-Castro Cuban Student Directorate in New Orleans in an apparent effort at infiltration. (He had previously formed the fictitious New Orleans chapter of the pro-Castro Fair Play for Cuba Committee and had passed as its secretary.) Shortly thereafter Oswald was arrested in a street fight that erupted when the directorate's New Orleans delegate found him handing out pro-Castro literature. Oswald was fined $10 for disturbing the peace.

Oswald sent his wife and child to live with Mrs. Ruth Paine, a Quaker friend, in Irving, Tex. Sept. 23, 1963. Their 2d daughter was born there in October. At about the same time he was hired as a $50-a-week warehouse employe in the Texas School Book Depository in Dallas, and he rented a room for himself in that city under the name of O. H. Lee.

The night before Pres. Kennedy's assassination Oswald went to the house in Irving, Tex. where his wife and children were staying to pick up his rifle. (He explained that the long, bulky package contained curtain rods for his Dallas apartment.) After his return to Dallas the next morning, Mrs. Oswald found his wedding ring and his wallet, containing $170, on her dresser.

Oswald Slain

Oswald was shot fatally at 11:21 a.m. CST Nov. 24, 1963 in the basement of Dallas' Police & Courts (municipal) Building. He had just been brought down in the elevator to be transferred

Wide World

*Jack Ruby, gun in hand, leaps forward in basement of
Dallas jail Nov. 24, 1963 just seconds before slaying
Lee Harvey Oswald.*

by armored car (to protect him) from the city jail to the Dallas County jail, about a mile away.

As Oswald was walking toward the car, Jack Ruby, a Dallas night-club operator, darted out suddenly from a group of newsmen watching Oswald's transfer. Ruby pushed a Colt .38 revolver into Oswald's left side and fired a single shot.

Oswald cried out and fell to the ground unconscious. A police ambulance rushed him to Parkland Memorial Hospital, where he died in surgery at 1:07 p.m. without regaining consciousness. At no time, from the moment of his capture to his death, did Oswald admit any connection with the assassination.

Ruby was seized immediately after he fired the shot and confined to a 5th-floor jail cell. Under interrogation he denied that his act was in any way connected with a conspiracy to assassinate Pres. Kennedy. He said that he had killed Oswald while in a state of rage and depression over the President's death. Later Nov. 24 Ruby was formally charged with Oswald's murder. A county grand jury indicted him for murder Nov. 26.

The shooting of Oswald took place before "live" TV cameras and was witnessed by TV viewers throughout the country.

Pres. Johnson ordered the Federal Bureau of Investigation (FBI) Nov. 24 to check into "every aspect" of Oswald's murder.

Ruby's Background

Jack L. Ruby, raised in a broken home in the Jewish ghettos of Chicago, was a man generally motivated by 2 extreme emotions—deep compassion for those he liked or who needed help, and violent rage directed at those he considered unfair or who in any way slurred his ethnic origin.

Ruby, originally named Jacob Rubenstein, was born in Chicago in 1911. (The exact date of his birth was unknown, but Ruby most frequently used Mar. 25, 1911 as his birthday.) He was the 5th of 8 living children born to Joseph Rubenstein, a carpenter, and the former Fannie Turek Rutkowski, Polish immigrants who had settled in Chicago in the early 1900s.

During the first 5 years of Ruby's life the family moved through a succession of homes in various parts of the Chicago Jewish ghettos. Family strife, believed traceable primarily to Ruby's father's excessive drinking and frequent unemployment and his mother's uncontrollable temper, resulted in the parents' separation in 1921. Ruby then became a school truant and, at age 11, was referred to a local truancy institution by the Jewish Social Service Bureau. His psychiatric report showed that Ruby was a "quick tempered," "disobedient" child who almost totally disregarded his mother because he felt her to be inferior. When the home situation worsened, Ruby, his 2 older brothers and his sister were placed in foster homes, where they remained intermittently for a few years beginning in about 1922. Ruby's mother, later found to be psychoneurotic, was committed to several mental institutions during 1937-8. At about the same time she was reconciled with her husband. She died of heart failure in 1944; Ruby's father died in 1958.

Except for periods during 1922-4 when he was involved with the Jewish relief agency, Ruby attended Chicago elementary schools through the 8th grade. An avid sports fan, he "scalped tickets" to sports events for extra money, an activity that led to his first trouble with the police. At 16 he left high school and moved out of his family's house.

In 1933 Ruby and several friends went to Los Angeles and San Francisco, where he sold "tip" sheets at the racetrack and then worked as a door-to-door salesman. He returned to Chicago in 1937 and became active in Local 20467 of the Scrap Iron & Junk Handlers Union, mainly through his friendship with the local's financial secretary, Leon Cooke. He worked as a union organizer and negotiator until 1940, when he quit after Cooke was shot to death by the union's president. Although it was suspected that Ruby was connected with Chicago's criminal elements, no evidence was found. Ruby spent the next year traveling for the Spartan Novelty Co., a firm he founded in 1941 with a friend, which sold punchboards (gambling devices).

After the Japanese bombed Pearl Harbor in Dec. 1941, Ruby returned to Chicago and began several commercial ventures to sell patriotic memorabilia (including busts of Franklin Roosevelt). At first deferred from military duty, Ruby continued daily physical "workouts" and his close relationships with such sports figures as boxer Barney Ross. During this time he and friends broke up several German-American Bund rallies; Ruby fought with anyone he suspected of being a Nazi or having anti-Semitic tendencies. He was drafted into the Army Air Forces in 1943 and trained as an aircraft mechanic. Stationed at various Southern bases, he attained the PFC rating and qualified as marksman and sharpshooter in carbine firing. He was honorably discharged Feb. 21, 1946.

Returning to Chicago, Ruby and his 3 brothers formed Earl Products, which manufactured novelty items. In 1947 he sold his share of the firm to 2 of his brothers and moved to Dallas to help his sister run a supper club after her husband was arrested on a narcotics charge. Later that same year he officially changed his name from Rubenstein to Ruby. Shortly thereafter his sister went to California and left Ruby in charge of the club. From then until 1963 Ruby owned or operated several nightclubs and dancehalls in Dallas, including the Vegas and Carousel clubs.

Although his pleasures—gambling, horse racing, card playing—put him in touch with numerous underworld figures, his 8 arrests—between 1949 and Nov. 24, 1963—were due to minor charges dealing with disturbing the peace, brawling and carrying concealed weapons. He was suspended by the Texas Liquor Control Board several times for obscenity in his nightclub shows. His relationship with the clubs' employes was generally poor because of his violent temper, and he was continually at odds with the American Guild of Variety Artists (AGVA) over his use of amateur strippers and other club policies.

Because of his acquaintance with many members of the Dallas press and with about 50 Dallas policemen, Ruby's presence in the basement of the Dallas municipal building before he shot Lee Harvey Oswald received no particular attention.

The Nation Mourns

Pres. Johnson Nov. 23, 1963 issued a proclamation designating Nov. 25, the day of John F. Kennedy's funeral, "to be a day of national mourning throughout the United States."

He asked Americans to assemble Nov. 25 at their places of worship, and he "invite[d] the people of the world who share our grief to join us in this day of mourning and rededication."

The U.S. government observed a national 30-day period of mourning from Nov. 22 to sundown Dec. 22. (Johnson took part in its ending at a candlelight service at the Lincoln Memorial in Washington Dec. 22. The ceremony, sponsored by the Inter-religious Committee on Race Relations, was attended by 7 Cabinet members, 2 Supreme Court justices and an estimated 14,000 other participants. Johnson declared in a brief speech at the service: "... We buried Abraham Lincoln and John Kennedy, but we did not bury their dreams or their visions. They are our dreams and our visions today, for Pres. Lincoln and John Kennedy moved towards those nobler dreams and those larger visions where the needs of the people dwell, where a fight for a better life for more people is their legacy to their countrymen.")

Sen. Edward M. Kennedy (D., Mass.), Pres. Kennedy's brother, had been presiding over the Senate Nov. 22 when the news of his brother's death was brought to him. Sen. Kennedy immediately left the chamber. A short time later the Senate recessed briefly, reconvened for prayers offered by the Senate chaplain, and then recessed until Nov. 25, when the Senate and House adopted resolutions of "profound regret and sorrow."

Increasingly heavily-attended religious and secular services were held throughout the U.S. Nov. 23-25 in tribute to the slain President. Proclamations declaring Nov. 25 a holiday were issued in many states.

In St. Louis, Mo. an estimated 35,000 persons, the largest crowd in the city's history, gathered Nov. 24 before the old St. Louis Courthouse to hear the mayor and religious leaders eulogize Kennedy at what previously had been scheduled as an interfaith procession for civil rights.

In Philadelphia Nov. 24, Gov. William W. Scranton of Pennsylvania and Gov. Richard J. Hughes of New Jersey spoke at a memorial service outside Independence Hall. More than 10,000 persons participated.

TV and radio networks and stations canceled all entertainment programs and commercial announcements Nov. 22-25 to devote their time almost exclusively to the assassination and related events.

Thousands of stores, government and business offices, theaters and other establishments were shut throughout the U.S. beginning at various times Nov. 22 and continuing through Nov. 25. In many offices that remained open Nov. 25, a moment of silence was observed about noontime. Several railroads ordered their trains to be halted for a minute or 2 in honor of the murdered President. Trading on the N.Y. Stock Exchange was halted at 2:07 p.m. Nov. 22 after news of the assassination resulted in a flood of "sell" orders that wiped $11 billion in paper value from listed stocks and caused the Dow-Jones industrial average to drop 21.16 points to 711.49. Other exchanges also closed and remained closed through Nov. 25.

A moratorium on partisan political activities during the 30-day official mourning period for Kennedy was declared by the Republican National Committee Nov. 25 and the Democratic National Committee Nov. 26.

(In one of his first political speaking tours after the moratorium ended, Republican Presidential candidate Barry M. Goldwater said at a party fund-raising dinner in Grand Rapids, Mich. Jan. 6, 1964, that it would be a "libel" of the American people and politics if anyone blamed "America for the tragedy that struck in Dallas." "It was not a mind nurtured by American philosophies that turned to violence," Sen. Goldwater said. "It was a mind fed by communism.")

One of the very few anti-Kennedy reactions to the President's death in the U.S. was a report that Dallas schoolchildren had applauded the news of the assassination.

Mrs. Kennedy, overwhelmed with messages of sympathy from 800,000 persons in every part of the world, expressed her thanks Jan. 14, 1964 in a TV statement made in the office of her brother-in-law, Atty. Gen. Robert F. Kennedy. Speaking publicly for the first time since the assassination, Mrs. Kennedy said that all the messages would be placed in the President John F. Kennedy Memorial Library being built in Cambridgé, Mass. (Harvard Pres. Nathan M. Pusey had announced in Boston Dec. 5 that articles of incorporation had been filed for the library-museum, a $6 million structure to be built on a 2-acre site donated by Harvard University.)

Atty. Gen. Kennedy had disclosed Jan. 13, 1964 that the library would not be restricted to Pres. Kennedy's own papers but would include a variety of materials from government sources on issues he had handled. Thousands of people who had worked with the late President were to record their recollections on tape for preservation in the library. Ex-World Bank Pres. Eugene Black agreed to serve as chairman of the library's board of trustees. (The *N.Y. Times* reported Aug. 17, 1970 that the first selection of the library's 15 million pages of documents and manuscripts had been opened to scholars and researchers. Included in the volumes were transcripts of 300 oral-history interviews.)

World Reaction

Outside the U.S. the news of Kennedy's assassination was generally greeted with expressions of shock, disbelief and profound sorrow. Messages of grief and sympathy poured into Washington from thousands of private citizens and government leaders of most nations.

Soviet Premier Nikita S. Khrushchev interrupted a tour of the USSR to rush back to Moscow when he was informed of Kennedy's death. Then, accompanied by Foreign Min. Andrei A. Gromyko, Khrushchev called at the residence of U.S. Amb.-to-USSR Foy D. Kohler Nov. 23, 1963 to express his grief in person. The premier and Mrs. Khrushchev sent personal messages of sympathy to Mrs. Kennedy, and Khrushchev and Soviet Pres. Leonid I. Brezhnev sent official messages to Pres. Johnson. Khrushchev said in his message to Johnson that Kennedy's death was "a hard blow to all people who cherish the cause of peace and Soviet-American cooperation."

The Soviet press, radio and TV lauded the late President, and many Americans in the USSR said that Soviet citizens went to great pains to express their regret at his death. Similar experiences were reported in other Soviet-bloc countries.

Pope Paul VI Nov. 23 dedicated his morning mass to Kennedy's eternal repose, and he cabled condolences to Mrs. Kennedy, to other members of the Kennedy family and to Pres. Johnson. Receiving agriculture ministers in Rome for a UN food and agriculture conference, the pope later Nov. 23 "reiterate[d] our prayerful wishes that his death may not hinder the cause of peace but serve as a sacrifice and an example for the good of all mankind." The pope dwelt on the assassination again Nov. 24 when he said to the crowd gathered in St. Peter's

Square for his Sunday benediction: "Our thoughts show us how much the capacity for hatred and evil yet remains in the world, how great the threat to civil order and peace still is...."

Premier Fidel Castro of Cuba declared in a TV address Nov. 23 that the assassination "is grave and bad news" despite the fact that the Eisenhower and Kennedy Administrations "have been characterized by a spirit of aggression and hostility." "Great responsibility" for acts of aggression against Cuba "fell on Pres. Kennedy," Castro asserted. But Cubans, he said, "don't hate men. We hate the imperialist and capitalist system.... The death of a man, although this man is an enemy, does not have to cause us joy."

UN delegates in New York reacted to the news of the assassination with expressions of shock. The Nov. 22 afternoon session of the UN General Assembly was adjourned after a moment's silent prayer and expressions of grief by UN Secy. Gen. U Thant and Dr. Carlos Sosa Rodriguez, Assembly president. The Assembly Nov. 26 held a memorial meeting at which Sosa, Thant and delegates eulogized the assassinated President.

Mrs. Ngo Dinh Nhu, widow of South Vietnam's slain security chief and sister-in-law of its slain president, sent Mrs. Kennedy an English-language telegram from Rome Nov. 24 in which she expressed "profound sympathy." She added: The "ordeal might seem to you even more unbearable because of your habitually well-sheltered life"; Kennedy's murder would "prove to the world that even power or extreme graciousness with communism still does not protect from its traitorous blows."

Chinese Communist Premier Chou En-lai Dec. 20 described the assassination as a "despicable shameful act." The Chinese leader, in Cairo on a 2-month tour of Africa, said that Communists opposed any kind of assassination, "even if the one assassinated is hostile to China."

World Leaders Attend Funeral

The body of John Kennedy was brought to the White House early Nov. 23, 1963 after an autopsy had been performed at Bethesda (Md.) Naval Hospital. The closed, flag-draped coffin was placed in the East Room of the White House on a black catafalque similar to the one that had supported the body of Abraham Lincoln after his assassination. A ceremonial military honor guard kept vigil over the body as members of the Kennedy family and then government officials and foreign dignitaries entered to pay their respects.

Early in the afternoon of Nov. 24 the casket was borne on a horse-drawn caisson up Pennsylvania Avenue to the Capitol Rotunda for pubic viewing. Crowds estimated at hundreds of thousands of people somberly lined the streets to watch the procession, in which members of all U.S. armed forces marched as guards of honor.

At the Capitol, the late President was eulogized by Senate majority leader Mike Mansfield (D., Mont.), House Speaker John W. McCormack (D., Mass.) and Chief Justice Earl Warren in a brief ceremony attended by the Kennedy family, Pres. and Mrs. Johnson, former Pres. Harry S. Truman and hundreds of government officials. The Rotunda was then opened to the public, and hundreds of thousands of persons filed past the closed coffin Nov. 24 and early Nov. 25.

The funeral took place Nov. 25 with monarchs, presidents, premiers and other high-ranking officials representing 92 countries joining the Kennedy family and other American mourners. In late morning Nov. 25 the coffin was drawn on its caisson from the Capitol to the White House, where it was met by throngs of mourners, including the foreign dignitaries, who walked behind the caisson to St. Matthews Roman Catholic Cathedral. At the church, Richard Cardinal Cushing of Boston, a long-time friend of the Kennedys, celebrated a pontifical low mass, and the Most Rev. Philip M. Hannan, auxiliary bishop of Washington, delivered the funeral eulogy. The cortege then continued to Arlington National Cemetery. As the casket was carried to the burial ground, 50 jet planes, one for each state, and *Air Force One,* the Presidential plane, flew overhead.

At the graveside, Cardinal Cushing intoned the burial service. A 21-gun salute and 3 musket volleys shook the air; a bugler played taps, and Mrs. Kennedy was presented with the flag that had covered the coffin. Then she and the late President's 2 brothers lit a symbolic "eternal flame" that was to burn at the head of the grave.

John Kennedy was buried in the Memorial Area in front of Arlington Mansion (the Custis-Lee House). No other graves were in the immediate vicinity.*

Among the 220 foreign representatives who attended the funeral in Washington were: Pres. Charles de Gaulle and Foreign Min. Maurice Couve de Murville of France, Emperor Haile Selassie of Ethiopia, the Duke of Edinburgh (Prince Philip of Britain),British Prime Min. Sir Alec Douglas-Home, Queen Frederika of Greece, King Baudouin I of Belgium, Crown Princess Beatrix and Prince Bernhard of the Netherlands, Prince Bertil and Premier Tage Erlander of Sweden, Crown Prince Harald of Norway, Crown Prince George and Premier Jens Krag of Denmark, UN Secy. Gen. U Thant, West German Pres. Heinrich Luebke and Chancellor Ludwig Erhard, Mayor Willy Brandt of West Berlin, Canadian Prime Min. Lester B. Pearson, Pres. Eamon de Valera of Ireland, Prince Jean, hereditary grand duke of Luxembourg, Premier Ismet Inonu of Turkey, First Deputy Premier Anastas I. Mikoyan of the USSR, Austrian Chancellor Alfons Gorbach, Pres. Zalman Shazar and Foreign Min. Golda Meir of Israel, Premier Hayato Ikeda of Japan, Pres. Chung Hee Park of South Korea, Pres. Diosdado Macapagal of the Philippines, ex-Pres. Luis Somoza de Bayle of Nicaragua, Prime Min. Alexander Bustamante of Jamaica, Premier-designate Sir Roland Symonette of the Bahamas, ex-European Coal & Steel Community Pres. Jean Monnet, Foreign Min. Koca Popovic of Yugoslavia, Foreign Min. Zulfikar Ali Bhutto of Pakistan, Foreign Min. Thanat Khoman of Thailand, Foreign Min. Manuel Tello of Mexico, Prince Moulay Abdullah of Morocco, Foreign Min. Mongi Slim of Tunisia, Foreign Min. Mahmoud Fawzi of the United Arab Republic.

---

* Pres. Kennedy's 2 dead children were reburied next to the late President Dec. 4, 1963. The children were an unnamed girl, stillborn Aug. 23, 1956, who had been buried in Newport, R.I., and Patrick Bouvier Kennedy, who had died Aug. 9, 1963, only 2 days after birth, and had been buried in Brookline, Mass. Mrs. Jacqueline Kennedy rejected a U.S. Army plan, announced Dec. 5, 1963, to set aside 3.2 acres surrounding her husband's grave as a burial plot for the Kennedy family. She said the family would need only enough land around the grave for family graves and a monument.

Kennedy's Final Speeches

On the day before his death Pres. Kennedy Nov. 21, 1963 had dedicated the Aerospace Medical Health Center at Brooks Air Force Base outside San Antonio and then had flown to Houston, where he spoke that evening at a testimonial dinner for Rep. Albert Thomas (D., Tex.).

The Presidential party flew to Ft. Worth the night of Nov. 21, and Kennedy made his last speech at a Chamber of Commerce breakfast in Ft. Worth Nov. 22. He was killed before he could deliver the address he had prepared for the Trade Mart in Dallas.

Excerpts from the final Kennedy speeches:

San Antonio—"The conquest of space must and will go ahead.... There will be setbacks and frustrations and disappointments. There will be pressures for our country to do less and temptations to do something else. But this research must and will go on...."

Ft. Worth—"As a result of the effort which this country has made in the last 3 years, we are 2d to none [in military strength]. In the past 3 years we have increased the defense budget ... by over 20%, ... increased the tactical nuclear forces deployed in Western Europe by over 60%, ... and increased our special counter-insurgency forces which are engaged now in South Vietnam by 600%.

"... This requires sacrifice by the people of the United States. But this is a very dangerous and uncertain world.... On 3 separate occasions in the last 3 years the United States has had a direct confrontation. No one can say when it will come again.... Without the United States, South Vietnam ..., the SEATO Alliance ... [and] the CENTO Alliance would collapse overnight ..., there would be no NATO, and gradually Europe would drift into neutralism and indifference. Without the effort of the United States and the Alliance for Progress, the Communist advance onto the mainland of South America would long ago have taken place....

"... We would like to live as we once lived, but history will not permit it.... We are still the keystone in the arch of freedom. And I think we'll continue to do as we have done in our past—our duty...."

Dallas (undelivered speech) —"This nation's strength and security are not easily or cheaply obtained.... There are many kinds of strength, and no one kind will suffice. Overwhelming nuclear strength cannot stop a guerrilla war. Formal pacts of alliance cannot stop internal subversion. Displays of material wealth cannot stop the disillusionment of diplomats subjected to discrimination....

"... American military might should not and need not stand alone against ... international communism. Our security and strength ... directly depend on the security and strength of others—and that is why our ... assistance plays such a key role in enabling those who live on the periphery of the Communist world to maintain their independence of choice.

"... Our assistance makes possible the stationing of 3.5 million allied troops along the Communist frontier at $\frac{1}{10}$ the cost of maintaining a comparable number of American soldiers.... About 70% of our military assistance goes to 9 key countries located on or near the borders of the Communist bloc ...—Vietnam, free China, Korea, India, Pakistan, Thailand, Greece, Turkey and Iran....

"... In today's world, freedom can be lost without a shot being fired, by ballots as well as bullets. The success of our leadership is dependent ... on a clearer recognition of the virtues of freedom as well as the evils of tyranny. That is why our information agency has doubled the shortwave broadcasting power of the Voice of America and increased the number of broadcasting hours by 30%.... And that is also why we have regained the initiative in the exploration of outer space—making an annual effort greater than the combined total of all space activities undertaken during the '50s ... and making it clear to all that the United States of America has no intention of finishing 2d in space....

"... America today is stronger than ever before. Our adversaries have not abandoned their ambitions—our dangers have not diminished—our vigilance cannot be relaxed. But now we have the military, the scientific and the economic strength to do whatever must be done for the preservation and promotion of freedom...

"That strength will never be used in pursuit of aggressive ambitions. It will always be used in pursuit of peace....

"We in this country, in this generation, are—by destiny rather than choice—the watchmen on the walls of world freedom. We ask, therefore, that we may be worthy of our power and responsibility—that we may exercise our strength with wisdom and restraint—and that we may achieve in our time and for all time the ancient vision of peace on earth, good will toward men. That must always be our goal—and the righteousness of our cause must always underlie our strength. For as was written long ago: 'Except the Lord keep the city, the watchman waketh but in vain.'"

Johnson Continues Kennedy Programs

Pres. Johnson spoke briefly with many of the foreign leaders in Washington following the Kennedy funeral.

Pres. Charles de Gaulle of France, the first foreign leader to confer privately with Johnson, met with him for about 15 minutes during a Presidential reception for the foreign visitors at the State Department Nov. 25, 1963 following the funeral. Johnson also met privately with Prime Min. Lester B. Pearson of Canada and Premier Hayato Ikeda of Japan.

Johnson met Nov. 26 with Emperor Haile Selassie of Ethiopia, British Prime Min. Sir Alec Douglas-Home, Pres. Diosdado Macapagal of the Philippines, Premier Ismet Inonu of Turkey, Soviet First Deputy Premier Anastas I. Mikoyan, Chancellor Ludwig Erhard and Pres. Heinrich Luebke of West Germany, and Pres. Eamon de Valera of Ireland.

Johnson's first public foreign-policy statement as President was addressed to Latin Americans to "reaffirm" the Alliance for Progress and "pledge all the energies of my government to our common goals." Johnson met privately with 100 representatives of Latin America Nov. 26 in the East Room of the White House, where the late Kennedy had made his first major foreign-policy speech in proposing the Alliance. Johnson urged his visitors to make the Alliance a "living memorial" to Kennedy.

In his first appearance before Congress since assuming the Presidency, Johnson told a joint session of the Senate and House of Representatives Nov. 27 that he wished for the "earliest possible passage of civil rights and tax-cut legislation." (Johnson had revealed his intention to press for this Kennedy-proposed legislation Nov. 25 in a talk with about 30 governors who attended the Kennedy funeral.)

Johnson opened his address with the assertion that: "All I have I would have given gladly not to be standing here today. The greatest leader of our time has been struck down by the foulest deed of our time."

Johnson continued: "Today, in this moment of new resolve, I would say to all my fellow Americans, let us continue" the work Kennedy had urged the country to begin. "The time has come for Americans of all races and creeds and political beliefs to understand and to respect one another. . . . So, let us put an end to the teaching and the preaching of hate and evil and violence. Let us turn away from the fanatics, from the far left and the far right, from the apostles of bitterness and bigotry, from those defiant of law and those who pour venom into our nation's bloodstream."

The President asserted his belief in Congress' "independence," "integrity," "capacity" and "ability   ..., despite the divisions of opinions which characterize our nation, to act." "The need is here," he declared. "The need is now. I ask your [Congress'] help. . . . John Kennedy's death commands what his life conveyed—that America must move forward." "No memorial oration or eulogy could more eloquently honor Pres. Kennedy's memory" than prompt enactment of a civil rights bill, he said. "We have talked long enough in this country about equal rights. We have talked for a hundred years or more. It is time now to write the next chapter, and to write it in the books of law."

Johnson expressed his determination "to continue the forward thrust of America" begun by Kennedy—the "dreams" of conquering space, of partnership across the Atlantic and Pacific, of a Peace Corps, of education "for all of our children," of jobs "for all who seek them and need them," of care for "our elderly," of "an all-out attack on mental illness" and, "above all, the dream of equal rights for all Americans whatever their races or color."

The new President pledged that "this nation will keep its commitments from South Vietnam to West Berlin," "will be unceasing in the search for peace." He said the U.S. "must recognize the obligation to match national strength with national restraint," "must be ready to defend the national interest and to negotiate the common interest."

"We will demonstrate anew that the strong can be just in the use of strength, and the just can be strong in the defense of justice," Johnson said. "Let all the world know that I rededicate this government to the unswerving support of the United Nations—to the honorable and determined execution of our commitments to our allies—to the maintenance of military strength 2d to none—to the defense of the strength and the stability of the dollar—to the expansion of our foreign trade—to the reinforcement of our programs of mutual assistance and cooperation in Asia and Africa—and to our Alliance for Progress in this hemisphere."

Johnson closed his address with these words: "So let us here highly resolve that John Fitzgerald Kennedy did not live—or die—in vain."

(The Administration's tax bill was passed by the House Feb. 25, 1964 and the Senate Feb. 26, 1964. 6 hours after the Senate action was completed Johnson signed the bill into law. Then the President and his wife visited Mrs. Jacqueline Kennedy and her children to give them 3 of the pens he had used to sign the bill.)

A pledge "to work for a new American greatness" was made by Johnson in a Thanksgiving Day address televised to the nation from the White House Nov. 28, 1963.

Johnson said: "Let us today renew our dedication to the ideals that are American. Let us pray for His divine wisdom in banishing from our land any injustice or intolerance or oppression to any of our fellow Americans whatever their opinion, whatever the color of their skins, for God made all of, not some of us, in His image. All of us, not just some of us, are His children."

The new President urged "all Americans in reverence to think" of their responsibility "to make our society well and whole for the tests ahead. . . ." "It is this work," he said, "that I most want us to do—to banish rancor from our words and malice from our hearts—to close down the poison springs of hatred and intolerance and fanaticism—to perfect our unity North and South, East and West, to hasten the day when bias of race, religion and region is no more. . . ."

"A great leader is dead, a great nation must move on," Johnson said. "Yesterday is not ours to recover, but tomorrow is ours to win or to lose. I am resolved that we shall win the tomorrows before us.... The service of our public institutions and our public men is the salvation of us all.... And how much better would it be, how much more sane it would be, how much more decent an America it would be if all Americans could give their time, and spend their energies helping our system and its servants to solve your problems instead of pouring out the venom, and the hate that stalemate us in progress."

White House Press Secy. Pierre Salinger announced Dec. 2, 1963 that he and 3 other close Kennedy advisers—special counsel Theodore C. Sorensen, appointments secretary P. Kenneth O'Donnell and Congressional liaison aide Lawrence F. O'Brien—would remain in their posts "at the pleasure of the President." Johnson had disclosed Nov. 30 that he had asked Charles A. Horsky to remain as White House adviser on District of Columbia affairs.

Johnson met with the heads of 16 federal regulatory agencies Dec. 3 and told them that the Kennedy Administration policies would be continued. He urged them to weigh any pressures exerted on them: "When those pressures are honorable, respect them; when they are not, reject them."

Johnson met separately with 20 members of the AFl-CIO executive council and 90 members of the Business Council Dec. 4 and asked both groups to help the Administration in its economic programs. Both pledged their support. Johnson specifically asked them to back the tax bill and the drive to eliminate bias in employment.

A pledge of "loyal support and cooperation" to the new President was adopted by acclamation by 1,200 members of the National Association of Manufacturers (NAM) at the 68th annual Congress of American Industry in New York Dec. 4. A letter from Johnson asking for cooperation had been read to the group by NAM Pres. W. P. Gullander.

The Johnson family officially took up residence in the White House Dec. 7, 1963. Johnson told reporters at his first Presidential news conference that day that his primary task as President was to try "to establish a continuity in government." 2d, he said, was an attempt to "give a sense of unity in the country and in the world.... Finally,... we have embraced the

programs that we helped to fashion which are now pending
before the Congress...."

In telegrams to the 50 state governors Jan. 2, 1964,
Johnson thanked them for their support through the "tragic
period in which our system of government faced its greatest
test." The telegrams said: "Let us begin the new year resolved
to forge in this country a deeper sense of unity regardless of
political party or persuasion."

Johnson announced Dec. 5, 1963 that he and House
Speaker John W. McCormack, 71, had made an agreement on
temporary succession to the Presidency should Johnson become
disabled.

McCormack, next in line to the Presidency, was to be
notified, if possible by Johnson, of Johnson's inability to serve;
McCormack then would serve as Acting President until
Johnson could return. If Johnson could not notify McCormack,
McCormack, "after such consultation as seems to him
appropriate under the circumstances," would decide whether to
assume the duties of Acting President. In either event, Johnson
was to determine when he would resume his full duties as
President.

Similar agreements had been made by the President and
Vice President in the Eisenhower and Kennedy
Administrations.

The White House had announced Dec. 3: "To assure the
continuity of the government in the event of any contingency,
the President has given instructions that the Speaker ... be kept
continuously and appropriately informed on national security
matters and be invited to ... [National Security Council] or
other key decision-making meetings...."

John Connally's Story

Still hospitalized in Dallas, Gov. John Connally had told his
version of the story of the assassination in an NBC interview
Nov. 27, 1963.

Connally said: As the Presidential party rode in the
motorcade in Dallas, "we heard a shot. I turned ..., and the
President had slumped. He said nothing. As I turned, I was
hit.... Then there was a 3d shot, and the President was hit

again. When he was hit, she [Mrs. Kennedy] said 'Oh, my God, they have killed my husband—Jack, Jack!' "

Connally speculated that "maybe" Kennedy "has been asked to do something in death that he could not do in life, that is to so shock and so stun the nation, the people of the world, of what is happening to us, of the cancerous growth that is being permitted to expand and enlarge upon the world and the society in which we live, that breeds hatred and bigotry and intolerance, indifference and lawlessness, and is an outward manifestation of what occurred here in Dallas, which could have occurred in any other city in America. This is an open manifestation of extremism on both sides that is the genesis of our own self-destruction if we are ever going to be destroyed."

Connally agreed that "we should have a memorial" to Kennedy but expressed hope that Americans would not build one "in the sense of absolving themselves ... for a lack of tolerance, lack of understanding, the passion, the prejudice, the hate and the bigotry which permeates the whole society in which we live and which manifested itself here on Friday [Nov. 22]. This was only one facet of it. We see it in the bombing of the 5 little children in Birmingham...." (Connally was referring to the bombing of a Negro Baptist church in Birmingham, Ala. during Sunday School services Sept. 15, 1963. 4 Negro girls were killed in the explosion. The incident took place during a desegregation drive in Birmingham.)

Autopsy Findings

Nate Haseltine reported in the *Washington Post* Dec. 18, 1963 that Kennedy had been killed by the 2d of the 2 bullets that hit him "and could readily have survived the first bullet, which was found deep in his shoulder."

Haseltine said that according to the findings of "pathologists who performed the autopsy ... the night of Nov. 22" at Bethesda Naval Hospital, the 2d bullet "tore off the right rear portion of his [Kennedy's] head" and created destruction "completely incompatible with life." A fragment of this bullet, Haseltine wrote, "passed out the front of his throat, causing an erroneous belief he may have been shot from 2 angles."

Both bullets hit the President in the back, the first bullet entering "in the back shoulder, 5 to 7 inches below the collar line," Haseltine reported. (The Dallas doctors who had attended the President were surprised when they later learned of this injury because Kennedy had been on his back the entire time he was in the Dallas hospital, and the shoulder wound, therefore, was not discovered there.)

The 2 bullets that hit Kennedy were reported to be the first and 3d fired. The 2d injured Gov. Connally.

According to Haseltine, investigations showed that all 3 shots "had trajectories that would line them up with the 6th-floor window of the Texas School Book Depository Building, where the assassin had been traced." Haseltine reported that ballistics tests showed that both bullets that hit the President had been fired from the rifle found in the book depository building but that the one that hit Connally could not be subjected to similar tests because it had been too fragmented, one fragment even striking the windshield of the car the 2 victims had been riding in.

Kennedy's Will

John F. Kennedy's will was filed for probate in Boston Dec. 23, 1963. It directed that the bulk of his estate (value undisclosed) be "divide[d] into 2 equal shares," one of which was to be held in trust for his wife, the other to be held in trust for his 2 surviving children, Caroline, 6, and John Jr., 3. Mrs. Kennedy, who was to be an executor of the estate and a trustee of the trusts (along with Kennedy's 2 brothers, Robert and Edward), was to receive the net income from her trust.

The Senate Dec. 10 completed the passage of a bill giving Mrs. Kennedy Secret Service protection, a temporary secretarial staff (at a total cost of $50,000), office space and free mailing privileges for life. As a President's widow, she was already entitled to a pension of $10,000 a year for life or until she remarried. (Mrs. Kennedy was remarried Oct. 20, 1968 to Greek shipping magnate Aristotle Socrates Onassis, 62.)

Mrs. Kennedy and her 2 children had moved out of the White House Dec. 6 and had taken up residence in a house in the Georgetown section of Washington lent to her by State Undersecy. and Mrs. W. Averell Harriman. It was disclosed

Dec. 11 that Mrs. Kennedy had bought a 169-year-old, 3-story, 14-room brick home in Georgetown across the street from the Harriman house.

Black Muslims & Teamsters

Malcolm X, New York and Washington leader of the Black Muslim movement, widely regarded as the sect's 2d in command, had been disciplined by the head of the movement Dec. 4, 1963 for a speech in which he indicated that he was "glad" at Kennedy's assassination.

Elijah Muhammad, leader of the Black Muslims, said in a statement released in Chicago Dec. 4 that Malcolm X's remarks did not reflect Muslim thinking. "We are very shocked at the assassination of our President," Muhammad declared. He said in a phone interview from his winter home in Phoenix, Ariz. Dec. 4 that "Malcolm is still a minister, but he will not be permitted to speak in public."

Malcolm X had been quoted as saying at a rally in Manhattan Center in New York Dec. 1: Kennedy had been "twiddling his thumbs" when South Vietnamese Pres. Ngo Dinh Diem and Diem's brother were killed; Kennedy's own assassination was a case of the "chickens coming home to roost"; "being an old farm boy myself, chickens coming home to roost never did make me sad; they've always made me glad."

Harold J. Gibbons and 4 other top aides to Teamsters Pres. James R. Hoffa were reported to have submitted their resignations Dec. 4 from posts with the international union over a dispute dealing with Kennedy's death. Gibbons reportedly resigned as Hoffa's executive assistant while retaining his post as 11th vice president of the union and as the elected president of Joint Council 13 in St. Louis, Mo.

The other resignees: Lawrence Steinberg and Richard Kavner, personal assistants to Hoffa; Ferguson Keathley, an assistant in the Teamsters' national warehouse division; Keathley's wife, Yuki, Hoffa's Washington secretary.

According to the *Wall Street Journal* Dec. 9, the resignations stemmed from Hoffa's opposition (a) to Gibbons' and Steinberg's attempt to issue a press release extending condolences to the Kennedy family, and (b) to their decision to

close the Teamsters' Washington headquarters on the day of
Kennedy's funeral.

Hoffa denied that the 5 had resigned or that he had
objected to their sympathetic reaction to Kennedy's death. He
said his aides had merely "asked to be relieved" of their duties.
A statement from Hoffa following the assassination said the
late President's brother, Atty. Gen. Robert F. Kennedy, would
be "just another lawyer" as a result of the slaying.

(Both John and Robert Kennedy had been investigators
for the Senate Rackets Committee which had probed Hoffa and
the Teamsters in 1957-9.)

THE WARREN COMMISSION

Warren Commission Investigates

Pres. Johnson Nov. 29, 1963 appointed a special commission, headed by Chief Justice Earl Warren, to investigate Pres. Kennedy's assassination and the murder of Lee Harvey Oswald.* The White House said Johnson had instructed the commission "to satisfy itself that the truth is known as far as it can be discovered and to report its findings and conclusions to him, to the American people and to the world." The Congressional leadership of both parties was consulted about the commission, the White House said.

Commission members appointed by Johnson to serve with Warren were Sen. Richard B. Russell (D., Ga.), Sen. John Sherman Cooper (R., Ky.), Rep. Hale Boggs (D., La.), Rep. Gerald R. Ford (R., Mich.), ex-Central Intelligence Agency director Allen W. Dulles and John J. McCloy, who had served as World Bank president and disarmament adviser to Pres. Kennedy.

The White House had announced Nov. 25 that Johnson had ordered the Justice Department and FBI "to conduct a prompt and thorough investigation of all the circumstances" surrounding the assassination and Oswald's death. He "directed all federal agencies to cooperate." Material uncovered in this inquiry and any other material from federal, state or other sources were to be examined by the Warren Commission.

Texas Atty. Gen. Waggoner Carr announced in Washington Dec. 6 that he was postponing indefinitely a state court of inquiry into the assassination. He said he was acting in line with Chief Justice Warren's warning that "a public inquiry in Texas at this time might be more harmful than helpful. . . ."

---

* Warren, too, had been a frequent target of right-wing abuse. About 75 pickets shouting "Impeach Earl Warren" had met the Chief Justice in New York Oct. 29, 1963 as he arrived at a meeting at which he was made an honorary member of the N.Y. City Bar Association. Warren told the bar group: "It is a great thing that they [the pickets] can do this in this country. . . ." Leaflets and signs were thrown at him when he left.

Congress voted Dec. 9 to give the Warren Commission subpoena power and authority to grant immunity from prosecution as a means of compelling testimony from reluctant witnesses. The commission had requested such powers Dec. 5.

The commission Dec. 10 announced the appointment of ex-U.S. Solicitor Gen. James Lee Rankin, 56, as its general counsel.

(The Communist Party of the U.S.A. said in New York Dec. 23 that it had forwarded its correspondence with Oswald to the Warren Commission. The party's public relations director, Arnold Johnson, asserted at the same time that Oswald "was never a Communist or a Marxist.")

Rankin announced Jan. 11, 1964 that the inquiry had been divided into 6 main areas, each of which would be handled by a senior lawyer assisted by a younger lawyer.

The 6 areas of the inquiry: (1) All activities of Oswald the day of the assassination. (2) Oswald's life and background, his associations, ideas and psychology. (3) Oswald's Marine Corps service and his life in the Soviet Union. (4) The murder of Oswald by Jack Ruby. (5) Ruby's story. (6) What was done to protect Kennedy.

Rankin was named as one of the senior lawyers in charge of one of the 6 topics. 4 of the remaining 5 senior lawyers were: Francis W. H. Adams, 59, a former N.Y. City police commissioner (1954-5); Joseph A. Ball, 61, of Los Angeles, a University of Southern California Law School professor and member of the Supreme Court's Advisory Committee on the Federal Rules of Criminal Procedure; William T. Coleman Jr., 43, of Philadelphia, a Negro, who had served as a law clerk to Justice Felix Frankfurter 1948-9; Albert E. Jenner Jr., 56, of Chicago, vice chairman of the National Joint Committee on the Administration of Justice. Leon D. Hubert Jr. of New Orleans, La. was appointed the 6th senior lawyer Jan. 21.

Mrs. Marguerite Oswald, Lee Harvey Oswald's mother, announced in Ft. Worth, Tex. Jan. 14 that she had retained ex-N.Y. Assemblyman Mark Lane as an unpaid attorney to represent Oswald before the Warren Commission. She said she would fight to prove Oswald's innocence.

Rankin had indicated Jan. 11 that the commission would not appoint a lawyer to represent Oswald because "the commission is not engaged in determining the guilt of anybody;

it is a fact-finding body." But the commission Feb. 25 appointed Pres. Walter E. Craig of the American Bar Association as an "independent lawyer" to protect Oswald's interests in the investigation.

Mrs. Marina Oswald, 22, Oswald's widow, was the first witness called before the Warren Commission. She testified in closed session in Washington Feb. 3-6, 1964. Her testimony was not disclosed. (Mrs. Oswald, interviewed on TV in Dallas Jan. 27 said that "facts tell me that Lee shot Kennedy." In a TV interview in Washington Feb. 7 she said Oswald had "never" said "anything bad" about Kennedy or Gov. John Connally.)

Mrs. Marguerite Oswald, 56, Oswald's mother, testified in secret before the commission Feb. 10-12. (She told newsmen after completing her testimony Feb. 12 that "I still believe my son ... is innocent." She said she thought Oswald was a Central Intelligence Agency [CIA] "agent" who had been "set up to take the blame" while the real killer remained "still at large." CIA chief John McCone asserted in a statement issued through a CIA spokesman Feb. 13 that Oswald "was never directly or indirectly linked with the CIA.")

FBI Calls Oswald the Killer

An FBI report on its investigation of Pres. Kennedy's assassination had been turned over to the Warren Commission by the Justice Department Dec. 9, 1963. (The FBI had given the report to Deputy Atty. Gen. Nicholas deB. Katzenbach Dec. 5.)

Although the Warren Commission decided that the report would not be made public until it had reviewed it and decided on its course of action, it was disclosed that the report (a) named Lee Harvey Oswald as Kennedy's assassin, (b) concluded that Oswald had acted alone and had not conspired with anybody in assassinating the President, and (c) asserted that there had been no connection between Oswald and Jack Ruby until the latter suddenly killed Oswald as he was being transferred from one jail to another. (The Soviet press and some newspapers in Western countries had expressed suspicions that Oswald had been involved in a conspiracy and had been silenced by Ruby to protect the other conspirators.)

It had been reported Dec. 6 that the FBI was investigating the possibility that Oswald might have fired a rifle shot that barely missed ex-Maj. Gen. Edwin A. Walker in his home in Dallas Apr. 10, 1963. According to the report, Oswald's wife had told the investigators that Oswald had come home that night and had told her of his unsuccessful attempt to kill Walker.

Commission's Findings

The Warren Commission's final report on the assassination of Pres. Kennedy was presented to Pres. Johnson by Chief Justice Warren Sept. 24, 1964.

The 296,000-word document, made public Sept. 27, concluded that Oswald had "acted alone" in assassinating Kennedy Nov. 22, 1963 and that Jack Ruby similarly had acted alone in slaying Oswald 2 days later. The 7-member commission was unanimous in its denial that either Oswald or Ruby was "part of any conspiracy, domestic or foreign, to assassinate Pres. Kennedy." It found no evidence of any "direct or indirect relationship" between Oswald and Ruby or between either of them and Dallas Police Patrolman J. D. Tippit, whom Oswald had gunned down some 45 minutes after he killed the President.

The report was written after the commission, assisted by a 27-member staff, had gone over the result of investigations conducted by the FBI and other federal, state and local agencies and had considered the testimony of 552 witnesses, most of whom were questioned by the commission or by its staff.

As an indication of the scope and detail of the inquiry, the commission reported that "more than 80 additional FBI personnel were transferred to the Dallas office" to aid the investigation, that the FBI "conducted approximately 25,000 interviews and reinterviews," that the FBI "submitted over 2,300 reports totaling approximately 25,400 pages to the commission" and that "the Secret Service conducted approximately 1,550 interviews and submitted 800 reports totaling some 4,600 pages."

In addition to its 888-page report, the commission compiled, for later publication, more than 20 volumes of about 500 pages each. This material included the complete record of the questioning of all witnesses.

Among statements made by the commission in the report:

No conspiracy found —Thorough investigation had turned up "no credible evidence that Lee Harvey Oswald was part of a conspiracy to assassinate Pres. Kennedy."

"Examination of the facts of the assassination itself revealed no indication that Oswald was aided in the planning or execution of his scheme. Review of Oswald's life and activities since 1959 ... did not produce any meaningful evidence of a conspiracy. The commission discovered no evidence that the Soviet Union or Cuba were involved in the assassination.... Nor did the commission's investigation of Jack Ruby produce any grounds for believing that Ruby's killing of Oswald was part of a conspiracy. The conclusion that there is no evidence of a conspiracy was also reached independently by Dean Rusk, the Secretary of State; Robert S. McNamara, the Secretary of Defense; C. Douglas Dillon, the Secretary of the Treasury; Robert F. Kennedy, the Attorney General; J. Edgar Hoover, the director of the FBI; John A. McCone, the director of the CIA; and James J. Rowley, the chief of the Secret Service, on the basis of the information available to each of them."

Oswald's motive unclear —The commission could not identify "any one motive or group of motives" for Oswald's action in killing Kennedy.

"Many factors were undoubtedly involved." "It is apparent, however, that Oswald was moved by an overriding hostility to his environment. He does not appear to have been able to establish meaningful relationships with other people. He was perpetually discontented with the world around him. Long before the assassination he expressed his hatred for American society and acted in protest against it. Oswald's search for what he conceived to be the perfect society was doomed from the start. He sought for himself a place in history—a role as the 'great man' who would be recognized as having been in advance of his times...."

The commission isolated these contributing factors: "(a) His [Oswald's] deep-rooted resentment of all authority which was expressed in a hostility toward every society in which he lived; (b) his inability to enter into meaningful relationships with people, and a continuous pattern of rejecting his environment in favor of new surroundings; (c) his urge to try to find a place in history and despair at times over failure in his various undertakings; (d) his capacity for violence as evidenced by his attempt to kill Gen. [Edwin A.] Walker [the commission confirmed that Oswald had fired Apr. 10, 1963 at Walker, a controversial right-wing leader]; (e) his [Oswald's] avowed commitment to Marxism and communism, as he understood the terms and developed his own interpretation of them...."

'Myths' disproved—"Myths have traditionally surrounded the dramatic assassinations of history." The commission had investigated—and disproved—most of "the various hypotheses, rumors and speculations that have arisen" around the Kennedy case. In addition to finding "no credible evidence" of a conspiracy or of a connection between Oswald and Ruby, the commission had disproved, among other theories, "speculations":

● That "the shots that killed the President" came from a railroad overpass near the assassination scene, that the overpass had been "unguarded," that "there were witnesses who alleged that the shots came from the overpass" and that "a rifle cartridge was recovered on the overpass."

● That "more than 3 shots ... were fired," that "at least 4 or 5 bullets have been found," that "a bullet was found on the stretcher used for Pres. Kennedy at the Parkland Hospital" and that Dallas County Deputy Sheriff E. R. Walthers found "a bullet ... on the grass near the scene of the assassination shortly afterward."

●That, as evidence a shot was fired from in front of the death car (Oswald's 3 shots came from a 6th-floor window of the Texas School Book Depository Building behind the car), "the Presidential car had a small, round bullet hole in the front windshield," and "doctors at Parkland Hospital [where Kennedy died]" had said that "the throat wound sustained by the President was the result of a shot fired from the front."

● That the route of the Kennedy motorcade was changed after a map of the route had been printed in Dallas newspapers.

● That a photo taken 10 minutes before the assassination "showed 2 silhouettes" at the window used by the assassin.

● That a photo showed Oswald standing on the steps of the depository building "shortly before the President's motorcade passed by."

● That the President's car was moving at 12-20 mph. and thus presented an extremely difficult target, that Oswald could not have fired the 3 shots in the time he had and that "Oswald did not have the marksmanship ability demonstrated by the rifleman who fired the shots."

● That "a 2d rifle" was found on the depository building's roof or on the overpass.

● That the FBI had denied to newsmen that Oswald's palmprint had been found on the rifle.

● That "after firing the shots, Oswald could not have disposed of the rifle and descended the stairs to the [depository building's] lunchroom in time to get a drink from a soft-drink machine and be there when Patrolman [Marrion L.] Baker came in" shortly after the assassination, and that "police were sealing off all exits from the building by the time Oswald got to the 2d floor."

● That "Oswald did not have time for all the movements imputed to him between his departure from the Texas School Book Depository and his encounter with Tippit."

● That "an unidentified woman" witnessed Tippit's slaying, "was interviewed by the FBI," "was never called as a witness" by the Warren Commission and "is alleged to have stated that she saw 2 men involved in the shooting and that they ran off in opposite directions afterward."

● That "Oswald was the victim of police brutality."

● That "Oswald was trained by the Russians in a special school for assassins at Minsk."

● That during a trip Oswald had made to Mexico City in Sept.-Oct. 1963, he "made a clandestine flight to Havana and back" and "came back from Mexico City with $5,000."

● That Cuban Premier Fidel Castro had admitted surreptitious visits by Oswald to Cuba by saying, while "under the influence of liquor" during a Nov. 27, 1963 speech: "The first time that Oswald was in Cuba...."

● That "Oswald was an informant of either the FBI or the CIA" and had been recruited by a U.S. government agency and "sent to Russia in 1959."

● That "the FBI interviewed Oswald 10 days before the assassination."

● That "the Dallas police suspected Oswald and Ruby of being involved in an attack on Gen. Walker and planned to arrest the 2 when the FBI intervened at the request of Atty. Gen. Robert F. Kennedy, and asked the police not to do so for reasons of state."

● That "Oswald received money by Western Union telegraph from time to time for several months before the assassination."

● That Mrs. Marguerite Oswald, Oswald's mother, "was shown a photograph of Jack Ruby by an FBI agent the night before Ruby killed her son."

● That "the headquarters detachment of the U.S. Army, under orders from [Defense Secy. Robert S.] McNamara's office, began to rehearse for the funeral more than a week before the assassination."

All the above "myths" and many other rumors concerning the assassination were investigated and proven untrue.

Federal Agencies Criticized

The Warren Commission report criticized the Secret Service and the FBI for inadequacies in protecting Pres. Kennedy at the time of his fatal visit to Dallas. It recommended thoroughgoing improvements in Presidential-protection practices and in "liaison between all federal agencies responsible for Presidential protection."

The commission proposed that "a Cabinet-level committee or the National Security Council" be given "the responsibility to review and oversee the protective activities of the Secret Service and the other federal agencies that assist in safeguarding the President."

The commission recommended that the Treasury Secretary "appoint a special assistant [of high stature and experience] with the responsibility of supervising the [Secret] Service."

It also recommended legislation that would make a federal crime: "the murder or manslaughter of, attempt or conspiracy to murder, kidnaping of and assault upon the President, Vice

President, or other officer next in the order of succession to the office of President, the President-elect and the Vice President-elect...."

The commission said that "the complexities of the Presidency have increased so rapidly ... that the Secret Service has not been able to develop or to secure adequate resources of personnel and facilities to fulfill its important assignment." It asserted that "the criteria and procedures of the Secret Service designed to identify and protect against persons considered threats to the President were not adequate prior to the assassination." "Although the Secret Service treated the direct threats against the President adequately, it failed to recognize other potential sources of danger to his security."

The commission also "concluded that there was insufficient liaison and coordination of information between the Secret Service and other federal agencies necessarily concerned with Presidential protection." "Although the FBI, in the normal exercise of its responsibility, had secured considerable information about Lee Harvey Oswald, it had no official responsibility, under the Secret Service criteria existing at the time of the President's trip to Dallas, to refer to the Secret Service the information it had about Oswald." But the commission held that "the FBI took an unduly restrictive view of its role in preventive intelligence work prior to the assassination. A more carefully coordinated treatment of the Oswald case by the FBI might well have resulted in bringing Oswald's activities to the attention of the Secret Service."

Summary of Warren Report

The following is the official "Summary and Conclusions" of the Warren Commission Report:

The assassination of John Fitzgerald Kennedy on Nov. 22, 1963 was a cruel and shocking act of violence directed against a man, a family, a nation, and against all mankind. A young and vigorous leader whose years of public and private life stretched before him was the victim of the 4th Presidential assassination in the history of a country dedicated to the concepts of reasoned argument and peaceful political change. This commission was created on Nov. 29, 1963, in recognition of the right of people everywhere to full and truthful knowledge concerning these events. This report endeavors to fulfill that right and to appraise this tragedy by the light of reason and the standard of fairness. It has been prepared with a deep awareness of the commission's responsibility to present to the American people an objective report of the facts relating to the assassination.

NARRATIVE OF EVENTS

At 11:40 a.m., CST, on Friday, Nov. 22, 1963 Pres. John F. Kennedy, Mrs. Kennedy and their party arrived at Love Field, Dallas, Tex. Behind them was the first day of a Texas trip planned 5 months before by the President, Vice Pres. Lyndon B. Johnson, and John B. Connally Jr., governor of Texas. After leaving the White House on Thursday morning, the President had flown initially to San Antonio where Vice Pres. Lyndon B. Johnson joined the party and the President dedicated new research facilities at the U.S. Air Force School of Aerospace Medicine. Following a testimonial dinner in Houston for U.S. Rep. Albert Thomas, the President flew to Ft. Worth where he spent the night and spoke at a large breakfast gathering on Friday.

Planned for later that day were a motorcade through downtown Dallas, a luncheon speech at the Trade Mart, and a flight to Austin where the President would attend a reception and speak at a Democratic fund-raising dinner. From Austin he would proceed to the Texas ranch of the Vice President. Evident on this trip were the varied roles which an American President performs—Head of State, Chief Executive, party leader, and, in this instance, prospective candidate for reelection.

The Dallas motorcade, it was hoped, would evoke a demonstration of the President's personal popularity in a city which he had lost in the 1960 election. Once it had been decided that the trip to Texas would span 2 days, those responsible for planning, primarily Gov. Connally and Kenneth O'Donnell, a special assistant to the President, agreed that a motorcade through Dallas would be desirable. The Secret Service was told on Nov. 8 that 45 minutes had been allotted to a motorcade procession from Love Field to the site of a luncheon planned by Dallas business and civic leaders in honor of the President. After considering the facilities and security problems of several buildings, the Trade Mart was chosen as the luncheon site. Given this selection, and in accordance with the customary practice of affording the greatest number of people an opportunity to see the President, the motorcade route selected was a natural one. The route was approved by the local host committee and White House representatives on Nov. 18 and publicized in the local papers starting on Nov. 19. This advance publicity made it clear that the motorcade would leave Main Street and pass the intersection of Elm and Houston streets as it proceeded to the Trade Mart by way of the Stemmons Freeway.

By midmorning of Nov. 22, clearing skies in Dallas dispelled the threat of rain and the President greeted the crowds from his open limousine without the "bubbletop," which was at that time a plastic shield furnishing protection only against inclement weather. To the left of the President in the rear seat was Mrs. Kennedy. In the jump seats were Gov. Connally, who was in front of the President, and Mrs. Connally at the governor's left. Agent William R. Greer of the Secret Service was driving, and Agent Roy H. Kellerman was sitting to his right.

Directly behind the Presidential limousine was an open "followup" car with 8 Secret Service agents, 2 in the front seat, 2 in the rear and 2 on each running board. These agents, in accordance with normal Secret Service procedures, were instructed to scan the crowds, the roofs and windows of buildings, overpasses and crossings for signs of trouble. Behind the "followup" car was the Vice-Presidential car carrying the Vice President and

Mrs. Johnson and Sen. Ralph W. Yarborough. Next were a Vice-Presidential "followup" car and several cars and buses for additional dignitaries, press representatives and others.

The motorcade left Love Field shortly after 11:50 a.m., and proceeded through residential neighborhoods, stopping twice at the President's request to greet well-wishers among the friendly crowds. Each time the President's car halted, Secret Service agents from the "followup" car moved forward to assume a protective stance near the President and Mrs. Kennedy. As the motorcade reached Main Street, a principal east-west artery in downtown Dallas, the welcome became tumultuous. At the extreme west end of Main Street the motorcade turned right on Houston Street and proceeded north for one block in order to make a left turn on Elm Street, the most direct and convenient approach to the Stemmons Freeway and the Trade Mart. As the President's car approached the intersection of Houston and Elm streets, there loomed directly ahead on the intersection's northwest corner a 7-story, orange brick warehouse and office building, the Texas School Book Depository. Riding in the Vice President's car, Agent Rufus W. Youngblood of the Secret Service noticed that the clock atop the building indicated 12:30 p.m., the scheduled arrival time at the Trade Mart.

The President's car, which had been going north, made a sharp turn toward the southwest onto Elm Street. At a speed of about 11 miles per hour, it started down the gradual descent toward a railroad overpass under which the motorcade would proceed before reaching the Stemmons Freeway. The front of the Texas School Book Depository was now on the President's right, and he waved to the crowd assembled there as he passed the building. Dealey Plaza—an open, landscaped area marking the western end of downtown Dallas—stretched out to the President's left. A Secret Service agent riding in the motorcade radioed the Trade Mart that the President would arrive in 5 minutes.

Seconds later shots resounded in rapid succession. The President's hands moved to his neck. He appeared to stiffen momentarily and lurch slightly forward in his seat. A bullet had entered the base of the back of his neck slightly to the right of the spine. It traveled downward and exited from the front of the neck, causing a nick in the left lower portion of the knot in the President's necktie. Before the shooting started, Gov. Connally had been facing toward the crowd on the right. He started to turn toward the left and suddenly felt a blow on his back. The governor had been hit by a bullet which entered at the extreme right side of his back at a point below his right armpit. The bullet traveled through his chest in a downward and forward direction, exited below his right nipple, passed through his right wrist which had been in his lap, and then caused a wound to his left thigh. The force of the bullet's impact appeared to spin the governor to his right, and Mrs. Connally pulled him down into her lap. Another bullet then struck Pres. Kennedy in the rear portion of his head, causing a massive and fatal wound. The President fell to the left into Mrs. Kennedy's lap.

Secret Service Agent Clinton J. Hill, riding on the left running board of the "followup" car, heard a noise which sounded like a firecracker and saw the President suddenly lean forward and to the left. Hill jumped off the car and raced toward the President's limousine. In the front seat of the Vice-Presidential car, Agent Youngblood heard an explosion and noticed unusual movements in the crowd. He vaulted into the rear seat and sat on the Vice President in order to protect him. At the same time Agent Kellerman in the front seat of the Presidential limousine turned to observe the President. Seeing that the President was struck, Kellerman instructed the driver, "Let's get out of here; we are hit." He radioed ahead to the lead car, "Get us to the hospital immediately." Agent Greer immediately accelerated the Presidential car. As it gained speed, Agent Hill managed to pull himself onto the back of the car where Mrs. Kennedy had climbed. Hill pushed her back into the rear seat and shielded the stricken President and Mrs. Kennedy as the President's car proceeded at high speed to Parkland Memorial Hospital, 4 miles away.

At Parkland, the President was immediately treated by a team of physicians who had been alerted for the President's arrival by the Dallas Police Department as the result of a radio message from the motorcade after the shooting. The doctors noted irregular breathing movements and a possible heartbeat, although they could not detect a pulsebeat. They observed the extensive wound in the President's head and a small wound approximately $\frac{1}{4}$ inch in diameter in the lower 3d of his neck. In an effort to facilitate breathing, the physicians performed a tracheotomy by enlarging the throat wound and inserting a tube. Totally absorbed in the immediate task of trying to preserve the President's life, the attending doctors never turned the President over for an examination of his back. At 1 p.m., after all heart activity ceased and the Last Rites were administered by a priest, Pres. Kennedy was pronounced dead. Gov. Connally underwent surgery and ultimately recovered from his serious wounds.

Upon learning of the President's death, Vice Pres. Johnson left Parkland Hospital under close guard and proceeded to the Presidential plane at Love Field. Mrs. Kennedy, accompanying her husband's body, boarded the plane shortly thereafter. At 2:38 p.m., in the central compartment of the plane, Lyndon B. Johnson was sworn in as the 36th President of the U.S. by Federal District Court Judge Sarah T. Hughes. The plane left immediately for Washington, D.C., arriving at Andrews AFB, Md., at 5:58 p.m., EST. The President's body was taken to the National Naval Medical Center, Bethesda, Md., where it was given a complete pathological examination. The autopsy disclosed the large head wound observed at Parkland and the wound in the front of the neck which had been enlarged by the Parkland doctors when they performed the tracheotomy. Both of these wounds were described in the autopsy report as being "presumably of exit." In addition the autopsy revealed a small wound of entry in the rear of the President's skull and another wound of entry near the base of the back of the neck. The autopsy report stated the cause of death as "Gunshot wound, head," and the bullets which struck the President were described as having been fired "from a point behind and somewhat above the level of the deceased."

At the scene of the shooting, there was evident confusion at the outset concerning the point of origin of the shots. Witnesses differed in their accounts of the direction from which the sound of the shots emanated. Within a few minutes, however, attention centered on the Texas School Book Depository Building as the source of the shots. The building was occupied by a private corporation, the Texas School Book Depository Co., which distributed school textbooks of several publishers and leased space to representatives of the publishers. Most of the employees in the building worked for these publishers. The balance, including a 15-man warehousing crew, were employees of the Texas School Book Depository Co. itself.

Several eyewitnesses in front of the building reported that they saw a rifle being fired from the southeast corner window on the 6th floor of the Texas School Book Depository. One eyewitness, Howard L. Brennan, had been watching the parade from a point on Elm Street directly opposite and facing the building. He promptly told a policeman that he had seen a slender man, about 5 feet 10 inches, in his early 30s, take deliberate aim from the 6th floor corner window and fire a rifle in the direction of the President's car. Brennan thought he might be able to identify the man since he had noticed him in the window a few minutes before the motorcade made the turn onto Elm Street. At 12:34 p.m., the Dallas police radio mentioned the Depository Building as a possible source of the shots, and at 12:45 p.m., the police radio broadcast a description of the suspected assassin based primarily on Brennan's observations.

When the shots were fired, a Dallas motorcycle patrolman, Marrion L. Baker, was riding in the motorcade at a point several cars behind the President. He had turned right from Main Street onto Houston Street and was about 200 feet south of Elm Street when he heard a shot. Baker, having recently returned from a week of deer hunting, was certain the shot came from a high-powered rifle. He looked up and saw pigeons scattering in the air from their perches on the Texas School Book Depository Building. He raced his motorcycle to the building, dismounted, scanned the area to the west and pushed his way through the spectators toward the entrance. There he encountered Roy Truly, the building superintendent, who offered Baker his help. They entered the building, and ran toward the 2 elevators in the rear. Finding that both elevators were on an upper floor, they dashed up the stairs. Not more than 2 minutes had elapsed since the shooting.

When they reached the 2d-floor landing on their way up to the top of the building, Patrolman Baker thought he caught a glimpse of someone through the small glass window in the door separating the hall area near the stairs from the small vestibule leading into the lunchroom. Gun in hand, he rushed to the door and saw a man about 20 feet away walking toward the other end of the lunchroom. The man was empty handed. At Baker's command, the man turned and approached him. Truly, who had started up the stairs to the 3d floor ahead of Baker, returned to see what had delayed the patrolman. Baker asked Truly whether he knew the man in the lunchroom. Truly replied that the man worked in the building, whereupon Baker turned from the man and proceeded, with Truly, up the stairs. The man they encountered had started working in the Texas School Book Depository Building on Oct. 16, 1963. His fellow workers described him as very quiet—a "loner." His name was Lee Harvey Oswald.

Within about one minute after his encounter with Baker and Truly, Oswald was seen passing through the 2d-floor offices. In his hand was a full "Coke" bottle which he had purchased from a vending machine in the lunchroom. He was walking toward the front of the building where a passenger elevator and a short flight of stairs provided access to the main entrance of the building on the first floor. Approximately 7 minutes later, at about 12:40 p.m., Oswald boarded a bus at a point on Elm Street 7 short blocks east of the Depository Building. The bus was traveling west toward the very building from which Oswald had come. Its route lay through the Oak Cliff section in southwest Dallas, where it would pass 7 blocks east of the roominghouse in which Oswald was living, at 1026 North Beckley Avenue. On the bus was Mrs. Mary Bledsoe, one of Oswald's former landladies who immediately recognized him. Oswald stayed on the bus approximately 3 or 4 minutes, during which time it proceeded only 2 blocks because of the traffic jam created by the motorcade and the assassination. Oswald then left the bus.

A few minutes later he entered a vacant taxi 4 blocks away and asked the driver to take him to a point on North Beckley Avenue several blocks beyond his roominghouse. The trip required 5 or 6 minutes. At about 1 p.m. Oswald arrived at the roominghouse. The housekeeper, Mrs. Earlene Roberts, was surprised to see Oswald at midday and remarked to him that he seemed to be in quite a hurry. He made no reply. A few minutes later Oswald emerged from his room zipping up his jacket and rushed out of the house.

Approximately 14 minutes later, and just 45 minutes after the assassination, another violent shooting occurred in Dallas. The victim was Patrolman J. D. Tippit of the Dallas police, an officer with a good record during his more than 11 years with the police force. He was shot near the intersection of 10th Street and Patton Avenue, about $\%_{10}$ of a mile from Oswald's roominghouse. At the time of the assassination, Tippit was alone in his patrol car, the routine practice for most police patrol cars at this time of day. He had been ordered by radio at 12:45 p.m. to proceed to the central Oak Cliff area as part of a concentration of patrol car activity around the center of the city following the assassination. At 12:54 Tippit radioed that he had moved as directed and would be available for any emergency. By this time the police radio had broadcast several messages alerting the police to the suspect described by Brennan at the scene of the assassination—a slender white male, about 30 years old, 5 feet 10 inches and weighing about 165 pounds.

At approximately 1:15 p.m. Tippit was driving slowly in an easterly direction on East 10th Street in Oak Cliff. About 100 feet past the intersection of 10th Street and Patton Avenue, Tippit pulled up alongside a man walking in the same direction. The man met the general description of the suspect wanted in connection with the assassination. He walked over to Tippit's car, rested his arms on the door on the righthand side of the car, and apparently exchanged words with Tippit through the window. Tippit opened the door on the left side and started to walk around the front of his car. As he reached the front wheel on the driver's side, the man on the sidewalk drew a revolver and fired several shots in rapid succession, hitting Tippit 4 times and killing him instantly. An automobile repairman, Domingo Benavides, heard the shots and stopped his pickup truck on the opposite side of the street about 25 feet in front of Tippit's car. He observed the gunman start back toward Patton Avenue, removing the empty cartridge cases from the gun as he went. Benavides rushed to Tippit's side. The patrolman, apparently dead, was lying on his revolver, which was out of its holster. Benavides promptly reported the shooting to police headquarters over the radio in Tippit's car. The message was received shortly after 1:16 p.m.

As the gunman left the scene, he walked hurriedly back toward Patton Avenue and turned left, heading south. Standing on the northwest corner of 10th Street and Patton Avenue was Helen Markham, who had been walking south on Patton Avenue and had seen both the killer and Tippit cross the intersection in front of her as she waited on the curb for traffic to pass. She witnessed the shooting and then saw the man with a gun in his hand walk back toward the corner and cut across the lawn of the corner house as he started south on Patton Avenue.

In the corner house itself, Mrs. Barbara Jeanette Davis and her sister-in-law, Mrs. Virginia Davis, heard the shots and rushed to the door in time to see the man walk rapidly across the lawn shaking a revolver as if he were emptying it of cartridge cases. Later that day each woman found a cartridge case near the house. As the gunman turned the corner he passed alongside a taxicab which was parked on Patton Avenue, a few feet from 10th Street. The driver, William W. Scoggins, had seen the slaying and was now crouched behind the cab on the street side. As the gunman cut through the shrubbery on the lawn, Scoggins looked up and saw the man approximately 12 feet away. In his hand was a pistol and he muttered words which sounded to Scoggins like "poor dumb cop" or "poor damn cop."

After passing Scoggins, the gunman crossed to the west side of Patton Avenue and ran south toward Jefferson Boulevard, a main Oak Cliff thoroughfare. On the east side of Patton, between 10th Street and Jefferson Boulevard, Ted Callaway, a used-car salesman, heard the shots and ran to the sidewalk. As the man with the gun rushed past, Callaway shouted "What's going on?" The man merely shrugged, ran on to Jefferson Boulevard and turned right. On the next corner was a gas station with a parking lot in the rear. The assailant ran into the lot, discarded his jacket and then continued his flight west on Jefferson.

In a shoe store a few blocks farther west on Jefferson, the manager, Johnny Calvin Brewer, heard the siren of a police car moments after the radio in his store announced the shooting of the police officer in Oak Cliff. Brewer saw a man step quickly into the entranceway of the store and stand there with his back toward the street. When the police car made a U-turn and headed back in the direction of the Tippit shooting, the man left and Brewer followed him. He saw the man enter the Texas Theatre, a motion picture house about 60 feet away, without buying a ticket. Brewer pointed this out to the cashier, Mrs. Julia Postal, who called the police. The time was shortly after 1:40 p.m.

At 1:29 p.m. the police radio had noted the similarity in the descriptions of the suspects in the Tippit shooting and the assassination. At 1:45 p.m., in response to Mrs. Postal's call, the police radio sounded the alarm: "Have information a suspect just went in the Texas Theatre on West Jefferson." Within minutes the theater was surrounded. The house lights were then turned up. Patrolman M. N. McDonald and several other policemen approached the man, who had been pointed out to them by Brewer.

McDonald ordered the man to his feet and heard him say, "Well, it's all over now." The man drew a gun from his waist with one hand and struck the officer with the other. McDonald struck out with his right hand and grabbed the gun with his left hand. After a brief struggle McDonald and several other police officers disarmed and handcuffed the suspect and drove him to police headquarters, arriving at approximately 2 p.m.

Following the assassination, police cars had rushed to the Texas School Book Depository in response to the many radio messages reporting that the shots had been fired from the Depository Building. Inspector J. Herbert Sawyer of the Dallas Police Department arrived at the scene shortly after hearing the first of these police radio messages at 12:34 p.m. Some of the officers who had been assigned to the area of Elm and Houston Streets for the motorcade were talking to witnesses and watching the building when Sawyer arrived. Sawyer entered the building and rode a passenger elevator to the 4th floor, which was the top floor for this elevator. He conducted a quick search, returned to the main floor and, between approximately 12:37 and 12:40 p.m., ordered that no one be permitted to leave the building.

Shortly before 1 p.m. Capt. J. Will Fritz, chief of the homicide and robbery bureau of the Dallas Police Department, arrived to take charge of the investigation. Searching the 6th floor, Deputy Sheriff Luke Mooney noticed a pile of cartons in the southeast corner. He squeezed through the boxes and realized immediately that he had discovered the point from which the shots had been fired. On the floor were 3 empty cartridge cases. A carton had apparently been placed on the floor at the side of the window so that a person sitting on the carton could look down Elm Street toward the overpass and scarcely be noticed from the outside. Between this carton and the half-open window were 3 additional cartons arranged at such an angle that a rifle resting on the top carton would be aimed directly at the motorcade as it moved away from the building. The high stack of boxes, which first attracted Mooney's attention, effectively screened a person at the window from the view of anyone else on the floor.

Mooney's discovery intensified the search for additional evidence on the 6th floor, and at 1:22 p.m., approximately 10 minutes after the cartridge cases were found, Dep. Sheriff Eugene Boone turned his flashlight in the direction of 2 rows of boxes in the northwest corner near the staircase. Stuffed between the 2 rows was a bolt-action rifle with a telescopic sight. The rifle was not touched until it could be photographed. When Lt. J. C. Day of the police identification bureau decided that the wooden stock and the metal knob at the end of the bolt contained no prints, he held the rifle by the stock while Capt. Fritz ejected a live shell by operating the bolt. Lt. Day promptly noted that stamped on the rifle itself was the serial number "C2766" as well as the markings "1940" "MADE ITALY" and "CAL. 6.5." The rifle was about 40 inches long and when disassembled it could fit into a handmade paper sack which, after the assassination, was found in the southeast corner of the building within a few feet of the cartridge cases.

As Fritz and Day were completing their examination of this rifle on the 6th floor, Roy Truly, the building superintendent, approached with information which he felt should be brought to the attention of the police. Earlier, while the police were questioning the employees, Truly had observed that Lee Harvey Oswald, one of the 15 men who worked in the warehouse, was missing. After Truly provided Oswald's name, address and general description, Fritz left for police headquarters. He arrived at headquarters shortly after 2 p.m. and asked 2 detectives to pick up the employe who was missing from the Texas School Book Depository. Standing nearby were the police officers who had just arrived with the man arrested in the Texas Theatre. When Fritz mentioned the name of the missing employe, he learned that the man was already in the interrogation room. The missing School Book Depository employe and the suspect who had been apprehended in the Texas Theatre were one and the same—Lee Harvey Oswald.

The suspect Fritz was about to question in connection with the assassination of the President and the murder of a policeman was born in New Orleans on Oct. 18, 1939, 2 months after the death of his father. His mother, Marguerite Claverie Oswald, had 2 older children. One, John Pic, was a half-brother to Lee from an earlier marriage which had ended in divorce. The other was Robert Oswald, a full brother to Lee and 5 years older. When Lee Oswald was 3, Mrs. Oswald placed him in an orphanage where his brother and half-brother were already living, primarily because she had to work.

In Jan. 1944, when Lee was 4, he was taken out of the orphanage, and shortly thereafter his mother moved with him to Dallas, Tex., where the older boys joined them at the end of the school year. In May of 1945 Marguerite Oswald married her 3d husband, Edwin A. Ekdahl. While the 2 older boys attended a military boarding school, Lee lived at home and developed a warm attachment to Ekdahl, occasionally accompanying his mother and stepfather on business trips around the country. Lee started school in Benbrook, Tex., but in the fall of 1946, after a separation from Ekdahl, Marguerite Oswald reentered Lee in the first grade in Covington, La. In Jan. 1947, while Lee was still in the first grade, the family moved to Ft. Worth, Tex., as the result of an attempted reconciliation between Ekdahl and Lee's mother. A year and a half later, before Lee was 9, his mother was divorced from her 3d husband as the result of a divorce action instituted by Ekdahl. Lee's school record during the next 5½ years in Ft. Worth was average, although generally it grew poorer each year. The comments of teachers and others who knew him at that time do not reveal any unusual personality traits or characteristics.

Another change for Lee Oswald occurred in Aug. 1952, a few months after he completed the 6th grade. Marguerite Oswald and her 12-year-old son moved to New York City where Marguerite's oldest son, John Pic, was stationed with the Coast Guard. The ensuing year and one-half in New York was marked by Lee's refusals to attend school and by emotional and psychological problems of a seemingly serious nature. Because he had become a chronic school truant, Lee underwent psychiatric study at Youth House, an institution in New York for juveniles who have had truancy problems or difficulties with the law, and who appear to require psychiatric observation, or other types of guidance. The social worker assigned to his case described him as "seriously detached" and "withdrawn" and noted "a rather pleasant, appealing quality about this emotionally starved, affectionless youngster." Lee expressed the feeling to the social worker that his mother did not care for him and regarded him as a burden. He experienced fantasies about being all-powerful and hurting people, but during his stay at Youth House he was apparently not a behavior problem. He appeared withdrawn and evasive, a boy who preferred to spend his time alone, reading and watching television. His tests indicated that he was above average in intelligence for his age group. The chief psychiatrist of Youth House diagnosed Lee's problem as a "personality pattern disturbance with schizoid features and passive-aggressive tendencies." He concluded that the boy was "an emotionally quite disturbed youngster" and recommended psychiatric treatment.

In May 1953, after having been at Youth House for 3 weeks, Lee Oswald returned to school where his attendance and grades temporarily improved. By the following fall, however, the probation officer reported that virtually every teacher complained about the boy's behavior. His mother insisted that he did not need psychiatric assistance. Although there was apparently some improvement in Lee's behavior during the next few months, the court recommended further treatment. In Jan. 1954, while Lee's case was still pending, Marguerite and Lee left for New Orleans, the city of Lee's birth.

Upon his return to New Orleans, Lee maintained mediocre grades but had no obvious behavior problems. Neighbors and others who knew him outside of school remembered him as a quiet, solitary and introverted boy who read a great deal and whose vocabulary made him quite articulate. About one month after he started the 10th grade and 11 days before his 16th birthday in Oct. 1955, he brought to school a note purportedly written by his mother, stating that the family was moving to California. The note was written by Lee. A few days later he dropped out of school and almost immediately tried to join the Marine Corps. Because he was only 16, he was rejected.

After leaving school Lee worked for the next 10 months at several jobs in New Orleans as an office messenger or clerk. It was during this period that he started to read Communist literature. Occasionally, in conversations with others, he praised communism and expressed to his fellow employes a desire to join the Communist Party. At about this time, when he was not yet 17, he wrote to the Socialist Party of America, professing his belief in Marxism.

Another move followed in July 1956 when Lee and his mother returned to Ft. Worth. He reentered high school but again dropped out after a few weeks and enlisted in the Marine Corps on Oct. 24, 1956, 6 days after his 17th birthday. On Dec. 21, 1956, during boot camp in San Diego, Oswald fired a score of 212 for record with the M-1 rifle—2 points over the minimum for a rating of "sharpshooter" on a marksman/sharpshooter/expert scale. After his basic training, Oswald received training in aviation fundamentals and then in radar scanning.

Most people who knew Oswald in the Marines described him as a "loner" who resented the exercise of authority by others. He spent much of his free time reading. He was court-martialed once for possessing an unregistered privately owned weapon and, on another occasion, for using provocative language to a noncommissioned officer. He was, however, generally able to comply with Marine discipline, even though his experiences in the Marine Corps did not live up to his expectations.

Oswald served 15 months overseas until Nov. 1958, most of it in Japan. During his final year in the Marine Corps he was stationed for the most part in Santa Ana, Calif., where he showed a marked interest in the Soviet Union and sometimes expressed politically radical views with dogmatic conviction. Oswald again fired the M-1 rifle for record on May 6, 1959, and this time he shot a score of 191 on a shorter course than before, only one point over the minimum required to be a "marksman." According to one of his fellow marines, Oswald was not particularly interested in his rifle performance, and his unit was not expected to exhibit the usual proficiency. During this period he expressed strong admiration for Fidel Castro and an interest in joining the

Cuban army. He tried to impress those around him as an intellectual, but his thinking appeared to some as shallow and rigid.

Oswald's Marine service terminated on Sept. 11, 1959, when at his own request he was released from active service a few months ahead of his scheduled release. He offered as the reason for his release the ill health and economic plight of his mother. He returned to Ft. Worth, remained with his mother only 3 days and left for New Orleans, telling his mother he planned to get work there in the shipping or import-export business. In New Orleans he booked passage on the freighter SS *Marion Lykes,* which sailed from New Orleans to Le Havre, France, on Sept. 20, 1959.

Lee Harvey Oswald had presumably planned this step in his life for quite some time. In March of 1959 he had applied to the Albert Schweitzer College in Switzerland for admission to the spring 1960 term. His letter of application contained many blatant falsehoods concerning his qualifications and background. A few weeks before his discharge he had applied for and obtained a passport, listing the Soviet Union as one of the countries which he planned to visit. During his service in the Marines he had saved a comparatively large sum of money, possibly as much as $1,500, which would appear to have been accomplished by considerable frugality and apparently for a specific purpose.

The purpose of the accumulated fund soon became known. On Oct. 16, 1959, Oswald arrived in Moscow by train after crossing the border from Finland, where he had secured a visa for a 6-day stay in the Soviet Union. He immediately applied for Soviet citizenship. On the afternoon of Oct. 21, 1959, Oswald was ordered to leave the Soviet Union by 8 p.m. that evening. That same afternoon in his hotel room Oswald, in an apparent suicide attempt, slashed his left wrist. He was hospitalized immediately. On Oct. 31, 3 days after his release from the hospital, Oswald appeared at the American embassy, announced that he wished to renounce his U.S. citizenship and become a Russian citizen, and handed the embassy officer a written statement he had prepared for the occasion. When asked his reasons, Oswald replied, "I am a Marxist." Oswald never formally complied with the legal steps necessary to renounce his American citizenship. The Soviet government did not grant his request for citizenship, but in Jan. 1960 he was given permission to remain in the Soviet Union on a year-to-year basis. At the same time Oswald was sent to Minsk where he worked in a radio factory as an unskilled laborer. In Jan. 1961 his permission to remain in the Soviet Union was extended for another year. A few weeks later, in Feb. 1961, he wrote to the American embassy in Moscow expressing a desire to return to the U.S.

The following month Oswald met a 19-year-old Russian girl, Marina Nikolaevna Prusakova, a pharmacist, who had been brought up in Leningrad but was then living with an aunt and uncle in Minsk. They were married on Apr. 30, 1961. Throughout the following year he carried on a correspondence with American and Soviet authorities seeking approval for the departure of himself and his wife to the U.S. In the course of this effort, Oswald and his wife visited the U.S. embassy in Moscow in July of 1961. Primarily on the basis of an interview and questionnaire completed there, the embassy concluded that Oswald had not lost his citizenship, a decision subsequently ratified by the Department of State in Washington, D.C. Upon their return to Minsk, Oswald and his wife filed with the Soviet authorities for permission to leave together. Their formal application was made in July 1961, and on Dec. 25, 1961, Marina Oswald was advised it would be granted.

A daughter was born to the Oswalds in Feb. 1962. In the months that followed they prepared for their return to the U.S. On May 9, 1962, the U.S. Immigration & Naturalization Service, at the request of the Department of State, agreed to waive a restriction under the law which would have prevented the issuance of a U.S. visa to Oswald's Russian wife until she had left the Soviet Union. They finally left Moscow on June 1, 1962, and were assisted in meeting their travel expenses by a loan of $435.71 from the U.S. Department of State. 2 weeks later they arrived in Ft. Worth, Tex.

For a few weeks Oswald, his wife and child lived with Oswald's brother Robert. After a similar stay with Oswald's mother, they moved into their own apartment in early August. Oswald obtained a job on July 16 as a sheet metal worker. During this period in Ft. Worth, Oswald was interviewed twice by agents of the FBI. The report of the first interview, which occurred on June 26, described him as arrogant and unwilling to discuss the reasons why he had gone to the Soviet Union. Oswald denied that he was involved in Soviet intelligence activities and promised to advise the FBI if Soviet representatives ever communicated with him. He was interviewed again on Aug. 16, when he displayed a less belligerent attitude and once again agreed to inform the FBI of any attempt to enlist him in intelligence activities.

In early Oct. 1962 Oswald quit his job at the sheet metal plant and moved to Dallas. While living in Ft. Worth the Oswalds had been introduced to a group of Russian-speaking people in the Dallas-Ft. Worth area. Many of them assisted the Oswalds by providing small amounts of food, clothing and household items. Oswald himself was disliked by almost all of this group whose help to the family was prompted primarily by sympathy for Marina Oswald and the child. Despite the fact that he had left the Soviet Union, disillusioned with its government, Oswald seemed more firmly committed than ever to his concepts of Marxism. He showed disdain for democracy, capitalism and American society in general. He was highly critical of the Russian-speaking group because they seemed devoted to American concepts of democracy and capitalism and were ambitious to improve themselves economically.

In Feb. 1963 the Oswalds met Ruth Paine at a social gathering. Ruth Paine was temporarily separated from her husband and living with her 2 children in their home in Irving, Tex., a suburb of Dallas. Because of an interest in the Russian language and sympathy for Marina Oswald, who spoke no English and had little funds, Ruth Paine befriended Marina and, during the next 2 months, visited her on several occasions.

On Apr. 6, 1963, Oswald lost his job with a photography firm. A few days later, on Apr. 10, he attempted to kill Maj. Gen. Edwin A. Walker (resigned, U.S. Army), using a rifle which he had ordered by mail one month previously under an assumed name. Marina Oswald learned of her husband's act when she confronted him with a note which he had left, giving her instructions in the event he did not return. That incident and their general economic difficulties impelled Marina Oswald to suggest that her husband leave Dallas and go to New Orleans to look for work.

Oswald left for New Orleans on Apr. 24, 1963. Ruth Paine, who knew nothing of the Walker shooting, invited Marina Oswald and the baby to stay with her in the Paines' modest home while Oswald sought work in New Orleans. Early in May, upon receiving word from Oswald that he had found a job, Ruth Paine drove Marina Oswald and the baby to New Orleans to rejoin Oswald.

During the stay in New Orleans, Oswald formed a fictitious New Orleans Chapter of the Fair Play for Cuba Committee. He posed as secretary of this organization and represented that the president was A. J. Hidell. In reality, Hidell was a completely fictitious person created by Oswald, the organization's only member. Oswald was arrested on Aug. 9 in connection with a scuffle which occurred while he was distributing pro-Castro leaflets. The next day, while at the police station, he was interviewed by an FBI agent after Oswald requested the police to arrange such an interview. Oswald gave the agent false information about his own background and was evasive in his replies concerning Fair Play for Cuba activities. During the next 2 weeks Oswald appeared on radio programs twice, claiming to be the spokesman for the Fair Play for Cuba Committee in New Orleans.

On July 19, 1963, Oswald lost his job as a greaser of coffee processing machinery. In September, after an exchange of correspondence with Marina Oswald, Ruth Paine drove to New Orleans and on Sept. 23 transported Marina, the child and the family belongings to Irving, Tex. Ruth Paine suggested that Marina Oswald, who was expecting her 2d child in October, live at the Paine house until after the baby was born. Oswald remained behind, ostensibly to find work either in Houston or some other city. Instead, he departed by bus for Mexico, arriving in Mexico City on Sept. 27, where he promptly visited the Cuban and Russian embassies. His stated objective was to obtain official permission to visit Cuba, on his way to the Soviet Union. The Cuban government would not grant his visa unless the Soviet government would also issue a visa permitting his entry into Russia. Oswald's efforts to secure these visas failed, and he left for Dallas, where he arrived on Oct. 3, 1963.

When he saw his wife the next day, it was decided that Oswald would rent a room in Dallas and visit his family on weekends. For one week he rented a room from Mrs. Bledsoe, the woman who later saw him on the bus shortly after the assassination. On Oct. 14, 1963, he rented the Beckley Avenue room and listed his name as O. H. Lee. On the same day, at the suggestion of a neighbor, Mrs. Paine phoned the Texas School Book Depository and was told that there was a job opening. She informed Oswald who was interviewed the following day at the depository and started to work there on Oct. 16, 1963.

On Oct. 20 the Oswalds' 2d daughter was born. During October and November Oswald established a general pattern of weekend visits to Irving, arriving on Friday afternoon and returning to Dallas Monday morning with a fellow employe, Buell Wesley Frazier, who lived near the Paines. On Friday, Nov. 15, Oswald remained in Dallas at the suggestion of his wife who told him that the house would be crowded because of a birthday party for Ruth Paine's daughter. On Monday, Nov. 18, Oswald and his wife quarreled bitterly during a telephone conversation, because she learned for the first time that he was living at the rooming house under an assumed name. On Thursday, Nov. 21, Oswald told Frazier that he would like to drive to Irving to pick up some curtain rods for an apartment in Dallas. His wife and Mrs. Paine were quite surprised to see him since it was a Thursday night. They thought he had returned to make up after Monday's quarrel. He was conciliatory, but Marina Oswald was still angry.

Later that evening, when Mrs. Paine had finished cleaning the kitchen, she went into the garage and noticed that the light was burning. She was certain that she had not left it on, although the incident appeared unimportant at the time. In the garage were most of the Oswalds' personal possessions. The following morning Oswald left while his wife was still in bed feeding the baby. She did not see him leave the house, nor did Ruth Paine. On the dresser in their room he left his wedding ring which he had never done before. His wallet containing $170 was left intact in a dresser-drawer.

Oswald walked to Frazier's house about ½ a block away and placed a long bulky package, made out of wrapping paper and tape, into the rear seat of the car. He told Frazier that the package contained curtain rods. When they reached the depository parking lot, Oswald walked quickly ahead. Frazier followed and saw Oswald enter the Depository Building carrying the long bulky package with him.

During the morning of Nov. 22, Marina Oswald followed Pres. Kennedy's activities on television. She and Ruth Paine cried when they heard that the President had been shot. Ruth Paine translated the news of the shooting to Marina Oswald as it came over television, including the report that the shots were probably fired from the building where Oswald worked. When Marina Oswald heard this, she recalled the Walker episode and the fact that her husband still owned the rifle. She went quietly to the Paine's garage where the rifle had been concealed in a blanket among their other belongings. It appeared to her that the rifle was still there, although she did not actually open the blanket.

At about 3 p.m. the police arrived at the Paine house and asked Marina Oswald whether her husband owned a rifle. She said that he did and then led them into the garage and pointed to the rolled up blanket. As a police officer lifted it, the blanket hung limply over either side of his arm. The rifle was not there.

Meanwhile, at police headquarters, Capt. Fritz had begun questioning Oswald. Soon after the start of the first interrogation, agents of the FBI and the U.S. Secret Service arrived and participated in the questioning. Oswald denied having anything to do with the assassination of Pres. Kennedy or the murder of Patrolman Tippit. He claimed that he was eating lunch at the time of the assassination, and that he then spoke with his foreman for 5 to 10 minutes before going home. He denied that he owned a rifle and when confronted, in a subsequent interview, with a picture showing him holding a rifle and pistol, he claimed that his face had been superimposed on someone else's body. He refused to answer any questions about the presence in his wallet of a selective service card with his picture and the name "Alek J. Hidell."

During the questioning of Oswald on the 3d floor of the police department, more than 100 representatives of the press, radio and television were crowded into the hallway through which Oswald had to pass when being taken from his cell to Capt. Fritz' office for interrogation. Reporters tried to interview Oswald during these trips. Between Friday afternoon and Sunday morning he appeared in the hallway at least 16 times. The generally confused conditions outside and inside Capt. Fritz' office increased the difficulty of police questioning. Advised by the police that he could communicate with an attorney, Oswald made several telephone calls on Saturday in an effort to procure representation of his own choice and discussed the matter with the president of the local bar association, who offered to obtain counsel. Oswald declined the offer, saying that he would first try to obtain counsel by himself. By Sunday morning he had not yet engaged an attorney.

At 7:10 p.m. on Nov. 22, 1963, Lee Harvey Oswald was formally advised that he had been charged with the murder of Patrolman J. D. Tippit. Several witnesses to the Tippit slaying and to the subsequent flight of the gunman had positively identified Oswald in police lineups. While positive firearm identification evidence was not available at the time, the revolver in Oswald's possession at the time of his arrest was of a type which could have fired the shots that killed Tippit.

The formal charge against Oswald for the assassination of Pres. Kennedy was lodged shortly after 1:30 a.m., on Saturday, Nov. 23. By 10 p.m. of the day of the assassination, the FBI had traced the rifle found on the 6th floor of the Texas School Book Depository to a mail-order house in Chicago which had purchased it from a distributor in New York. Approximately 6 hours later the Chicago firm advised that this rifle had been ordered in Mar. 1963 by an A. Hidell for shipment to post office box 2915, in Dallas, Tex., a box rented by Oswald. Payment for the rifle was remitted by a money order signed by A. Hidell. By 6:45 p.m. on Nov. 23, the FBI was able to advise the Dallas police that, as a result of handwriting analysis of the documents used to purchase the rifle, it had concluded that the rifle had been ordered by Lee Harvey Oswald.

Throughout Friday and Saturday, the Dallas police released to the public many of the details concerning the alleged evidence against Oswald. Police officials discussed important aspects of the case, usually in the course of impromptu and confused press conferences in the 3d-floor corridor. Some of the information divulged was erroneous. Efforts by the news media representatives to reconstruct the crime and promptly report details frequently led to erroneous and often conflicting reports. At the urgings of the newsmen, Chief of Police Jesse E. Curry, brought Oswald to a press conference in the police assembly room shortly after midnight of the day Oswald was arrested. The assembly room was crowded with newsmen who had come to Dallas from all over the country. They shouted questions at Oswald and flashed cameras at him. Among this group was a 52-year-old Dallas nightclub operator—Jack Ruby.

On Sunday morning, Nov. 24, arrangements were made for Oswald's transfer from the city jail to the Dallas County jail, about one mile away. The news media had been informed on Saturday night that the transfer of Oswald would not take place until after 10 a.m. on Sunday. Earlier on Sunday, between 2:30 and 3 a.m., anonymous telephone calls threatening Oswald's life had been received by the Dallas office of the FBI and by the office of the county sheriff. Nevertheless, on Sunday morning, television, radio and newspaper representatives crowded into the basement to record the transfer. As viewed through television cameras, Oswald would emerge from a door in front of the cameras and proceed to the transfer vehicle. To the right of the cameras was a "down" ramp from Main Street on the north. To the left was an "up" ramp leading to Commerce Street on the south.

The armored truck in which Oswald was to be transferred arrived shortly after 11 a.m. Police officials then decided, however, that an unmarked police car would be preferable for the trip because of its greater speed and maneuverability. At approximately 11:20 a.m. Oswald emerged from the basement jail office flanked by detectives on either side and at his rear. He took a few steps toward the car and was in the glaring light of the television cameras when a man suddenly darted out from an area on the right of the cameras where newsmen had been assembled. The man was carrying a Colt .38 revolver in his right hand and, while millions watched on television, he moved quickly to within a few feet of Oswald and fired one shot into Oswald's abdomen. Oswald groaned with pain as he fell to the ground and quickly lost consciousness. Within 7 minutes Oswald was at Parkland Hospital where, without having regained consciousness, he was pronounced dead at 1:07 p.m.

The man who killed Oswald was Jack Ruby. He was instantly arrested and, minutes later, confined in a cell on the 5th floor of the Dallas police jail. Under interrogation, he denied that the killing of Oswald was in any way connected with a conspiracy involving the assassination of Pres. Kennedy. He maintained that he had killed Oswald in a temporary fit of depression and rage over the President's death. Ruby was transferred the following day to the county jail without notice to the press or to police officers not directly involved in the transfer. Indicted for the murder of Oswald by the State of Texas on Nov. 26, 1963, Ruby was found guilty on Mar. 14, 1964, and sentenced to death. As of Sept. 1964, his case was pending on appeal.

CONCLUSIONS

This commission was created to ascertain the facts relating to the preceding summary of events and to consider the important questions which they raised. The commission has addressed itself to this task and has reached certain conclusions based on all the available evidence. No limitations have been placed on the commission's inquiry; it has conducted its own investigation, and all Government agencies have fully discharged their responsibility to cooperate with the commission in its investigation. These conclusions represent the reasoned judgment of all members of the commission and are presented after an investigation which has satisfied the commission that it has ascertained the truth concerning the assassination of Pres. Kennedy to the extent that a prolonged and thorough search makes this possible.

1. The shots which killed Pres. Kennedy and wounded Gov. Connally were fired from the 6th-floor window at the southeast corner of the Texas School Book Depository. This determination is based upon the following:

(a) Witnesses at the scene of the assassination saw a rifle being fired from the 6th-floor window of the Depository Building, and some witnesses saw a rifle in the window immediately after the shots were fired.

(b) The nearly whole bullet found on Gov. Connally's stretcher at Parkland Memorial Hospital and the 2 bullet fragments found in the front seat of the Presidential limousine were fired from the 6.5-millimeter Mannlicher-Carcano rifle found on the 6th floor of the Depository Building to the exclusion of all other weapons.

(c) The 3 used cartridge cases found near the window on the 6th floor at the southeast corner of the building were fired from the same rifle which fired the above-described bullet and fragments, to the exclusion of all other weapons.

(d) The windshield in the Presidential limousine was struck by a bullet fragment on the inside surface of the glass, but was not penetrated.

(e) The nature of the bullet wounds suffered by Pres. Kennedy and Gov. Connally and the location of the car at the time of the shots establish that the bullets were fired from above and behind the Presidential limousine, striking the President and the governor as follows:

(1) Pres. Kennedy was first struck by a bullet which entered at the back of his neck and exited through the lower front portion of his neck, causing a wound which would not necessarily have been lethal. The President was struck a 2d time by a bullet which entered the right-rear portion of his head, causing a massive and fatal wound.

(2) Gov. Connally was struck by a bullet which entered on the right side of his back and traveled downward through the right side of his chest; exiting below his right nipple. This bullet then passed through his right wrist and entered his left thigh, where it caused a superficial wound.

(f) There is no credible evidence that the shots were fired from the Triple Underpass, ahead of the motorcade or from any other location.

2. The weight of the evidence indicates that there were 3 shots fired.

3. Although it is not necessary to any essential findings of the commission to determine just which shot hit Gov. Connally, there is very persuasive evidence from the experts to indicate that the same bullet which pierced the President's throat also caused Gov. Connally's wounds. However, Gov. Connally's testimony and certain other factors have given rise to some difference of opinion as to this probability but there is no question in the mind of any member of the commission that all the shots which caused the President's and Gov. Connally's wounds were fired from the 6th-floor window of the Texas School Book Depository.

4. The shots which killed Pres. Kennedy and wounded Gov. Connally were fired by Lee Harvey Oswald. This conclusion is based upon the following:

(a) The Mannlicher-Carcano 6.5-millimeter Italian rifle from which the shots were fired was owned by and in the possession of Oswald.

(b) Oswald carried this rifle into the Depository Building on the morning of Nov. 22, 1963.

(c) Oswald, at the time of the assassination, was present at the window from which the shots were fired.

(d) Shortly after the assassination, the Mannlicher-Carcano rifle belonging to Oswald was found partially hidden between some cartons on the 6th floor and the improvised paper bag in which Oswald brought the rifle to the depository was found close by the window from which the shots were fired.

(e) Based on testimony of the experts and their analysis of films of the assassination, the commission has concluded that a rifleman of Lee Harvey Oswald's capabilities could have fired the shots from the rifle used in the assassination within the elapsed time of the shooting. The commission has concluded further that Oswald possessed the capability with a rifle which enabled him to commit the assassination.

(f) Oswald lied to the police after his arrest concerning important substantive matters.

(g) Oswald had attempted to kill Maj. Gen. Edwin A. Walker (resigned, U.S. Army) on Apr. 10, 1963, thereby demonstrating his disposition to take human life.

5. Oswald killed Dallas Police Patrolman J. D. Tippit approximately 45 minutes after the assassination. This conclusion upholds the finding that Oswald fired the shots which killed Pres. Kennedy and wounded Gov. Connally and is supported by the following:

(a) 2 eyewitnesses saw the Tippit shooting and 7 eyewitnesses heard the shots and saw the gunman leave the scene with revolver in hand. These 9 eyewitnesses positively identified Lee Harvey Oswald as the man they saw.

(b) The cartridge cases found at the scene of the shooting were fired from the revolver in the possession of Oswald at the time of his arrest to the exclusion of all other weapons.

(c) The revolver in Oswald's possession at the time of his arrest was purchased by and belonged to Oswald.

(d) Oswald's jacket was found along the path of flight taken by the gunman as he fled from the scene of the killing.

6. Within 80 minutes of the assassination and 35 minutes of the Tippit killing Oswald resisted arrest at the theatre by attempting to shoot another Dallas police officer.

7. The commission has reached the following conclusions concerning Oswald's interrogation and detention by the Dallas police:

(a) Except for the force required to effect his arrest, Oswald was not subjected to any physical coercion by any law enforcement officials. He was advised that he could not be compelled to give any information and that any statements made by him might be used against him in court. He was advised of his right to counsel. He was given the opportunity to obtain counsel of his own choice and was offered legal assistance by the Dallas Bar Association, which he rejected at that time.

(b) Newspaper, radio and television reporters were allowed uninhibited access to the area through which Oswald had to pass when he was moved from his cell to the interrogation room and other sections of the building, thereby subjecting Oswald to harassment and creating chaotic conditions which were not conducive to orderly interrogation or the protection of the rights of the prisoner.

(c) The numerous statements, sometimes erroneous, made to the press by various local law enforcement officials, during this period of confusion and disorder in the police station, would have presented serious obstacles to the obtaining of a fair trial for Oswald. To the extent that the information was erroneous or misleading, it helped to create doubts, speculations and fears in the mind of the public which might otherwise not have arisen.

8. The commission has reached the following conclusions concerning the killing of Oswald by Jack Ruby on Nov. 24, 1963;

(a) Ruby entered the basement of the Dallas Police Department shortly after 11:17 a.m. and killed Lee Harvey Oswald at 11:21 a.m.

(b) Although the evidence on Ruby's means of entry is not conclusive, the weight of the evidence indicates that he walked down the ramp leading from Main Street to the basement of the police department.

(c) There is no evidence to support the rumor that Ruby may have been assisted by any members of the Dallas Police Department in the killing of Oswald.

(d) The Dallas Police Department's decision to transfer Oswald to the county jail in full public view was unsound. The arrangements made by the police department on Sunday morning, only a few hours before the attempted transfer, were inadequate. Of critical importance was the fact that news media representatives and others were not excluded from the basement even after the police were notified of threats to Oswald's life. These deficiencies contributed to the death of Lee Harvey Oswald.

9. The commission has found no evidence that either Lee Harvey Oswald or Jack Ruby was part of any conspiracy, domestic or foreign, to assassinate Pres. Kennedy. The reasons for this conclusion are:

(a) The commission has found no evidence that anyone assisted Oswald in planning or carrying out the assassination. In this connection it has thoroughly investigated, among other factors, the circumstances surrounding the planning of the motorcade route through Dallas, the hiring of Oswald by the Texas School Book Depository Co. on Oct. 15, 1963, the method by which the rifle was brought into the building, the placing of cartons of books at the window, Oswald's escape from the building and the testimony of eyewitnesses to the shooting.

(b) The commission has found no evidence that Oswald was involved with any person or group in a conspiracy to assassinate the President, although it has thoroughly investigated, in addition to other possible leads, all facets of Oswald's associations, finances and personal habits, particularly during the period following his return from the Soviet Union in June 1962.

(c) The commission has found no evidence to show that Oswald was employed, persuaded or encouraged by any foreign government to assassinate Pres. Kennedy or that he was an agent of any foreign government, although the commission has reviewed the circumstances surrounding Oswald's defection to the Soviet Union, his life there from October of 1959 to June of 1962 so far as it can be reconstructed, his known contacts with the Fair Play for Cuba Committee, and his visits to the Cuban and Soviet embassies in Mexico City during his trip to Mexico from Sept. 26 to Oct. 3, 1963, and his known contacts with the Soviet Embassy in the U.S.

(d) The commission has explored all attempts of Oswald to identify himself with various political groups, including the Communist Party, U.S.A., the Fair Play for Cuba Committee and the Socialist Workers Party, and has been unable to find any evidence that the contacts which he initiated were related to Oswald's subsequent assassination of the President.

(e) All of the evidence before the commission established that there was nothing to support the speculation that Oswald was an agent, employee, or informant of the FBI, the CIA, or any other governmental agency. It has thoroughly investigated Oswald's relationships prior to the assassination with all agencies of the U.S. government. All contacts with Oswald by any of these agencies were made in the regular exercise of their different responsibilities.

(f) No direct or indirect relationship between Lee Harvey Oswald and Jack Ruby has been discovered by the commission, nor has it been able to find any credible evidence that either knew the other, although a thorough investigation was made of the many rumors and speculations of such a relationship.

(g) The commission has found no evidence that Jack Ruby acted with any other person in the killing of Lee Harvey Oswald.

(h) After careful investigation the commission has found no credible evidence either that Ruby and Officer Tippit, who was killed by Oswald, knew each other or that Oswald and Tippit knew each other.

Because of the difficulty of proving negatives to a certainty, the possibility of others being involved with either Oswald or Ruby cannot be established categorically, but if there is any such evidence it has been beyond the reach of all the investigative agencies and resources of the United States and has not come to the attention of this commission.

10. In its entire investigation the commission has found no evidence of conspiracy, subversion, or disloyalty to the U.S. government by any federal, state, or local official.

11. On the basis of the evidence before the commission, it concludes that Oswald acted alone. Therefore, to determine the motives for the assassination of Pres. Kennedy, one must look to the assassin himself. Clues to Oswald's motives can be found in his family history, his education or lack of it, his acts, his writings and the recollections of those who had close contacts with him throughout his life. The commission has presented with this report all of the background information bearing on motivation which it could discover. Thus, others may study Lee Oswald's life and arrive at their own conclusions as to his possible motives.

The commission could not make any definitive determination of Oswald's motives. It has endeavored to isolate factors which contributed to his character and which might have influenced his decision to assassinate Pres. Kennedy. These factors were:

(a) His deep-rooted resentment of all authority which was expressed in a hostility toward every society in which he lived;

(b) His inability to enter into meaningful relationships with people, and a continuous pattern of rejecting his environment in favor of new surroundings;

(c) His urge to try to find a place in history and despair at times over failures in his various undertakings;

(d) His capacity for violence as evidenced by his attempt to kill Gen. Walker;

(e) His avowed commitment to Marxism and communism, as he understood the terms and developed his own interpretation of them; this was expressed by his antagonism toward the United States, by his defection to the Soviet Union, by his failure to be reconciled with life in the United States even after his disenchantment with the Soviet Union, and by his efforts, though frustrated, to go to Cuba.

Each of these contributed to his capacity to risk all in cruel and irresponsible actions.

12. The commission recognizes that the varied responsibilities of the President require that he make frequent trips to all parts of the United States and abroad. Consistent with their high responsibilities Presidents can never be protected from every potential threat. The Secret Service's difficulty in meeting its protective responsibility varies with the activities and the nature of the occupant of the Office of President and his willingness to conform to plans for his safety. In appraising the performance of the Secret Service it should be understood that it has to do its work within such limitations. Nevertheless, the commission believes that recommendations for improvements in Presidential protection are compelled by the facts disclosed in this investigation.

(a) The complexities of the Presidency have increased so rapidly in recent years that the Secret Service has not been able to develop or to secure adequate resources of personnel and facilities to fulfill its important assignment. This situation should be promptly remedied.

(b) The commission has concluded that the criteria and procedures of the Secret Service designed to identify and protect against persons considered threats to the President, were not adequate prior to the assassination.

(1) The Protective Research Section of the Secret Service, which is responsible for its preventive work, lacked sufficient trained personnel and the mechanical and technical assistance needed to fulfill its responsibility.

(2) Prior to the assassination the Secret Service's criteria dealt with direct threats against the President. Although the Secret Service treated the direct threats against the President adequately, it failed to recognize the necessity of identifying other potential sources of danger to his security. The Secret Service did not develop adequate and specific criteria defining those persons or groups who might present a danger to the President. In effect, the Secret Service largely relied upon other federal or state agencies to supply the information necessary for it to fulfill its preventive responsibilities, although it did ask for information about direct threats to the President.

(c) The commission has concluded that there was insufficient liaison and coordination of information between the Secret Service and other federal agencies necessarily concerned with Presidential protection. Although the FBI, in the normal exercise of its responsibility, had secured considerable information about Lee Harvey Oswald, it had no official responsibility, under the Secret Service criteria existing at the time of the President's trip to Dallas, to refer to the Secret Service the information it had about Oswald. The commission has concluded, however, that the FBI took an unduly restrictive view of its role in preventive intelligence work prior to the assassination. A more carefully coordinated treatment of the Oswald case by the FBI might well have resulted in bringing Oswald's activities to the attention of the Secret Service.

(d) The commission has concluded that some of the advance preparations in Dallas made by the Secret Service, such as the detailed security measures taken at Love Field and the Trade Mart, were thorough and well executed. In other respects, however, the commission has concluded that the advance preparations for the President's trip were deficient.

(1) Although the Secret Service is compelled to rely to a great extent on local law enforcement officials, its procedures at the time of the Dallas trip did not call for well-defined instructions as to the respective responsibilities of the police officials and others assisting in the protection of the President.

(2) The procedures relied upon by the Secret Service for detecting the presence of an assassin located in a building along a motorcade route were inadequate. At the time of the trip to Dallas, the Secret Service as a matter of practice did not investigate, or cause to be checked, any building located along the motorcade route to be taken by the President. The responsibility for observing windows in these buildings during the motorcade was divided between local police personnel stationed on the streets to regulate crowds and Secret Service agents riding in the motorcade. Based on its investigation the commission has concluded that these arrangements during the trip to Dallas were clearly not sufficient.

(e) The configuration of the Presidential car and the seating arrangements of the Secret Service agents in the car did not afford the Secret Service agents the opportunity they should have had to be of immediate assistance to the President at the first sign of danger.

(f) Within these limitations, however, the commission finds that the agents most immediately responsible for the President's safety reacted promptly at the time the shots were fired from the Texas School Book Depository Building.

RECOMMENDATIONS

Prompted by the assassination of Pres. Kennedy, the Secret Service has initiated a comprehensive and critical review of its total operations. As a result of studies conducted during the past several months, and in cooperation with this commission, the Secret Service has prepared a planning document dated Aug. 27, 1964, which recommends various programs considered necessary by the Service to improve its techniques and enlarge its resources. The commission is encouraged by the efforts taken by the Secret Service since the assassination and suggests the following recommendations:

1. A committee of Cabinet members including the Secretary of the Treasury and the Attorney General, or the National Security Council, should be assigned the responsibility of reviewing and overseeing the protective activities of the Secret Service and the other federal agencies that assist in safeguarding the President. Once given this responsibility, such a committee would insure that the maximum resources of the federal government are fully engaged in the task of protecting the President, and would provide guidance in defining the general nature of domestic and foreign dangers to Presidential security.

2. Suggestions have been advanced to the commission for the transfer of all or parts of the Presidential protective responsibilities of the Secret Service to some other department or agency. The commission believes that if there is to be any determination of whether or not to relocate these responsibilities and functions, it ought to be made by the Executive and the Congress, perhaps upon recommendations based on studies by the previously suggested committee.

3. Meanwhile, in order to improve daily supervision of the Secret Service within the Department of the Treasury, the commission recommends that the Secretary of the Treasury appoint a special assistant with the responsibility of supervising the Secret Service. This special assistant should have sufficient stature and experience in law enforcement, intelligence, and allied fields to provide effective continuing supervision, and to keep the Secretary fully informed regarding the performance of the Secret Service. One of the initial assignments of this special assistant should be the supervision of the current effort by the Secret Service to revise and modernize its basic operating procedures.

4. The commission recommends that the Secret Service completely overhaul its facilities devoted to the advance detection of potential threats against the President. The commission suggests the following measures:

(a) The Secret Service should develop as quickly as possible more useful and precise criteria defining those potential threats to the President which should be brought to its attention by other agencies. The criteria should, among other additions, provide for prompt notice to the Secret Service of all returned defectors.

(b) The Secret Service should expedite its current plans to utilize the most efficient data-processing techniques.

(c) Once the Secret Service has formulated new criteria delineating the information it desires, it should enter into agreements with each federal agency to insure its receipt of such information.

5. The commission recommends that the Secret Service improve the protective measures followed in the planning and conducting of Presidential motorcades. In particular, the Secret Service should continue its current efforts to increase the precautionary attention given to buildings along the motorcade route.

6. The commission recommends that the Secret Service continue its recent efforts to improve and formalize its relationships with local police departments in areas to be visited by the President.

7. The commission believes that when the new criteria and procedures are established, the Secret Service will not have sufficient personnel or adequate facilities. The commission recommends that the Secret Service be provided with the personnel and resources which the Service and the Department of the Treasury may be able to demonstrate are needed to fulfill its important mission.

8. Even with an increase in Secret Service personnel, the protection of the President will continue to require the resources and cooperation of many federal agencies. The commission recommends that these agencies, specifically the FBI, continue the practice as it has developed, particularly since the assassination, of assisting the Secret Service upon request by providing personnel or other aid, and that there be a closer association and liaison between the Secret Service and all federal agencies.

9. The commission recommends that the President's physician always accompany him during his travels and occupy a position near the President where he can be immediately available in case of any emergency.

10. The commission recommends to Congress that it adopt legislation which would make the assassination of the President and Vice President a federal crime. A state of affairs where U.S. authorities have no clearly defined jurisdiction to investigate the assassination of a President is anomalous.

11. The commission has examined the Department of State's handling of the Oswald matters and finds that it followed the law throughout. However, the commission believes that the department in accordance with its own regulations should in all cases exercise great care in the return to this country of defectors who have evidenced disloyalty or hostility to this country or who have expressed a desire to renounce their American citizenship and that when such persons are so returned, procedures should be adopted for the better dissemination of information concerning them to the intelligence agencies of the Government.

12. The commission recommends that the representatives of the bar, law enforcement associations and the news media work together to establish ethical standards concerning the collection and presentation of information to the public so that there will be no interference with pending criminal investigations, court proceedings, or the right of individuals to a fair trial.

Reaction to the Report

Pres. Johnson Sept. 27, 1964 appointed a 4-man committee "to advise him on the execution of the recommendations of the Warren Commission." The committee's members: Treasury Secy. Douglas Dillon, Acting Atty. Gen. Nicholas deB. Katzenbach, CIA Director John A. McCone and McGeorge Bundy, special assistant to the President for national security affairs.

FBI Director J. Edgar Hoover Nov. 18, 1964 assailed the Warren Commission report during a 3-hour meeting with a group of 20 Washington newswomen who met periodically with Washington officials. Hoover, 69, called the report's criticism of the FBI "unfair and unjust" and "a classic example of Monday morning quarterbacking."

Hoover was especially critical of the report's assertion that the FBI had been remiss in not giving the Secret Service the information it had that might have shown Lee Harvey Oswald to be a potential assassin. Hoover said that since the Warren report had been released, the FBI had begun supplying the White House security detail with lists of thousands of names of potentially dangerous persons in cities where Pres. Johnson traveled whenever he left Washington. Hoover held that this requirement "charged the FBI with the obligations of a psychiatrist." He said the Secret Service was "hopelessly undermanned and ill-equipped to do the job it is supposed to do." (Hoover had warned in testimony before the Warren Commission that overly strict safety precautions around the President might become tantamount almost to "totalitarian security.")

Hoover did, however, back other findings of the report. In a statement issued Nov. 25, 1966 the FBI director said that "all available evidence and facts point to one conclusion—that Oswald acted alone in his crime."

Shortly after its release, the Warren Commission report was widely praised by officials and the press in most Western countries, but observers said that it had done little to diminish popularly held views that Kennedy had been the victim of a conspiracy. The Communist press asserted that allegedly justified "doubts and suspicions" remained.

Among Congressional leaders who indorsed the report: Rep. Carl Albert (Okla.), House Democratic leader, said Nov. 22, 1966 that "the commission answered the basic questions." House Republican leader Gerald R. Ford (Mich.), a member of the Warren Commission, said Nov. 22, 1966 that he had not "seen any new evidence whatsoever" concerning the assassination, and "at such time as I see any new evidence I would be glad to examine it or to have responsible authorities or some group other than the Warren Commission consider that." Rep. Hale Boggs (La.), House Democratic whip, who also served on the Warren Commission, said Nov. 27, 1966 that he "would have grave questions about" any new assassination inquiry "if the objective is to answer some of the things that have been raised up to the present." But he made an exception for autopsy X-rays not seen by the commission. "... If it would please anyone," Boggs said, "if it would help to clarify any doubts, ... then I would say that if the Attorney General or some appropriate authority wants to appoint a totally objective group—of doctors and others—to look into these ,X-rays, maybe it should be done."

Atty. Gen. Robert F. Kennedy had declared at a meeting with about 20 students and civic leaders at the Cracow, Poland municipal building June 29, 1964 that "there is no question" but that his brother's assassination was the act of only one man, Lee Harvey Oswald. He said Oswald "was anti-social and felt that the only way to take out his strong feelings against life

and society was by killing the President of the United States."
Kennedy made the remarks while on a tour of West Germany
and Poland.

Report Challenged

Life magazine, in its Nov. 25, 1966 issue, called for a new
official inquiry into the assassination on the ground that there
was "reasonable—and disturbing—doubt" that Lee Harvey
Oswald had acted alone. The statement followed a new
examination by Texas Gov. John B. Connally Jr. of motion
pictures taken by Abraham Zapruder of Dallas as the
assassination took place.

Life quoted Connally as saying after he and his wife
studied the film: "There is my absolute knowledge, and Nellie's
[Mrs. Connally] too, that one bullet caused the President's first
wound, and that an entirely separate shot struck me." Connally
and his wife had said this to the Warren Commission at the
time of the inquiry.

Life said that based on calculations of (a) the commission's
findings of the time needed between shots of the assassination
weapon (2.3 seconds), (b) the speed of Zapruder's camera and (c)
Connally's identification of the movie frame that probably
showed him being hit, 1.3 seconds must have elapsed between
the time Kennedy was hit and the time Connally was hit. Such
an interval, *Life* declared, would require firing from more than
one gun.

At a special news conference in Austin, Tex. Nov. 23, 1966,
Connally asserted that he accepted the Warren Commission
report on the assassination and that a new investigation was
"neither warranted, justified or desirable." Connally said he
was satisfied that Oswald had fired the shot that hit him and
that there was only one person involved in the shooting. But he
reiterated his belief that the shot that hit him did not hit
Kennedy. This was his sole disagreement with the Warren
Commission's findings, he said, but he did not believe this
disagreement affected the validity of the commission's over-all
findings.

Shortly after the Warren Commission report was issued a
rash of books appeared disclaiming most of its findings. Among
the books:

● *Who Killed Kennedy?* by Thomas G. Buchanan, published Nov. 25, 1964 by G. P. Putnam. The author asserted that Kennedy's assassination was the result of a plot.

● *Inquest: The Warren Commission and the Establishment of Truth,* by Edward Jay Epstein, published June 29, 1966 by Viking. Based on the author's graduate thesis at Cornell University, this book claimed that the Warren Commission had been created to establish the "political truth" rather than the literal truth of the events surrounding the assassination. According to Epstein, the commission sought and reached the conclusion that Oswald had acted as a lone assassin because this was the only conclusion that could end rumors of a conspiracy and soothe the public.

● *The Oswald Affair: An Examination of the Contradictions and Omissions of the Warren Report,* by Leo Sauvage, published Sept. 6, 1966 by World. Sauvage, the American correspondent of the Paris newspaper *Le Figaro,* argued that the commission should have employed more independent non-governmental investigators and that it should have been composed of full-time experts rather than part-time dignitaries. The author was sharply critical of the Dallas police and the FBI for what he charged had been incompetent handling of the case. He suggested that there might have been police acquiescence in the murder of Oswald. He also postulated the possibility that the assassination was the work of a conspiracy.

● *Rush to Judgment: A Critique of the Warren Commission's Inquiry into the Murders of President John F. Kennedy, Officer J. D. Tippit and Lee Harvey Oswald,* by Mark Lane, published Sept. 8, 1966 by Holt, Rinehart & Winston. Lane, the New York attorney who had been prevented from representing Oswald at the Warren Commission hearings, presented the case he had prepared for the commission. While Lane did not claim that Oswald was innocent, he did charge that the commission had committed errors serious enough to undermine its conclusions.

● *Whitewash: The Report on the Warren Commission,* by Harold Weisberg, published in Dec. 1966 by the author. Weisberg, a former Senate Civil Liberties Subcommittee investigator, questioned virtually every specific finding related to Oswald and the assassination. (In a book entitled *Photographic Whitewash: Suppressed Kennedy Assassination*

Pictures, published the week of July 9, 1967, Weisberg charged that the panel had failed to examine photos that might show Oswald standing in the doorway of the Texas School Book Depository and not at the building's 6th-floor window from which the commission said the fatal shot was fired.)

● *The Assassination of John F. Kennedy: The Reasons Why,* by Albert H. Newman, published May 21, 1970 by Clarkson N. Potter, Inc. The author contended that Oswald shot Kennedy because of the latter's opposition to Fidel Castro's regime in Cuba and that the same motivation was responsible for Oswald's hatred of Richard M. Nixon and ex-Maj. Gen. Edwin A. Walker.

Then 2 plays dealing with various aspects of the assassination opened in New York's Off-Broadway theater district during 1967:

● *Macbird,* a satire by Barbara Garson, opened Feb. 22, 1967 at the Village Gate Theater. In it a thinly disguised Pres. Johnson is accused of plotting Kennedy's death in a parallel to Shakespeare's *Macbeth.* The play, staged by Roy Levine, starred Stacy Keach.

● *The Trial of Lee Harvey Oswald,* by Amram Ducovny and Leon Friedman, based on an idea by Harold Steinberg and Ducovny, opened Nov. 6, 1967 at the ANTA Theater. In it Oswald testified in the case against him. The play was staged by Tunc Yalman and starred Peter Masterson.

Archives Gets Evidence; Suppression Charged

The family of the late John F. Kennedy placed in the National Archives in Washington Oct. 31, 1966 the photos and X-rays of the autopsy performed on the assassinated President's body Nov. 22, 1963. The Justice Department Nov. 1, 1966 turned over to the Archives all the physical evidence examined by the Warren Commission in its investigation.

The Justice Department reportedly had asked the Kennedy family to give the 14 X-rays, 25 black-and-white negatives and 26 4-by-5-inch color transparencies to the government after critics of the Warren report charged that the pictures had been suppressed to conceal flaws in the commission's conclusions. (Neither the photos nor the X-rays had been seen by the full commission, but Chief Justice Earl Warren had viewed them.

The undeveloped film and X-rays had been turned over to Secret Service agents, who had delivered them to the Kennedy family. The Kennedys reportedly withheld them for reasons of taste.)

Strict limitations on access to the pictures and X-rays were set forth in a written agreement between the Justice Department and the executors of Pres. Kennedy's estate. (A federal law regarding Presidential libraries provided that papers and other items could be deposited in the Archives subject to limitations and restrictions imposed by the donors.) The agreement barred all but official government investigative bodies and private experts approved by the Kennedy family from examining the material until Oct. 29, 1971. After that time, "any recognized expert in the field of pathology or related areas of science or technology, for serious purposes relevant to the investigation of matters relating to the death of the late President," would be permitted to see the 65 photos and X-rays. No public display or release would be permitted. The limitations would remain effective during the life of the late President's immediate family.

Ex-Asst. Atty. Gen. Burke Marshall, the Kennedy family's lawyer who had drawn up the agreement, said in New York Nov. 2 that he would grant no requests from journalists, historians, biographers or researchers for at least 5 years.

(The text of the agreement was made public by Robert H. Bahmer, director of the National Archives, in Washington Jan. 5, 1969. It was embodied in a letter to Lawson B. Knott Jr., administrator of the General Services Administration, the government agency responsible for maintaining records and property.)

Capt. James J. Humes and Dr. J. Thornton Boswell, 2 of the 3 physicians who had performed the autopsy, authenticated the pictures and X-rays Nov. 1, 1966 and said they had corroborated their testimony before the Warren Commission. The doctors had testified that their examination of Kennedy's body indicated that a bullet had struck him in the back of the neck and had passed out through his throat. This testimony was apparently crucial to the commission's conclusion that a single bullet, fired by Lee Harvey Oswald, had struck both Kennedy and Gov. John Connally. Dr. Boswell said: "The drawing we submitted" to the commission "was identical with the photographs."

Pres. Johnson defended the Warren Commission at a news conference Nov. 4, 1966. Asked why the material had not been turned over before and why it would not be available to non-government investigators for at least 5 years, Johnson said: "I think every American can understand the reason why we wouldn't want to have the garments, the records and everything paraded out in every sewing circle in the country to be exploited and used without serving any good or official purpose."

The clothing worn by Kennedy when he was assassinated was also turned over to the Archives by the government Oct. 31, 1966. Under the restrictions applicable to them, any government investigative body would have full access to them and any serious scholar would be permitted to see them, but public display was prohibited.

Acting Atty. Gen. Ramsey Clark Nov. 1, 1966 took title for the government to all the physical evidence considered by the commission and turned it over to the Archives. Among the articles were: "one 6.5-mm. Mannlicher-Carcano rifle, with telescopic sight, serial No. C2766, including sling and cartridge clip," the gun the commission said had killed Kennedy; a caliber-.38 special Smith & Wesson revolver owned by Oswald; hundreds of items found in Oswald's quarters.

A legal researcher in Chicago filed suit in federal district court Apr. 6, 1970 charging the National Archives with suppressing documents and data that he said showed Kennedy had died as a result of an intricate conspiracy. The researcher, Sherman Skolnick, said in his suit that 5 men had conspired to kill the President at the Army-Air Force football game in Chicago Nov. 2, 1963 but that when Kennedy cancelled his appearance because of a cold, the conspirators rescheduled their attempt for Dallas 3 weeks later.

Johnson Recalls Assassination

After leaving office, ex-Pres. Johnson gave his version of the events surrounding the assassination. He did so in a TV interview with correspondent Walter Cronkite. The program, broadcast by CBS News May 2, 1970, was the last segment of a

3-part conversation filmed at the Johnson ranch in Texas in the autumn of 1969.

Johnson recalled that while he had always been concerned about Kennedy's safety, he was especially uneasy about the Texas trip because of his own unpleasant experiences in Dallas in 1960 and because there still were "very ugly things being said" in his home state. But, he said, Kennedy had felt that "by going there personally and visiting these places that he could generate support and change the situation. And I think he did. I think he would have." * When Pres. Kennedy arrived in Dallas the morning of Nov. 22, 1963, Johnson said, "he was happy, smiling, and I think stimulated ... by the Fort Worth experience ... and by the previous day's" enthusiastic receptions in other Texas cities.

Shortly after the first assassination shot, which Johnson said was the only one he had heard, Secret Service Agent Rufus Youngblood shoved him to the bottom of the limousine and shielded him with his body. Johnson said he had not been aware that Kennedy had been hit until some time after they had gotten to Parkland Hospital; he learned about Kennedy's death from Presidential aide Kenneth O'Donnell. His first decision after hearing the news was to delay the public announcement of the President's death until both he and Mrs. Johnson were on their way back to *Air Force One* at Love Field. He did this, he said, to minimize the opportunity "to destroy our form of government and the leaders in that government" in case they were all victims of an international conspiracy. On the advice of Atty. Gen. Robert F. Kennedy, Johnson was sworn in as President so soon afterward so that the "country [would have] a man in charge and a man in a position to act and make decisions ..., that [everyone] here and abroad [would know] that we're not rudderless."

Johnson denied that he had been aware of any animosity between himself and the Kennedy staff on the trip back to Washington. "I think there must have been a calculated effort on someone's part, I don't know who," he said, "to try to make

---

* Johnson did not return to Dallas until Feb. 27, 1968, while he was still President, when he visited the city to address 10,000 persons at the National Rural Electric Cooperative Association's convention. Johnson's trip was not announced in advance, and he rode to and from the Memorial Auditorium in an unmarked car.

it appear that I didn't get along with the President's staff, although I employed them and asked them to continue to serve me and they did." He also denied rumors that Mrs. Jacqueline Kennedy had been aloof from him.

Discussing the transition of power, Johnson commented that he "had many problems in my conduct of the office being contrasted with Pres. Kennedy's conduct of the office, with my manner of dealing with things and his manner, with my accent and his accent, with my background and his background. He was a great public hero and anything that I did that someone didn't approve of, they would always feel that Pres. Kennedy wouldn't have done that—that he would have done it a different way, that he wouldn't have made that mistake."

In regard to the Warren Commission, Johnson said that he had appointed Chief Justice Earl Warren to the commission over the Justice's objections and that he (Johnson) believed not "a single man wanted to serve on that commission."

CBS had announced Apr. 28, 1970 that certain material "involving national security" had been deleted from the broadcast at Johnson's request. The deleted material reportedly dealt with the ex-President's doubts about the Warren Commission's finding that Oswald had acted alone in the assassination.

THE TRIAL OF JACK RUBY

Ruby Convicted of Oswald's Murder

Jack Ruby was convicted Mar. 14, 1964 of murdering Lee Harvey Oswald. The trial took place in Dallas after Texas District Judge Joseph Brantley Brown, 55, had ruled there Feb. 14 that Ruby must go on trial in Dallas. He had set Feb. 17 as the day the trial was to open.

Chief defense counsel Melvin M. Belli of San Francisco and associate defense counsel Joe H. Tonahill of Jasper, Tex. had presented 26 witnesses at a hearing before Brown Feb. 10-13 in an effort to prove their contention that the trial should be moved to a different city because Ruby could not get a fair trial in Dallas. Dallas County District Atty. Henry M. Wade, who was scheduled to prosecute the case before Brown, insisted throughout the hearing that a fair trial for Ruby was possible in Dallas.

Brown indicated in his ruling Feb. 14 that he might agree to move the trial to a different city if it proved impossible to impanel an acceptable jury in Dallas.

The trial opened Feb. 17, but the session was consumed by preliminaries. The questioning of prospective jurors did not start until Feb. 18, and the defense blocked the acceptance of any jurors until Feb. 20, when Belli agreed that the 24th prospective juror called was acceptable. A 2d juror was accepted Feb. 21, and the number accepted rose to 8 by Feb. 26.

The Texas Supreme Court Feb. 24 refused unanimously to hear a defense plea that Brown be ordered not to seat as a juror anybody who had seen Oswald shot on TV. Brown had held that seeing the crime committed on TV did not disqualify a viewer from becoming a juror unless he had developed an opinion so strong that evidence could not change it.

It took 14 days and the questioning of 162 prospective jurors to qualify the all-white all-Protestant jury of 8 men and 4 women. The delay was largely due to the defense contention that an impartial jury could not be found in Dallas. All but one of the 12 finally chosen had seen the TV coverage of Ruby shooting Oswald. The defense Feb. 28 had used up its 15th and last peremptory challenge—the right to reject a prospective juror without giving a reason—but Judge Brown then had allowed the defense 3 more challenges. The defense used up all 3 extra challenges, and the final 2 panelists were qualified Mar. 3 with Judge J. Frank Wilson substituting for Brown, who had gone to bed with a cold. But Brown was back Mar. 4 when District Atty. Henry Wade opened the case for the prosecution, and Brown presided during the entire trial.

66 witnesses were heard before the trial was ended. The defense made no attempt to dispute the fact (thoroughly proven by many eyewitnesses) that Ruby had shot Oswald in the basement of the Dallas municipal building Nov. 24, 1963. Instead the defense concentrated on a claim of insanity.

The defense produced a series of distinguished mental experts as witnesses: Dr. Roy Schafer, a Yale clinical psychologist, who testified Mar. 9; Dr. Manfred Guttmacher, a Baltimore psychiatrist, who testified Mar. 10; Dr. Martin L. Towler, a University of Texas neurologist, who testified Mar. 10; Dr. Walter Bromberg, a Katonah, N.Y. psychiatrist, who testified Mar. 12; Dr. Frederic A. Gibbs of Chicago, an authority on electroencephalograph examination of brain waves, who testified Mar. 13. All of the defense mental experts said Ruby was insane. Gibbs testified that in electroencephalographic examinations of Ruby's brain waves, administered by Towler, psychomotor variant epilepsy was unmistakable.

Mental experts who appeared as prosecution witnesses, however, rejected the insanity claims. Dr. Robert Stubblefield of Southwestern Medical School (Dallas) and Dr. John T. Holbrook of Dallas, both psychiatrists, testified Mar. 11 that Ruby had been sane when they and Towler had examined him in January. Dr. Peter Kellaway of the Baylor University School of Medicine, president of the American Electroencephalographic Society, and Dr. Earl A. Walker, neurological surgery professor at Johns Hopkins University School of Medicine, testified Mar. 11 that a diagnosis of organic brain damage could not be made on the basis of the electroencephalograph alone. But Walker added that such damage could be disclosed through the sort of psychological tests administered by Schafer. Dr. Shef Olinger, a Dallas neurologist, testified Mar. 11 that he did not diagnose Ruby as a psychomotor epileptic on the basis of Towler's tests. 3 other neurologists, Dr. Francis M. Forster of the University of

Wisconsin School of Medicine, Dr. Robert S. Schwab of Harvard Medical School and Dr. Roland Mackay of Northwestern University Medical School, testified Mar. 12 that the electroencephalograph alone could not support a psychomotor epilepsy diagnosis.

One of the witnesses at the trial was ex-welterweight boxing champion Barney Ross, who testified Mar. 9 that he and Ruby had been friends when they were teenagers in Chicago and that Ruby could often alternate between angry tantrums and subdued behavior.

District Atty. Henry Wade had reported in Dallas Jan. 6, 1964 that an inquiry had disclosed "no evidence whatever" of collusion between Ruby and Dallas police officers in Ruby's slaying of Oswald. The inquiry was conducted by a board appointed by Dallas Police Chief Jesse Curry. Wade said he had sent a copy of the board's report to the Warren Commission.

Ruby Sentenced to Death

Ruby was convicted Mar. 14 of the first-degree "murder with malice" of Oswald. The jury, which deliberated for 2 hours 19 minutes before announcing its verdict, directed that Ruby's punishment be death.

Chief defense counsel Belli, on hearing the verdict, said bitterly that he "thank[ed] this jury for a verdict that is a victory for bigotry." He shouted into radio-TV microphones and to newsmen that "this was a kangaroo court, a railroad court," that the Dallas "oligarchy wanted to send Ruby to the public abattoir ... to cleanse this city of its shame" but that "the jury has made this city a shame forevermore." He said Judge Brown had "committed 30 errors" and "went down the line for every motion the district attorney made."

Assistant defense counsel Tonahill told newsmen that the "jury had their minds made up when they started. One of them told his employer that he'd vote the death penalty. Another does public relations for the police department."

Ruby Ruled Sane

A Texas state court jury ruled in Dallas June 13, 1966 that Jack Ruby was sane.

The sanity trial had been ordered by the Texas Court of Criminal Appeals in order to determine Ruby's competence to hire and dismiss his lawyers. Ruby had attempted to hire a new team of lawyers to replace Melvin Belli and Joe Tonahill. The 2 competing sets of defense lawyers objected to the sanity hearing on the ground that a family request for such a hearing had been withdrawn.

Neither of the defense groups offered evidence or questioned 5 state witnesses—4 county jail guards and a doctor—who testified that Ruby was sane. One set of lawyers was led by Tonahill, the associate defense counsel in Ruby's 1964 murder trial, but Tonahill refused to be dismissed; he based his refusal on the ground that Ruby was insane. The 2d team of lawyers, hired by Ruby and his family, included Sam Houston Clinton Jr. of Austin, Tex., Phil Burleson of Dallas, Sol A. Dann of Detroit and William M. Kunstler of New York.

Conviction Reversed

Ruby's conviction of the murder of Oswald was reversed by the Texas Court of Criminal Appeals in Austin Oct. 5, 1966. The court also ordered the transfer of the case from Dallas County, where the shooting had occurred. The decision by Ruby's trial judge, Joseph Brown, to disqualify himself from further participation in the case was accepted by the court, which assigned the case to Judge Louis T. Holland of Montague, Tex.

The court's 3 judges issued separate opinions, all agreeing to reverse the conviction. Presiding Judge W. A. Morrison held that a state law requiring confessions to be voluntary and spontaneous had been violated in permitting as evidence testimony by a Dallas police officer that Ruby had told him that he had intended to kill Oswald if the opportunity arose. The admission was made about 40 minutes after the shooting, according to the officer, Detective Sgt. Patrick T. Dean.

U.S. Supreme Court decisions in the cases of Billie Sol Estes, convicted of fraud in Texas, and Dr. Samuel H. Sheppard, convicted of murder in Ohio, were cited by Morrison as precedents that an error had been made in holding the trial in Dallas County.

Appeals Judge W. T. McDonald, in his opinion, cited a Texas criminal code requirement that witnesses to the charged offense cannot serve as jurors. He said 10 of the 12 jurors who convicted Ruby had witnessed the shooting of Oswald on TV. But the 3d judge, K. K. Wooley, said "the majority does not hold that a juror who saw the shooting of the deceased on television is, for that reason alone, disqualified or subject to challenge for cause as being 'a witness in the case.'"

Ruby's case was handled without fee by 5 lawyers: Phil Burleson of Dallas; Sol A. Dann of Detroit, lawyer for Earl Ruby, the defendant's brother; Elmer Gertz of Chicago; William Kunstler of New York, member of the board of directors of the American Civil Liberties Union; Sam Houston Clinton Jr. of Austin, legal director of the Texas Civil Liberties Union.

Ruby Dies

Jack Ruby died in Parkland Memorial Hospital in Dallas Jan. 3, 1967 of a blood clot in the lungs. He had been admitted to Parkland Dec. 9, 1966, when it was thought he had pneumonia, but doctors discovered Dec. 10, 1966 that he had extensive adeno carcinoma cancer (the type that spreads through the body's ducts and cavities). Cancer was listed as a contributing cause of death.

Prior to his hospitalization Ruby had been in Dallas County jail awaiting retrial for Oswald's murder. District Atty. Henry Wade said Jan. 3 that the murder indictment would be dropped since he had died before coming to trial.

Judge Louis Holland formally dismissed the murder charges against Jack Ruby Jan. 30, 1967 in Wichita Falls, Tex.

(Ruby's demand that he be given a lie-detector test, to prove that he had acted alone in the slaying of Oswald, was denied because of his poor physical condition.)

Ruby Conversation Tapes Released

Capitol Records released in New York Jan. 3, 1967 a 3-minute tape-recorded conversation between Jack Ruby and his brother Earl. It had been made in Parkland Hospital in Dallas between Dec. 15 and 18, 1966.

In the recording Ruby said that although he knew Oswald
was to be transferred from the county jail at 10:00 a.m. (Nov.
24, 1963), his (Ruby's) presence at the jail was due to his having
made an "illegal turn" behind a bus and having wound up in the
jail parking lot. He said he had no recollection of the moment
he shot Oswald. "It happened in such a blur . . . , before I knew
it . . . the officers had me on the ground."

Asked whether Ruby had met Oswald before in his
nightclub, Ruby reportedly interrupted the interviewer and
said: "It's a fabrication." He had told his brother that he
"always carried a gun because of various altercations I had in
my club" and because he "carried a pretty large sum of money
at times."

JOHN F. KENNEDY HONORED

U.S. Memorials

Pres. Johnson announced Nov. 28, 1963 that Cape Canaveral, Fla. would be renamed Cape Kennedy and that its space installations would be called the John F. Kennedy Space Center. An Executive Order renaming the space center was issued Nov. 29; the cape was renamed effective Nov. 28. * It was reported that Mrs. Jacqueline Kennedy had asked Johnson for some memorial to her husband when the first Saturn rocket was scheduled to be launched from Canaveral (in Jan. 1964) because of Kennedy's great interest in space and devotion to the effort to make the U.S. the leader in space exploration.

Among numerous other steps taken to honor the late President:
● The Miami (Fla.) City Commission voted unanimously Nov. 29, 1963 to rename its Bayfront Park friendship torch (a symbol of U.S.-Latin American good-will) the John F. Kennedy Torch of Friendship.
● Pres. Johnson asked Congress Dec. 10, 1963 to approve the minting of 50¢ coins bearing a portrait of Kennedy. A bill to replace Alexander Hamilton's portrait on the $10 bill with one of Kennedy had been introduced in the House Nov. 29 by Rep. William S. Moorhead (D., Pa.). The initial stocks—26 million— of the 50¢ coins bearing the portrait of Kennedy went on sale Mar. 24, 1964.
● Sen. J. W. Fulbright (D., Ark.) and Rep. Carl Albert (D., Okla.) introduced in Congress Dec. 3, 1963 a Johnson Administration bill to name the proposed national cultural

---

* The city of Cape Canaveral, Fla. and the Cocoa Chamber of Commerce Dec. 4, 1963 adopted resolutions opposing the changing of the name of Cape Canaveral to Cape Kennedy. The Senate Committee on Interior & Insular Affairs heard testimony Nov. 24, 1969 from Florida Sens. Spessard L. Holland (D.) and Edward J. Gurney (R.) and 3 other Floridians that "the historic name [of] Canaveral ... should be restored ... to the Cape as a matter of law." The 5 testified that Johnson's action (to rename the Cape in 1963) was illegal since the President of the U.S. does not have the authority to rename geographic locations. They agreed, however, that the name John F. Kennedy Space Center should be retained. A bill to restore the name to Cape Canaveral died in the Senate Interior Committee Dec. 30, 1970.

center in Washington, D.C. the John Fitzgerald Kennedy Memorial Center and to appropriate matching funds for it. The center was subsequently renamed the John F. Kennedy Center for the Performing Arts.

● The new Ohio River bridge between Louisville, Ky. and Jeffersonville, Ind. was dedicated Dec. 6, 1963 as the John Fitzgerald Kennedy Memorial Bridge.

● Legislation changing the name of New York's International (Idlewild) Airport to John F. Kennedy International Airport was approved unanimously by the N.Y. City Council Dec. 10, 1963 and was signed by Mayor Robert F. Wagner Dec. 18. The airport was rededicated Dec. 24.

● Pres. Johnson dedicated the John F. Kennedy Educational, Civil & Cultural Center at Mitchel Field in Nassau County, N.Y. May 9, 1964.

● Kennedy's daughter, Caroline, 9, christened the aircraft carrier *John F. Kennedy* at Newport News, Va. May 27, 1967. Also present were Mrs. Jacqueline Kennedy, his widow, John Jr., his son, and Pres. Johnson.

● John F. Kennedy's birthplace, a gray frame house in Brookline, Mass., was dedicated as a national historic site May 29, 1969, the 52d anniversary of the late President's birth. Attending the ceremony were Mrs. Joseph P. (Rose) Kennedy, Sen. and Mrs. Edward M. Kennedy (D., Mass.) and Sen. Kennedy's sister, Mrs. Stephen Smith. The house, which had been purchased by the elder Kennedys shortly after their marriage in 1914, had been restored under the family's supervision to include many of the original furnishings.

● A cenotaph (empty tomb) memorial, designed by New York architect Philip Johnson, was dedicated to the memory of Kennedy in Dallas, Tex. June 24, 1970, just 200 yards from the site of his assassination.

(A bill to rename Texas' state school for the mentally retarded in Kennedy's honor had been rejected by the state legislature in May 1965 because of his unpopularity in Texas.)

Foreign Memorials

Among foreign memorials to Pres. Kennedy:
● Foreign Min. Thanat Khoman of Thailand announced Nov.

27, 1963 that his country was establishing a John F. Kennedy Foundation to provide scholarships.

● The square before West Berlin's city hall, where the late President had made his *"Ich bin ein Berliner* I am a Berliner]" declaration June 26, 1963, was dedicated as John F. Kennedy Platz Nov. 30, 1963 at a ceremony attended by more than 250,000 West Berliners.

The late President's brother, Atty. Gen. Robert F. Kennedy, unveiled a bronze memorial plaque to John F. Kennedy on the facade of West Berlin's city hall (Schoenberger Rathaus) June 26, 1964.

Bonn's Rhine bridge was renamed the Kennedy-Bruecke Dec. 2, 1963.

● Rue Clemenceau, a main street in Beirut, Lebanon, was renamed Kennedy Street Nov. 30, 1963.

● A monument honoring Kennedy was dedicated by Queen Elizabeth of Great Britain May 14, 1965 at Runnymede, England, where King John had signed the Magna Carta in 1215. The site was bequeathed in perpetuity to the U.S. The inscription on the monument read: "This acre of English ground was given to the United States of America by the people of Britain in memory of John F. Kennedy. . . ." (The memorial was found heavily damaged by a bomb Oct. 27, 1968. Police speculated that the blast was connected with an anti-Vietnamese war march held in London the same day.)

● A memorial to the late President was dedicated 5 miles west of Jerusalem July 4, 1966 by Israeli and U.S. leaders, among them U.S. Chief Justice Earl Warren. The memorial marked the site of a planned Kennedy Peace Forest.

● Kennedy's mother, Rose Kennedy, who had been widowed Nov. 18, 1969, dedicated the John F. Kennedy Memorial Library at Haile Selassie University in Addis Ababa, Ethiopia July 23, 1970. The ceremony was part of a joint birthday celebration for Emperor Haile Selassie, who was 78 July 23, and for Mrs. Kennedy, who was 80 July 22.

Posthumous Awards

Among many awards honoring Pres. Kennedy posthumously:

● Sen. Abraham A. Ribicoff (D., Conn.) announced in New

York Dec. 1, 1963 that the annual peace award of the
Synagogue Council of America had been renamed the John
Fitzgerald Kennedy Peace Award. He said Mr. Kennedy had
been chosen its winner before his death.
● Pres. Johnson awarded posthumous Presidential Medals of
Freedom, the U.S.' highest civilian honor, to Kennedy and
Pope John XXIII (who had died June 3, 1963) in Washington,
D.C. Dec. 6, 1963. Kennedy's award was accepted by his
brother, Atty. Gen. Robert F. Kennedy, while Mrs. Jacqueline
Kennedy watched from an anteroom. Johnson had added the
names of the late President and the pope to the original list of
31 winners selected by Kennedy before his death.
● The 19th constitutional convention of the United Automobile
Workers, held in Atlantic City, N.J. Mar. 20-26, 1964, awarded
Kennedy the union's social justice award. It was accepted by
Atty. Gen. Kennedy Mar. 22.
● John F. Kennedy was awarded the 4 Freedoms Foundation
Award for 1964 for service to the ideals of Franklin D.
Roosevelt. The plaque was presented to Robert F. Kennedy in
New York May 25, 1965 by Commerce Undersecy. Franklin D.
Roosevelt Jr.
    (The broadcasting industry was awarded a special George
Foster Peabody Award [for achievement in radio and TV] Apr.
29, 1964 for their coverage of Kennedy's assassination and the
aftermath.)

Special Films

    Several special motion pictures dealing with Pres.
Kennedy's Administration and his assassination were released
during the first 2 years after his death. Among the films and
events involving them:
● Atty. Gen. Robert F. Kennedy was accorded a 16-minute
ovation by the delegates at the 34th Democratic National
Convention when he appeared to introduce *A Thousand Days,*
a film produced as a tribute to John F. Kennedy, at the final
session of the convention in Atlantic City, N.J. Aug. 27, 1964.
(Mrs. Jacqueline Kennedy, who did not attend any of the
convention sessions, greeted more than 5,000 persons at a
reception given in her honor in an Atlantic City hotel Aug. 27,

1964 by State Undersecy. W. Averell Harriman. Excerpts from
John F. Kennedy's favorite poetry were read.)

● *Four Days in November,* a documentary about the events
between the late President's assassination and his funeral, was
released to commercial motion picture theaters in New York
Oct. 7, 1964. The film, presented by David L. Wolper and
released through United Artists, had been produced and
directed by Mel Stuart. Its screenplay was written by Theodore
Strauss.

● *John F. Kennedy: Years of Lightning, Day of Drums,* a
documentary about the Presidency and death of John F.
Kennedy narrated by actor Gregory Peck, was released
commercially by Embassy Pictures in New York Apr. 10, 1966.
The film, written, directed and scored by Bruce Herschensohn,
had been produced by George Stevens Jr. for the U.S.
Information Agency's overseas program. It required an act of
Congress to make possible the release of the film to theaters in
the U.S. A resolution permitting its domestic distribution was
passed by the Senate Aug. 26, 1965 and by the House Oct. 7,
1965 and was signed by Pres. Johnson Oct. 20, 1965. All profits
from the film were to go to the John F. Kennedy Center for the
Performing Arts.

Biographical Books

   The personal and political life of Pres. Kennedy was
examined in several books published after his death. Many were
personal reminiscences by former members of his White House
staff. Among the books:

● *My Twelve Years with John F. Kennedy,* by Evelyn Lincoln,
published Aug. 30, 1965 by David McKay Co. The President's
longtime personal secretary told what it was like to work for
the Chief Executive.

● *Kennedy,* by Theodore C. Sorensen, published Oct. 5, 1965 by
Harper & Row. A close-up portrait of the late President by his
former friend and legislative aide.

● *John Fitzgerald Kennedy ... As We Remember Him,* edited
by Goddard Lieberson, published Nov. 9, 1965 by Atheneum.
Reflections on the late President by his relatives and associates;
many photos.

● *A Thousand Days: John F. Kennedy in the White House,* by
Arthur M. Schlesinger Jr., published Nov. 29, 1965 by
Houghton Mifflin. An informed view of the Kennedy
Administration by a historian who had served as the President's
special aide and speech writer.
● *With Kennedy,* by Pierre Salinger, published Sept. 6, 1966 by
Doubleday. Kennedy's press secretary's memoirs.
● *The Day Kennedy Was Shot,* by Jim Bishop, published Nov.
22, 1968 by Funk & Wagnalls. A detailed account of the
assassination day. (The late President's widow had urged
Bishop not to write the book, and the Kennedy family refused
any aid to the author.)
● *My Life With Jacqueline Kennedy,* by Mary B. Gallagher,
edited by Frances Spatz Leighton, published Sept. 15, 1969 by
David McKay Co. Memoirs of the former first lady's personal
secretary.
● *Ambassador's Journal. A Personal Account of the Kennedy
Years,* by John Kenneth Galbraith, published Oct. 20, 1969 by
Houghton Mifflin. Memoirs of the former U.S. ambassador to
India, a close Kennedy friend.

Manchester Book Controversy

Another book, *The Death of a President,* an account of the
assassination, written by William Raymond Manchester,
became the subject of controversy prior to its publication.

Mrs. Jacqueline Kennedy Dec. 16, 1966 took legal action
against William Manchester, Harper & Row Publishers, Inc.
and Cowles Communications, Inc. (the publishers of *Look*
magazine) to block book publication and magazine serialization
of *The Death of a President.* Mrs. Kennedy charged that the
defendants had violated her wishes, her contract with
Manchester and "the dignity and privacy which my children
and I have striven with difficulty to retain."

Manchester, 44, author in 1962 of a flattering book about
the late Kennedy, *Portrait of a President,* had been chosen by
Mrs. Kennedy in Mar. 1964 to write the authorized account of
the assassination. An 11-point memo stating the conditions of
publication was signed by Manchester and Robert F. Kennedy
Mar. 26, 1964. It said: (a) The Kennedy family would cooperate
exclusively with Manchester on the subject; (b) the completed

manuscript would be reviewed by Mrs. Kennedy and Robert Kennedy and "shall not be published unless and until approved by them"; (c) the book would "not be published before Nov. 22, 1968, unless Mrs. Kennedy designates a prior date."

Early in Apr. 1964 Manchester interviewed Mrs. Kennedy on 2 successive days and tape-recorded their conversations. In these sessions Mrs. Kennedy reportedly made "no attempt at self-censorship" and "revealed her deepest thoughts." Manchester worked on the book until late 1965; editing began early in 1966. At some point while manuscript changes were being negotiated with Kennedy representatives, Manchester reportedly expressed concern that the book might not be published. In July 1966 Robert Kennedy sent Manchester a telegram that, Manchester contended, left him free to publish the book. The telegram said, in part, that "members of the Kennedy family will place no obstacle in the way of publication of his book."

Mrs. Kennedy Dec. 14, 1966 served a summons (a notification of intention to pursue court action) on Harper & Row and *Look* magazine. Mrs. Kennedy's attorney, ex-Federal Judge Simon H. Rifkind, sued in N.Y. State Supreme Court Dec. 16 to enjoin publication of the manuscript. Mrs. Kennedy's complaint charged that publication of the book would cause her "great and irreparable injury" and "result in precisely the sensationalism and commercialism which we—Robert F. Kennedy and I—have sought so strenuously to avoid." The complaint said Manchester had exploited Mrs. Kennedy's emotional state when he recorded her recollections of the assassination.

Manchester Dec. 18 issued a statement denying that he had "broken faith." He said: "Mrs. Kennedy asked me to write this book; I did not seek the opportunity. Mrs. Kennedy gave me 10 hours of interviews; I did not, indeed could not, have conducted these interviews without her voluntary cooperation. Mrs. Kennedy herself did not ask to see the manuscript and still hasn't. If she had, I would, of course, have given it to her."

Cass Canfield, chairman of the executive committee of Harper & Row, issued a statement Dec. 19 defending the decision to publish the book in the "interest of historical accuracy and of the people's right to know the true facts...."

Robert Kennedy, vacationing in Sun Valley, Ida., said Dec. 18 that the publishers had forced a suit by withholding from the Kennedy family or its representatives, until after the lawsuit had been filed Dec. 16, the version of the manuscript planned for publication.

The dispute on the serialization of the book in *Look* (then scheduled to begin Jan. 10, 1967) was resolved Dec. 21, 1966 after *Look* agreed to delete 1,600 words that dealt with the personal life of Mrs. Kennedy and her children. Mrs. Kennedy then said, however, that neither she nor Robert Kennedy had "in any way approved or endorsed the material in the *Look* article...."

Mrs. Kennedy and Harper & Row agreed Dec. 27, 1966 (the date set for a N.Y. State Supreme Court hearing) to continue negotiations and to postpone the hearing to allow time for an out-of-court settlement.

Meanwhile, reports on the contents of the book, attributed to publishing sources who claimed to have read the manuscript, had said that Pres. Johnson would have had reason to be displeased by Manchester's portrayal of his actions immediately following the assassination. According to the Dec. 18, 1966 *N.Y. Times,* one source recalled that the book had pictured Johnson's behavior in the plane returning to Washington from Dallas as gauche and insensitive, especially in his desire to immediately assert his Presidential authority.

The first concrete expression of rumors that Johnson was unhappy about the Manchester book came in the Dec. 26, 1966 issue of *Newsweek* magazine. Attributing its information to "intimates" of the President, *Newsweek* reported that Johnson was hurt by the Manchester allegations and that his recollections differed in major respects from those reportedly contained in the book.

White House Press Secy. George Christian told newsmen in Austin, Tex. Dec. 26 that Johnson had not seen either the Manchester manuscript or the *Newsweek* article. He said that *Newsweek's* statements were "inaccurate and untrue." Christian denied that the President had given an interview to anyone on the matter and declared that he would not do so in the future.

Both Harper & Row and Manchester filed separate answers Jan. 5, 1967 to Mrs. Kennedy's suit in N.Y. Supreme Court. They denied charges that they had violated Mrs. Kennedy's dignity and privacy and insisted that they had received her consent and approval to go ahead with early publication of the book.

A settlement of the dispute was reached Jan. 16, 1967 when Harper & Row and Manchester agreed to a number of deletions and modifications in the text. Shortly after N.Y. State Supreme Court Justice Saul S. Streit signed a consent decree, the 3 parties to the suit issued a joint statement to the press. Declaring that they had resolved the dispute, they said: "Certain passages of concern to Mrs. Kennedy have been deleted or modified by mutual agreement of all the parties.... All parties agree that the historical record has not been censored in any way."

Although details of the modifications were not made public, Cass Canfield of Harper & Row said that the changes involved "a cumulative total of some 7 pages in a book of 654 pages of text...."

A statement made on behalf of Mrs. Kennedy said that the title page of each copy of the book would carry the following publisher's note: "Harper & Row wishes to make it clear that neither Mrs. Kennedy nor Sen. Robert F. Kennedy has in any way endorsed the material appearing in this book. The author, William Manchester, and the publishers assume complete responsibility."

These additional conditions were reported Jan. 17, 1967: (1) With the exception of one copy each for Harper & Row and Mrs. Kennedy and 2 copies for Manchester, all 45 copies of the original manuscript would be destroyed within 45 days; (2) Manchester's 10 hours of taped interviews with Mrs. Kennedy would be placed under seal at the Kennedy Memorial Library in Cambridge, Mass.; (3) Robert Kennedy would waive rights set down in the memo signed by him and Manchester Mar. 26, 1964; (4) U.S. news media was prohibited from publishing the excised parts of the original manuscript without the consent of Mrs. Kennedy; (5) the publication of letters from Pres. Johnson to Mrs. Kennedy and her children would not be permitted without the consent of the President; (6) Manchester would return all personal letters to Mrs. Kennedy; (7) the decree resolving the controversy would be "in full force and effect until the expiration of 100 years" from the time of signing.

(White House Press Secy. George Christian said Jan. 17, 1967 that Pres. Johnson was "content to leave entirely to Mrs. Kennedy the question of publication of letters he has written to her.")

The Death of a President: November 20—November 25, 1963 was finally published by Harper & Row Apr. 7, 1967.

THE GARRISON PROBE

Investigation Disclosed

A new public investigation into the assassination of Pres. Kennedy was launched early in 1967 by Jim (James) Garrison, 46, district attorney of New Orleans, La. The probe centered on the theory that Lee Harvey Oswald was a member of a relatively widespread conspiracy aimed at murdering the President. It rejected the Warren Commission's findings that Oswald had acted alone. As his inquiry progressed, Garrison was widely assailed as a publicity seeker acting for political motives, and a man he named as an important participant in the alleged assassination plot was acquitted in a conspiracy trial in 1969.

The story of the Garrison probe was revealed nationally through a copyrighted article published Feb. 17, 1967 by the *New Orleans States-Item.* The newspaper's disclosure was confirmed by Garrison at a New Orleans press conference Feb. 18. Garrison declared that his investigation, under way since Oct. 1966, already had shown that the Warren Commission report was inaccurate in its finding of no conspiracy. He said that "there were other people besides Lee Harvey Oswald involved" and that the conspiracy had centered on New Orleans, where Oswald "had spent 6 months ... shortly before the assassination."

Garrison declared: "We already have the names of the people in the initial planning.... Arrests will be made. Charges will be filed and convictions will be obtained."

In a skeptical editorial published Feb. 18, the *States-Item* implied that Garrison was principally interested in gaining "exposure in a national magazine." Garrison called a news conference Feb. 20 (local newspapers were barred) and replied that the arrests of those who had conspired to kill Kennedy "probably were just a few weeks away until the disclosures of the investigation by the local newspapers. Now they are most certainly months away."

In the weeks that followed the disclosure of the investigation, Garrison was reported to have assembled scores of persons as Kennedy assassination witnesses or suspects.

According to press reports, Garrison believed that Oswald had been part of a conspiracy originally directed at the assassination of Cuban Premier Fidel Castro. Garrison was said to have theorized that the plot had turned against Kennedy when Oswald was denied entry to Cuba. Witnesses collected by Garrison testified before a New Orleans grand jury in the next few weeks, but only one man was arrested and no date was set for his trial. By May, national news media were treating the investigation as a hoax.

(Garrison had first gained the attention of the press during a campaign that he had launched against vice and crime in New Orleans' French Quarter in 1962-3. When his request for additional funds for the probe was rejected by 8 New Orleans Criminal District Court judges late in 1962, Garrison was quoted as saying the action raised "interesting questions about racketeer influences." The statement led to a lawsuit, and Garrison was convicted Feb. 6, 1963 of defaming the 8 judges. He was sentenced to 4 months in prison and fined $1,000. The conviction was overturned by the U.S. Supreme Court Nov. 23, 1964.)

The Defense Department disclosed Dec. 29, 1967 that Garrison "was released from active [military] duty by reason of physical disability" Oct. 31, 1951 with the rank of captain in the National Guard. The Pentagon said Garrison was currently a lieutenant colonel in the U.S. Army Reserve. He had served in the National Guard on 4 separate occasions beginning in June 1939 and terminating with his resignation Feb. 28, 1967.

A copyrighted article in the *Chicago Tribune* Dec. 29, 1967 asserted that Garrison had been under psychiatric care from 1950 to 1955. The article said Garrison had been "discharged from the Army as totally unfit for military duty."

Details of the Investigation

5 days after the *States-Item's* initial disclosure of the investigation, David William Ferrie, 49, a former airline pilot and prime Garrison suspect, was found dead in his apartment in New Orleans Feb. 22, 1967.

The New Orleans coroner, Dr. Nicholas Chetta, said Ferrie had died of a ruptured blood vessel in the brain, and this was confirmed Feb. 23 by an autopsy. Garrison, however, disputed the autopsy finding. He had called a news conference Feb. 22 and said: "The apparent suicide of David Ferrie ends the life of a man who, in my judgment, was one of history's most important individuals. Evidence developed by our office had long since confirmed that he was involved in events culminating in the assassination of Pres. Kennedy. Apparently we waited too long." Garrison gave no details as to how Ferrie was involved in the alleged conspiracy.

(Ferrie was a former Eastern Airlines pilot who had been dismissed from the company because of a record of homosexual arrests. He had been questioned by the FBI in Nov. 1963 in connection with the assassination. Although he reportedly had been involved in anti-Castro activities, Ferrie had denied knowing Oswald, and no further FBI action was reported. Dr. Chetta said Feb. 24 that Ferrie's physician had reported that Ferrie had threatened to sue Garrison for trying to frame him.)

Documents made public by the National Archives Feb. 23-24 alleged that a connection had existed between Oswald and Ferrie. After the assassination, Jack S. Martin, 51, a New Orleans private detective and bishop of an obscure dissident Catholic sect in which he had ordained Ferrie, had told Garrison that Ferrie had known Oswald. Both were said to have been members of the same Civil Air Patrol unit, and Ferrie was said to have coached Oswald in the use of rifles with telescopic sights. Shortly thereafter, however, in statements to the Secret Service and the FBI, Martin confessed that the stories linking Oswald and Ferrie were "a figment of my imagination."

Garrison announced Feb. 24 that his staff had "solved" the assassination but that he would need months or years to "work on details of evidence" and to make arrests. He said: "We know what cities were involved, how it was done in the essential respects, and the individuals involved." "It's my personal belief that Oswald did not kill anyone that day."

In the days following Ferrie's death, the press reported that the investigation had centered on anti-Castro Cuban refugees. The *Washington Post* said Feb. 26 that Garrison was preparing to question Sergio Arcacha Smith, 44, who had been head of the local branch of the Frente Revolucinario Democratico, a Cuban liberation group. Arcacha, located in

Dallas, said that he had helped to organize the Bay of Pigs invasion although he had not taken part in it personally.

Garrison Mar. 1 ordered the arrest of Clay L. Shaw, 54, retired director of the International Trade Mart, a non-profit organization formed to promote trade through the port of New Orleans. Shaw was charged with "participation in a conspiracy to murder John F. Kennedy" and was released on $10,000 bond. In the application for a warrant to search Shaw's home, Garrison charged that Shaw, "alias Clay Bertrand," had met with Oswald and Ferrie in Ferrie's apartment to plan Pres. Kennedy's assassination.

Garrison credited his information to a "confidential informant" who had been given sodium pentothal, a "truth drug," and had corroborated his earlier story of overhearing the plotters. Garrison also subpoenaed James R. Lewallen, 38, a Boeing Co. employe, Mar. 1 and Dean Adams Andrews Jr., a lawyer and part-time district attorney of neighboring Jefferson Parish, Mar. 2. (In testimony before the Warren Commission, Andrews had linked Shaw and Oswald but later had said that his testimony was false.) Garrison Mar. 3 subpoenaed Dante Marachini, 42, who had worked for the same coffee-processing firm, though not in the same plant, as Oswald had in the summer of 1963. J. B. Dauenhauer, a former assistant to Clay Shaw, was subpoenaed Mar. 6.

U.S. Atty. Gen. Ramsey Clark Mar. 12 labeled the Garrison investigation "unfortunate." He said: "I find it curious and I find it disturbing and I find it saddening." Clark Mar. 2 had told newsmen that on the basis of FBI inquiries there was "no connection" between Clay Shaw and the assassination of Pres. Kennedy. (The Justice Department reported June 2 that Clay Shaw had not been investigated by the FBI after the assassination and that Clark's statement to the contrary had been "erroneous.")

In an unusual legal move, Garrison called a 12-member grand jury into preliminary session Mar. 9 to question witnesses 5 days ahead of its scheduled hearing.

A 3-judge panel convened Mar. 12 to rule on Garrison's claim to have sufficient evidence to try Clay Shaw without grand jury action. The judges Mar. 13 rejected a defense request to have the case heard by a single judge. They also refused defense requests to have access to daily transcripts of the preliminary hearing and to introduce the Warren Commission's report as evidence.

Perry Raymond Russo, 25, an insurance agent for the Equitable Life Assurance Society, testified Mar. 14 before the 3-judge panel that he had seen Ferrie, a "Leon Oswald" and someone called Clem Bertrand (whom he identified in the courtroom as Shaw) in Ferrie's apartment on 3 different occasions in Sept. 1963. Russo said he had overheard the 3 men discuss plans for the assassination of Pres. Kennedy.

Russo, however, admitted Mar. 15 that he had failed to recognize pictures of Lee Harvey Oswald as "Leon Oswald" until Garrison's investigators painted a beard on the photos. Russo also said that he had attended a party at Ferrie's with a girl named Sandra Moffett. He testified that Oswald then had shared Ferrie's apartment. (This statement on Oswald's place of residence had been contradicted by the Warren Commission.)

(In a Feb. 24, 1967 TV interview in New Orleans, Russo had said he had not met Oswald nor had he heard of him before the assassination. A sound track of the interview played in the courtroom Mar. 15 contradicted much of Russo's testimony. Steve Derby, 20, a friend of Russo's, said in Baton Rouge Mar. 15 that Russo had not spoken of the alleged conspiracy until he was placed under hypnosis by Garrison's investigators. Russo admitted Mar. 16 that the investigators had placed him under hypnosis 3 times before the hearing. Russo also said that he had seen Oswald in Oct. 1963 and that Oswald at that time was clean-shaven.)

Vernon W. Bundy Jr., 29, a former narcotics addict, testified Mar. 17 that he had seen Shaw and Oswald together on the shore of Lake Pontchartrain, near New Orleans, in the summer of 1963 just as he was preparing to inject the contents of 2 capsules of heroin in his arm.

At the conclusion of testimony Mar. 17, the 3 judges ruled that there was sufficient evidence to try Shaw.

The grand jury Mar. 16 indicted Dean Andrews on charges of perjury after he refused to identify Clay Shaw as the man he said had tried to hire him in Nov. 1963 to defend Lee Harvey Oswald after the assassination. (Andrews had advised Oswald on minor legal affairs when the latter lived in New Orleans early in 1963.) The perjury case was based on inconsistencies in Andrews' statements before the grand jury. Andrews, consequently suspended as district attorney of Jefferson Parish, pleaded not guilty at his arraignment Mar. 22. He filed a $100,000 damage suit against Garrison Apr. 18 because, he said, Garrison had "compelled me to answer questions designed to trap me." (A New Orleans jury convicted Andrews of perjury Aug. 14, 1967.)

The grand jury Mar. 22 indicted Clay Shaw, charging that he had been party to a conspiracy with Oswald, Ferrie "and others" between Sept. 1 and Oct. 10, 1963.

Garrison Mar. 23 issued subpoenas for Patrick L. Martens (or Layton Martens) and Donald Dooty. Mrs. Lillie-Mae McMaines, the former Sandra Moffett, was taken into custody Mar. 28 in Omaha on a fugitive-from-justice warrant. She had told the *Omaha World Herald* Mar. 26 that she had not attended a party at Ferrie's apartment with Russo and that she had first met Ferrie in 1965.

New Orleans Criminal Court Judge Matthew S. Braniff Mar. 23 issued a warrant for the arrest of Gordon Novel, 29, a former New Orleans night-club operator. Garrison had filed an affidavit with Braniff swearing that he had "good reason to believe" that Novel was a "most important" witness in the case.

Novel was arrested in Gahanna, O. Apr. 1; he appeared in municipal court in Columbus, O. Apr. 3 and was held in jail in lieu of $10,000 bond. He had been picked up at Garrison's request on a fugitive charge stemming from an accusation of conspiring to commit burglary. Freed on $10,000 bail Apr. 4, Novel said he could prove that the whole investigation was "a complete fabrication."

Novel said in Columbus Apr. 24 that Garrison's investigation was a "fraud" motivated by his political ambitions. Novel disclosed that in a lie-detector test given to him Mar. 25, he had said he had overheard Garrison plotting to brainwash Ferrie to make him confess to a role in the conspiracy.

At his formal arraignment in New Orleans Apr. 5 Clay Shaw pleaded not guilty. A New Orleans grand jury indicted Patrick Martens the same day on perjury charges for denying he knew Novel and Arcacha, the Cuban exile leader.

An article in the May 6 issue of the *Saturday Evening Post* (released Apr. 24) cited evidence that tended to discredit the testimony of Garrison's principal witness, Perry Russo. *Post* writer James Phelan said that Garrison had made available to him statements by Russo that revealed discrepancies in his accounts of the alleged connection between the accused conspirators. One document cited, a report to Garrison on Russo's initial interrogation, showed that he had made no mention of an assassination plot or of a party at Ferrie's apartment.

Phelan also said: "There was no positive identification of Lee Harvey Oswald as 'Leon' Oswald ..., [and] most striking of all, when shown a picture of Clay Shaw, Russo said nothing whatever ... about having known him as Clay Bertrand." Phelan reported evidence that Russo had remembered the party only when given sodium pentothal. He said that Dr. Esmond Fatter had placed Russo in an hypnotic state and had told him to picture a TV screen on which he would see "Bertrand, Ferrie and Oswald ..., and they are talking about assassinating somebody."

Andrew J. Sciambra, Russo's first interrogator, said in New Orleans Apr. 24 that Phelan was "purposely" trying "to mislead the American public by telling a half-truth and not showing the full picture." He said that Russo had mentioned the conspiracy in the first interview and that this had been verified to Phelan by Russo himself.

Writing in the May 15 issue of *Newsweek* magazine, Hugh Aynesworth charged that Garrison, in his "scheme to concoct a fantastic 'solution'," had offered Alvin Beaubouef, a friend of Ferrie's, $3,000 to testify that he had overheard the planning of the assassination. Aynesworth said that Beaubouef and his lawyer had tape-recorded the meetings with Garrison's men, who, on learning of the tape, allegedly had forced Beaubouef to sign an affidavit declaring he did not consider the $3,000 offer to be a bribe.

(*N.Y. Times* correspondent Gene Roberts reported June 11 that 2 Louisiana convicts had asserted that Garrison's office had offered them their freedom if they would cooperate in the investigation. Miguel Torres, a heroin addict in prison for burglary, reportedly said that he had also been offered heroin and a Florida vacation if he would cooperate by saying that he had known Shaw. Another convicted burglar, John Cancler, reportedly said that Garrison's investigators indicated that charges against him might be dropped if he would "put

something" in Shaw's house. Cancler, brought before the grand
jury, refused July 12 to confirm or deny his statement. Criminal
Court Judge Bernard J. Dagert held him in contempt and
immediately sentenced him to 6 months imprisonment and fined
him $500.)

Garrison announced May 8 that he had begun to
investigate the CIA and the FBI. He charged that both
organizations were withholding evidence about the
assassination.

Garrison May 10 subpoenaed CIA Director Richard Helms
to testify before the New Orleans grand jury. He also
announced that he possessed evidence that Oswald had been an
agent of the CIA. FBI agent Regis Kennedy was subpoenaed
by Garrison but refused May 10 to appear before the grand
jury. Kennedy had been instructed by Atty. Gen. Ramsey Clark
not to answer the subpoena. (Kennedy appeared May 17, but he
refused to answer questions on the assassination. A Justice
Department order prohibited officers or employes from
"producing or disclosing information on material contained in
the files of the Department of Justice.") Ex-FBI agent Warren
DeBrueys also was subpoenaed but did not appear.

Garrison announced May 12 that he had discovered Jack
Ruby's unlisted telephone number written in code in address
books belonging to Oswald and Shaw. (The *Dallas Times
Herald* reported May 17 that the number was the post-office
box number of a bullfight promoter in Dallas.)

Garrison declared May 22 that Oswald had not killed
Kennedy and that the CIA knew this fact as well as "the name
of every man involved and the name of the individuals who
pulled the triggers" to kill Kennedy. He said: "Purely and
simply it's a case of former employes of the CIA, a large
number of them Cubans, having a venomous reaction from the
1961 Bay of Pigs episode. Certain individuals with a fusion of
interests in regaining Cuba assassinated the President."

TV Networks Assail Garrison

Garrison's investigation of the Kennedy assassination was
sharply criticized in special telecasts broadcast by the National
Broadcasting Co. (NBC) and Columbia Broadcasting System
(CBS) in June 1967.

In the NBC telecast—*The JFK Conspiracy: The Case of Jim Garrison*—it was charged June 19 that Garrison had intimidated potential witnesses and offered them bribes to secure their cooperation. In a filmed interview, Fred Leemans, former operator of a New Orleans Turkish bath, claimed that Garrison and his investigators had offered him money to "remember" that Clay Shaw had frequented his establishment under the name Clay Bertrand and was accompanied by a young man named Lee.

During the NBC broadcast, it was alleged that lie-detector tests on 2 key Garrison witnesses had cast grave doubts on their testimony. It was reported that Vernon Bundy, a narcotics addict who had testified before a grand jury in March that Shaw used the name Bertrand, had been given a lie-detector test before his testimony and that despite its negative findings Garrison had used his testimony. It was also reported on the telecast that Bundy, currently in a prison hospital, had told a fellow inmate that he had testified for Garrison "because this is the only way I can get cut loose." Perry Russo, another witness who said Shaw used the name Bertrand, also had showed a "deceptive-criteria" in a lie-detector test, according to statements made on the telecast. It was reported that NBC investigators had located the real Clay Bertrand and that he was not Shaw but a New Orleans homosexual.

Garrison June 19 issued a statement in reply to the NBC broadcast. He said: "All of the screaming and hollering now being heard is evidence that we have caught a very large fish. It is obvious that there are elements in Washington, D.C. which are desperate because we are in the process of uncovering their hoax."

Russo said June 20 that NBC investigator Walter Sheridan had offered "to set me up in California, protect my job and guarantee that Garrison would never get me extradited back to Louisiana" if he would "side with NBC and the defense [of Shaw]." He said another NBC representative had threatened to wreck his reputation if he refused to cooperate. NBC spokesmen denied Russo's charges June 20.

Garrison was given 30 minutes of free broadcast time on NBC July 15 under the "equal time" rule to rebut the charges aired by the network. He said that at least 3 men had shot

Kennedy and that the Warren Commission's contention that Oswald had been a lone assassin was a "fairy tale."

The New Orleans district attorney's office July 7 charged Sheridan with bribing Russo. Richard Townley, an investigator for WDSU-TV, the NBC affiliate in New Orleans, was charged July 11 with bribery and intimidation in connection with the production of the network broadcast.

CBS presented its report on the assassination in 4 consecutive evening TV documentary reports beginning June 25, 1967. During the 2d broadcast, June 26, the surgeon in charge of the Kennedy autopsy said that X-rays of the President's body had refuted contentions that the wound in Kennedy's back was too low to support Warren Commission findings that the same bullet had wounded Gov. John Connally. (Critics of the commission had insisted that 2 separate bullets had caused the wounds.) Garrison said in a taped interview June 27, during the 3d broadcast, that Oswald had been used as a "decoy" by the real assassins in the hope he would be killed by the Dallas police. When this plan failed, Garrison contended, "it was necessary for one of the people involved [Jack Ruby] to kill him."

Speaking on the final CBS broadcast June 28, John J. McCloy, a lawyer and former diplomat who had served on the Warren Commission, expressed regret that the commission had not studied the photos and X-rays taken of Kennedy after the assassination. McCloy said the panel was "perhaps a little oversensitive to what we understood were the sensitivities of the Kennedy family." McCloy, however, fully defended the conclusions of the report. In its summation of the 4-part series, the network generally supported the Warren Commission report but was critical of the commission's decision to allow Federal agencies—the CIA, the FBI and the Secret Service—to investigate questions involving their own actions.

Garrison Aide Quits

William Gurvich, one of Garrison's key investigators, resigned June 26, 1967 and declared that he had found "no truth" in Garrison's allegations of a conspiracy in the murder of Kennedy. Gurvich urged the Orleans Parish grand jury to begin an immediate investigation into the conduct of the

Garrison inquiry. In a telegram to the grand jury, Gurvich offered "to give evidence of travesties of justice on the part of the district attorney in the case of Louisiana *vs.* Clay Shaw." Gurvich was reported to have told Sen. Robert F. Kennedy at a meeting June 8 that the investigation had "no basis in fact."

Garrison charged later June 26 that Gurvich's resignation was "the latest move from the Eastern headquarters of 'the Establishment' to attempt to discredit our investigation into the true facts of Pres. Kennedy's assassination." He insisted that despite Gurvich's claim to a key role in the investigation, his assignments "were limited to photography, chauffeuring and other technical work of a limited nature."

Gurvich said June 27 that Garrison had become so "obsessed" with the investigation that he had considered raiding the local FBI office for further evidence.

Garrison Continues Charges

Garrison said in an interview in the Oct. 1967 issue of *Playboy* magazine that "a team of at least 7 men, including anti-Castro adventurers and members of the para-military right" had participated in the Kennedy assassination. He said the conspirators were upset by the President's peace overtures to Cuba and the Soviet Union. Garrison asserted that conspirators had fired at the President from at least 3 places.

In taped interviews in New York Sept. 21, 1967, Garrison charged that members of the Dallas police force were "involved in the assassination and the protection of the assassins." He said the assassins were "big business, Texas style—a handful of tremendously oil-rich psychotic individuals." He charged that Sen. Robert F. Kennedy had "done everything he could to obstruct the investigation" because the "development of truth about the assassination" "would interfere with his political career."

On a copyrighted production on WFAA-TV in Dallas Dec. 9, Garrison said Kennedy had been killed by a bullet from a .45-caliber pistol that was shot by a man standing in a manhole that connected with a drainage system under Dealey Plaza. The assassin, he declared, had fled through the drainage system.

Garrison filed charges in New Orleans Dec. 20 against Edgar Eugene Bradley, 49, a regional representative of Dr. Carl McIntire, director of the American Council of Christian Churches, as a conspirator in the plot to assassinate Kennedy. A warrant for Bradley's arrest was issued Dec. 21. Bradley voluntarily surrendered to authorities in Los Angeles Dec. 27 and said that the charge was a case of mistaken identity.

Garrison issued subpoenas in New Orleans Dec. 29 for the arrest of 3 "material witnesses": Loran E. Hall of California, Lawrence J. Howard of Los Angeles and Thomas E. Beckham of Omaha.

Mrs. Marina Oswald Porter, widow of Lee Harvey Oswald (she had married electronics worker Kenneth Jess Porter June 1, 1965), was subpoenaed for grand jury testimony Jan. 23, 1968; she appeared before the jury Feb. 8 and was reportedly asked about Oswald's activities in New Orleans during the summer of 1963. Ex-CIA Director Allen W. Dulles was subpoenaed Feb. 16, 1968 on the basis that he "would have pertinent knowledge as to substantial reports that Lee Harvey Oswald was an agent and/or an employe of the CIA." A federal district judge Mar. 8 ordered Dulles to answer the subpoena, but he did not appear before the grand jury.

Also subpoenaed by Garrison were James Hicks (Jan. 4), a civilian employe at Vance Air Force Base in Enid, Okla., who was reportedly at the scene of the assassination, and Mrs. Ruth Paine, of Irving, Tex. (Mar. 25), who allegedly had carried Oswald's rifle (which the Warren Commission had identified as the assassination weapon) from New Orleans to Dallas in Sept. 1963.

In a TV interview Jan. 31, 1968 Garrison said that Jack Ruby had been seen near the scene of the assassination an hour before it occurred. Garrison reported that a Dallas resident, Julia Ann Mercer, had seen Ruby driving a truck from which a man carrying a rifle emerged; an affidavit, bearing her signature, had stated that she could not see the face of the driver, but she reportedly claimed that her signature had been forged. Garrison said she had identified Ruby's photo for the Dallas sheriff's office within 24 hours of the assassination and a day before Ruby shot Oswald.

Garrison asserted July 11, 1968 that he had exchanged information with a "military ally" of the U.S. that had "penetrated the forces involved in the assassination." The foreign government, which he declined to identify, had information and evidence about the killing, including "an interview with one of the assassins," he said. Garrison claimed that the evidence showed Kennedy had been assassinated "by elements of the Central Intelligence Agency."

The U.S. Supreme Court Dec. 9, 1968 affirmed a district court decision that refused to bar Garrison from prosecuting Clay L. Shaw on charges of conspiracy in the Kennedy assassination. Garrison had tried for more than 6 months to bring Shaw to trial. The Supreme Court's decision was issued without dissent (Chief Justice Earl Warren, chairman of the Warren Commission, abstained).

Shaw Acquitted

Clay L. Shaw, 55, brought to trial in New Orleans Jan. 21, 1969 on a charge of conspiring to assassinate Pres. Kennedy, was acquitted Mar. 1, 1969. An all-male jury in Criminal District Court heard the testimony of 66 witnesses and then delivered its unanimous verdict of not guilty.

The panel of 12 jurors and 2 alternates had been chosen in 2 weeks of careful questioning by Shaw's chief defense attorney, F. Irvin Dymond, and Garrison's chief assistant, James L. Alcock. Alcock conducted most of the prosecution with only brief appearances by Garrison. Criminal District Court Judge Edward A. Haggerty Jr.* had dismissed many prospective jurors as having "fixed" opinions about the case. About 1,400 prospective jurors were called before both sides agreed on the final 14 men. While questioning the prospective jurors, Alcock said repeatedly that the prosecution would not have to prove the murder of Kennedy in order to establish that

---

* Judge Haggerty was arrested in a New Orleans vice raid Dec. 17, 1969 and charged with soliciting for prostitution, obscenity and resisting arrest. Although he was later found not guilty, the incident and other allegations of his misconduct prompted the Louisiana Supreme Court, in a 6-to-1 ruling Nov. 23, 1970, to order Haggerty removed from office.

a conspiracy involving Shaw had taken place. Haggerty indicated to newsmen Feb. 5 that he would allow evidence about the actual assassination even though Shaw was charged only with conspiracy.

Before 200 spectators crowded into the small courtroom, Garrison said in his opening statement Feb. 6 that the state would prove that Kennedy's murder had been planned in New Orleans in the summer of 1963 by Shaw and others, including Oswald and David Ferrie. Garrison also said that Kennedy and Gov. Connally "were wounded as a result of gunshots fired by different guns at different locations."

Garrison's contention brought the first of many objections from the defense that Haggerty had established during the questioning of jurors that the Warren Commission report would not be an issue in the case. The judge disallowed this objection. Dymond, in his opening statement, said that the defense would prove not only that Shaw had not conspired with Oswald or Ferrie, but that "he never laid eyes on either one of these individuals." Dymond said that Perry Russo, who Garrison had said would be a chief prosecution witness, was a "notoriety-seeking liar."

Vernon Bundy repeated testimony that he had given to a panel of judges in 1967. Bundy told Alcock Feb. 7 that he had seen Shaw give Oswald a roll of money on the shore of a lake outside New Orleans. Bundy said he had gone there to "give myself a fix." Under cross-examination he denied that he had made up the story so that a jail sentence that he was serving would be reduced. 2 men who had been in jail with Bundy had quoted him as saying that the story was untrue.

Charles I. Spiesel, 50, a New York accountant, was one of the state's first major witnesses. He testified Feb. 7 that he had been at a party given by Shaw in the New Orleans French Quarter in June 1963 and had heard Shaw discuss with Ferrie and another man a hypothetical assassination of Pres. Kennedy. Under Dymond's cross-examination, however, Spiesel told of having been "hypnotized or tortured" by New York policemen, members of his accounting firm and other enemies as part of a Communist conspiracy. Spiesel said that he had a suit pending against his persecutors.

During 2 days of testimony Feb. 10-11, prosecution witness Russo, 27, an encyclopedia salesman, repeated statements he had made at a pre-trial session in 1967 that, at a party at Ferrie's apartment, he had heard discussion of a plan to assassinate Kennedy. Russo said that Oswald and a man introduced as Clem Bertrand were at the party but that the discussion of the assassination plan was dominated by Ferrie. In the courtroom Russo identified Shaw as the man introduced as Clem Bertrand. According to the prosecution, Shaw had used the Bertrand alias while conspiring to murder Kennedy.

Under cross-examination, Russo answered "yes" when Dymond asked whether the conversation he had heard could not "just as well have been an inconsequential bull session as anything serious." Dymond also questioned the witness on apparent inconsistencies between his testimony at the trial and his statements at the 1967 pre-trial session. Russo had said in 1967 that Sandra Moffett had accompanied him to the party. Miss Moffett (later Mrs. McMaines) had denied that she had been at the party; Russo told Dymond that he had mentioned her because "you kept pushing me" for names. When Dymond asked Russo about discrepancies between his current testimony and statements set down in a memo of a meeting between the witness and one of Garrison's assistants, Russo said that the memo was not complete—it contained no mention of a conversation about killing Kennedy. Russo said that he had not made a big point of the conversation, although he had mentioned it, and that the assistant apparently had not heard him or had thought it insignificant.

Dymond questioned Russo about Russo's statements to various people that he was unsure of his identification of Shaw as the man introduced to him as Bertrand. Russo replied that he had been "under terrible stress." Russo also said that he had been hypnotized 3 times before testifying at the preliminary hearing in 1967 and that the hypnosis had helped him remember Oswald and Shaw. Dymond suggested that the idea of the conspiracy might have been "implanted" in Russo's mind.*

---

* Russo and a companion, Carl Moore, 20, of Jefferson Parish, La., were arrested Aug. 22, 1970 on 3 counts of burglary and theft. Russo was convicted Sept. 24, 1970.

The prosecution Feb. 13 showed the jury color motion pictures of the assassination that had been filmed by Abraham Zapruder, a Dallas dress manufacturer. The state contended that the film, which seemed to show that Kennedy had been knocked backward against his seat when struck by a bullet, was partial proof that Kennedy had been hit by a bullet fired from the front. The Warren Commission had concluded that he had been hit only by bullets fired from the rear and that he had been forced backwards against his seat by the acceleration of the limousine. Over the objections of Dymond, who insisted that any testimony about the actual murder scene was irrelevant to the alleged conspiracy, the Zapruder film was shown a total of 11 times before the prosecution rested its case Feb. 21.

The defense opened its case Feb. 21 with testimony by Oswald's widow, Mrs. Marina Oswald Porter, that her husband had not known Shaw or Ferrie. An FBI firearms expert testified Feb. 22 that the shots fired at Kennedy had come from behind the President. An Army pathologist, who had assisted in the Kennedy autopsy, further upheld the findings of the Warren Commission Feb. 24. He testified that all available evidence, including X-rays made of the body,* disproved the prosecution's "cross-fire" theory.

The defense Feb. 25 presented testimony by Dean Andrews. Andrews' claim that he had been called by Clem Bertrand and asked to defend Oswald for the assassination of Kennedy had formed the basis for Garrison's investigation. Andrews said that he had made up the name Clem Bertrand. He testified that his whole story about Bertrand's request, which he had told the Warren Commission, had been a figment of his imagination.

The defense rested Feb. 27 after Shaw took the witness stand and denied that he had conspired to assassinate Kennedy.

In the week following Shaw's acquittal Garrison filed 3 charges related to the trial. Saying he had "just begun to fight," Garrison Mar. 3 charged Shaw with perjury. He said that Shaw had lied under oath Feb. 27 when he had testified that he had never known Oswald or Ferrie. Shaw was arrested on the charge but was released without having to post bond. Garrison

---

* Garrison had tried repeatedly through the courts to gain access to these X-rays and autopsy photos. The Justice Department successfully fought Garrison's efforts to subpoena the items deposited in the National Archives.

Mar. 4 ordered the arrest of Thomas Bethell, one of his former investigators, for allegedly giving the prosecution's trial plan to one of Shaw's attorneys in Aug. 1968. Dean Andrews was arrested Mar. 5 for perjury in connection with his testimony at the trial. He was charged with giving inconsistent statements to the Orleans Parish grand jury and to the Shaw trial jury. (Andrews had already been convicted in 1968 of lying to the grand jury.)

Clay Shaw Feb. 27, 1970 sued Garrison and several others involved in his prosecution for $5 million in damages. Later, in an effort to recoup some of the money he had spent on his defense, Shaw began a series of lecture tours of the nation's campuses. In a speech to several hundred students at American University in Washington in Sept. 1970, Shaw called his trial "one of the seediest and shabbiest episodes in American judicial history" and a case of "the truly terrifying power which the state has over an individual." Warning students of "a creeping erosion of individual rights in this country," he said, "the importance of the Garrison case is not that he failed. He might have succeeded. Had I lacked the money to defend myself properly, I would be in jail now instead of talking to you."

A Heritage of Stone, a book written by Jim Garrison about the Kennedy assassination, was published by G. P. Putnam's Sons Nov. 16, 1970. In it Garrison repeated his charges that Kennedy had been killed as a result of a CIA plot engineered in behalf of the U.S. military-industrial-intelligence complex that feared Kennedy was seeking a detente with the Soviet Union and an end to the Vietnamese war. Garrison also charged that the same forces were responsible for every other evil committed in the U.S. during the past 7 years, including the assassinations of Dr. Martin Luther King Jr. and Robert F. Kennedy.

THE ASSASSINATION

OF

MARTIN LUTHER KING JR.

Martin Luther King Jr.   Wide World Photo

MARTIN LUTHER KING JR. (1929-68)

The Rev. Dr. Martin (Michael) Luther King Jr. was born Jan. 15, 1929 in Atlanta, Ga. He was the first son and 2d of 3 children of 2 prominent Atlanta Negroes, Martin (Michael) Luther King Sr. and the former Alberta Christine Williams. Martin King Sr. became pastor of Atlanta's Ebenezer Baptist Church in 1932 after the death of his father-in-law, the Rev. Adam Daniel Williams. Mrs. King, his mother, was a former schoolteacher. Both parents had been early activists in the Southern civil rights movement. When Martin King Jr. was 6 his father changed both their first names from Michael to Martin in honor of Martin Luther, the Protestant Reformation leader.

Martin King entered Young Street Grade School, an all-Negro public elementary school in Atlanta, in 1935, then attended the private laboratory school at the University of Atlanta. He graduated from the public Booker T. Washington High School at 15, after skipping the 9th and 12th grades, and entered Atlanta's Negro Morehouse College expecting to study medicine or law. During his junior year, however, he came under the influence of Dr. Benjamin E. Mays, the college president, and George Kelsey, a philosophy professor, who, by their involvement with social justice, persuaded the young King that he could best serve humanity by entering the ministry.

Martin King graduated from Morehouse with a BA in 1948 (in 1957 he received an LHD from Morehouse) and entered Crozer Theological Seminary in Chester, Pa., where he was one of 6 Negroes among 100 students. An honor student and president of his senior class, Martin King received a BD in 1951. He was awarded a PhD in systematic theology (1955) and a DD (1959) from Boston University. While at Crozer he attended special philosophy classes at the University of Pennsylvania; while at Boston he took additional philosophy classes at Harvard University. During this period he was exposed to the writings of India's Mahatma Gandhi, whose theory of nonviolence King later espoused. "From my Christian background I gained my ideals and from Gandhi my operational techniques," he later recalled. Among his other academic degrees: DD Chicago Theological Seminary 1957,

117

LLD Howard University 1957, LLD Morgan State College 1958, LHD Central State College 1958.

Ordained a minister in his father's church in 1947, King remained there as assistant pastor until 1954, when he was named pastor of the Dexter Avenue Baptist Church in Montgomery, Ala. During his tenure at the latter church, he urged his parishioners to become registered voters and to join the National Association for the Advancement of Colored People (NAACP). He was elected president of the Montgomery Improvement Association in Dec. 1955.

King first gained national recognition in 1956 as the leader of a 382-day boycott against Montgomery's racially segregated public buses; the boycott resulted in a Nov. 1956 U.S. Supreme Court decision declaring the Alabama bus segregation law unconstitutional. During the campaign, in which King urged 50,000 Negroes to use passive resistance, King's home was bombed (Jan. 30, 1956) and he and 23 other ministers were arrested (Feb. 22, 1956) for violating Alabama anti-boycott laws. (The first of his 16 Southern arrests had been for a speeding violation Jan. 26, 1956.) Negroes and whites first rode desegregated buses in Montgomery Dec. 21, 1956. 2 days later the front door of King's home was damaged by shotgun blasts; 2 more attempts to bomb his house were made Jan. 10 and Jan. 27, 1957.

King met in Atlanta Jan. 1957 with Negro leaders of 10 Southern states to form the Southern Christian Leadership Conference (SCLC) and was elected the group's president in Feb. 1957. A month later he accepted an invitation from Kwame Nkrumah to attend Ghana's independence day ceremonies in Accra. From then until the end of 1957 he traveled 780,000 miles, made 208 speeches and wrote his first book, Stride Toward Freedom, *an autobiographical account of the Montgomery boycott, which was published in 1958. (Autographing copies of the book in Harlem, New York Sept. 19, 1958, King was attacked by a 42-year-old Negro woman, who, after explaining that she had "been after [King] for 5 years," plunged a Japanese letter opener into his chest; it barely missed his aorta. The woman, Mrs. Isola Curry, was later committed to a mental institution.) In 1959 King fulfilled a long-time desire to visit India. He accepted an invitation from the Gandhi Peace Foundation to make a speaking tour of the country. Although sorely disillusioned by India's immense poverty and discrimination, he became even more committed to Gandhi's principles of nonviolence and asceticism.*

King returned to Atlanta in Jan. 1960 to become co-pastor, with his father, of the Ebenezer Baptist Church. Later that year he began his first major passive nonviolence campaign, aimed primarily at desegregating lunch counters and restaurants. Calling for Negroes to begin "mass violation of immoral laws," he earned the title "father of the sit-in movement." It was during these demonstrations that the song "We Shall Overcome" was adopted as the anthem of the civil rights movement. (In Oct. 1960 Sen. John F. Kennedy, then a Presidential candidate, personally intervened to have King released from Georgia State Prison where he had been serving a 4-month sentence for a traffic violation.)

An early supporter and organizer of the Freedom Rides (protest actions designed to desegregate Southern interstate buses and terminals), King, aided by U.S. marshals deployed by Atty. Gen. Robert F. Kennedy, successfully stemmed the violence that erupted in Alabama in May 1961 to threaten the entire campaign.

A leader of the Apr. 1963 actions called to desegregate public facilities and end job bias in Birmingham, Ala., King was again arrested when he defied a court order barring demonstrations. While in prison he wrote "Letter From a Birmingham Jail," a response to 8 white Birmingham clergymen who had criticized him for his "unwise and untimely" action in the protest.

One of King's greatest triumphs occurred Aug. 28, 1963 when he delivered his "I Have A Dream" speech before an estimated 250,000 persons, 60,000 of them white, gathered in front of the Lincoln Memorial during a massive "March on Washington" in a demand for equal rights for Negroes. Excerpts from the address:

"So even though we face the difficulties of today and tomorrow, I still have a dream. I have a dream that one day this nation will rise up and live out the true meaning of its creed: 'We hold these truths to be self-evident, that all men are created equal.'

"I have a dream that one day on the red hills of Georgia the sons of former slaves and the sons of former slave owners will be able to sit down together at the table of brotherhood.

"I have a dream that one day even the state of Mississippi, a state sweltering with the people's injustice, sweltering with the heat of oppression, will be transformed into an oasis of freedom and justice.

"I have a dream that my 4 little children will one day live in a nation where they will not be judged by the color of their skin, but by the content of their character.

"I have a dream that one day every valley shall be exalted, every hill and mountain shall be made low, the rough places will be made plain, and the crooked places will be made straight, and the glory of the Lord shall be revealed and all flesh shall see it together.

"This is our hope. This is the faith with which I return to the South. With this faith we will be able to hew out of the mountain of despair a stone of hope ... transform the jangling discords of our nation into a beautiful symphony of brotherhood ... work together, to pray together, to struggle together, to go to jail together, to stand up for freedom together, knowing that we will be free one day."

His 2d book, Strength to Love, *a collection of 17 sermons, was published in 1963 and* Time *magazine chose him "Man of the Year."*

King's influence among Negroes began to wane in 1964 with the emergence of black militants. Chided as an "Uncle Tom" whose principles of nonviolence were antiquated ideals, King was unable to control the racial unrest that had spread to the Northern urban centers. For the first time he became active in politics, campaigning strongly against Republican Presidential candidate Barry M. Goldwater, whose election, he felt, would lead to unprecedented rioting in the U.S. He also became embroiled with FBI Director J. Edgar Hoover in a controversy over the effectiveness of the FBI in Southern civil rights cases. The incident prompted Hoover, in a Nov. 18, 1964 Washington press conference, to call King "the most notorious liar in the country."

For his "furtherance of brotherhood among men" King was awarded the Nobel Peace Prize in 1964. He was the 14th American, 3d Negro and youngest man to win it. Declaring *that the entire cash value of the prize (about $54,000) would be given to the civil rights movement, he accepted the honor in Oslo, Norway Dec. 10, 1964 "as a trustee ... on behalf of all men who love peace and brotherhood." King said he had been awarded the prize because of the recognition "that nonviolence is the answer to the crucial political and moral questions of our time—the need for man to overcome oppression and violence without resorting to violence and oppression."*

His 3d book, Why We Can't Wait, *an account of the 1963 Birmingham boycott, was published in 1964.*

A leader of the 1965 Selma-Montgomery (Ala.) voter registration march, King met with Pres. Lyndon B. Johnson and other government officials Feb. 9, 1965 in an effort to expedite legislation to extend Negro voting rights. He led SCLC's first large-scale civil rights campaign in a major Northern city in Chicago July 24-26, 1965 and succeeded in bringing together a record 10,000-20,000 persons to march to city hall in a demonstration against school discrimination. Later that year he took on another cause—to end the war in Vietnam. Blaming the Vietnamese conflict for many of the U.S.' domestic problems, King soon became a prime spokesman for the opposition, urging, among other things over the next 3 years, a national boycott of the war by draft-eligible youths, a halt in the bombing of North Vietnam and the end of draft inequities between Negroes and whites. He received the Judaism & World Peace Award of the Synagogue Council of America in Dec. 1965.

During 1966 King's efforts were divided primarily between an "open city" campaign against segregated housing in Chicago and the continuance of a Mississippi voting rights march begun by James Meredith. (Meredith had been shot halfway through the protest.) Both demonstrations were marked by violence, a direct result of white animosity provoked by the outspoken Black Power leaders who had gained significant influence among Negroes. A year later, in 1967, SCLC and several other rights groups campaigned to eliminate racial inequality in Cleveland, O. Naming his particular drive "Operation Breadbasket" because it centered on the city's bread industry, King succeeded in gaining more and better jobs for Cleveland's Negroes. Towards the end of 1967 he began plans for a massive "Poor People's Campaign" against poverty

to be held in Washington in 1968; but he died before he could
fully implement it. Just prior to his death, during Mar. 1968,
King led a protest march resulting in violence in support of
striking Negro sanitation workers in Memphis, Tenn.

King's last 2 books were Where Do We Go From Here?
Chaos or Community (1967), an examination of the future of
civil rights movements, and The Trumpet of Conscience (1968),
a collection of 5 lectures he had presented over the Canadian
Broadcasting Corp. in Nov.-Dec. 1967.

He married Coretta Scott of Marion, Ala. June 18, 1953 in
Perry County, Ala. They had 4 children—Yolanda Denise, born
in 1955, Martin Luther King 3d, born in 1957, Dexter Scott,
born in 1961, and Bernice Albertine, born in 1963.

ASSASSINATION & AFTERMATH

King Killed in Memphis

The Rev. Dr. Martin Luther King Jr., 39, foremost leader of the nonviolent civil rights movement in the U.S., was assassinated in Memphis, Tenn. Apr. 4, 1968. The murder of the nation's most noted Negro touched off a wave of racial strife throughout the nation. An international search for the killer finally ended June 8, 1968 in London in the arrest of an escaped convict named James Earl Ray, who ultimately pleaded guilty to King's murder.

King had gone to Memphis Apr. 3 to lead a 2d march in support of the city's striking Negro sanitation workers.

An earlier march, led by King Mar. 28, had resulted in an outbreak of violence and looting in which a 16-year-old youth was slain. Discouraged by the event and his inability to control the black activists who had produced the violence, King decided to withdraw from the protest and return to Atlanta. But at the insistence of his aides in the Southern Christian Leadership Conference (SCLC), who felt that he had conceded to the violent militants, he reconsidered and finally consented to lead a 2d Memphis march. His planned departure from Atlanta Apr. 3 was delayed, however, when airport officials received an anonymous phone call warning that bombs had been placed on King's plane.

After arriving in Memphis, King spoke at a rally at the Mason Street Temple that evening and cited the Atlanta bomb incident and other threats on his life. "But it really doesn't matter with me now," he said, "because I've been to the mountaintop, and I don't mind. Like anybody, I would like to live a long life. Longevity has its place. But I'm not concerned about that now. I just want to do God's will. And He's allowed me to go up to the mountain. And I've looked over, and I've seen the Promised Land. I may not get there with you, but I want you to know tonight that we as a people will get to the Promised Land. So I'm happy tonight. I'm not fearing any man. Mine eyes have seen the glory of the coming of the Lord."

In this Apr. 3 speech, his last, King sought with some apparent success to unite the militants and moderates in his audience. "It is no longer a question of violence or nonviolence in this day and age," he told them. "It is nonviolence or nonexistence."

King spent most of Apr. 4 conferring with aides in his room (Room 306) on the 2d floor of the Negro-owned Lorraine Motel* in Memphis. Before leaving for a dinner engagement, he went outside on the motel balcony to get some fresh air and chat with the Rev. Jesse Jackson and the Rev. Ralph Abernathy, 2 members of his staff.

As King leaned over the 2d-floor balcony railing, at 6:01 p.m. CST Apr. 4, 1968, a heavy-caliber bullet smashed through his lower right jaw and neck, severing his spinal cord and lifting him up and back against the motel wall. The single shot was fired from a rooming house only 50-100 yards away. But as the 30-odd Memphis policemen ordered to guard King and his entourage converged on the motel in response to the shot, the assassin escaped. King was rushed to St. Joseph's Hospital, 1½ miles away, and he was pronounced dead at 7:05 p.m. after emergency surgery failed to revive him.

Memphis Police Director Frank Hollomon said Apr. 4 that the fatal shot had been fired from a bathroom used by upstairs occupants of the rooming house at 420 South Main Street. FBI agents and Memphis police found a spent cartridge casing and a number of fingerprints in the lavatory. They also collected a small suitcase, a caliber-30.06 Remington pump rifle with a telescopic sight and a pair of binoculars found in a doorway near the rooming house. Witnesses reported that they had seen a white man run from the house immediately after the shooting and drive away in a white Mustang. Police chased a similar car out of the city for 22 minutes at speeds of up to 100 mph. but lost it.

Mrs. Bessie Brewer, manager of the rooming house, described the suspect to police as white, a dark-haired, well-dressed 6-footer, about 30-35 years old, who called himself John

* During his first trip to Memphis a week earlier, King had stayed in a $29-a-day room at the Rivermont, a Holiday Inn motel on the east bank of the Mississippi. But in reaction to criticism from the local press on his luxurious living style, on his 2d trip King checked into a $12-a-day room at the Lorraine, a 2d-rate motel near Beale Street in the city's Negro sector.

Willard. She said he had purposely chosen a room that faced the Lorraine Motel and had paid her a week's rent, $8.50, with a new $20 bill.

Atty. Gen. Ramsey Clark flew to Memphis Apr. 5 with Justice Department officials on Pres. Johnson's orders. Clark said at a news conference that the FBI was looking for the assassin in several states. He reported that "all the evidence indicates that this was the act of a single individual."

President Urges Unity

The news of King's assassination evoked expressions of dismay and shock throughout the U.S. It also precipitated one of the worst waves of racial riots and violence in the nation's history.

Pres. Johnson, reflecting the country's grief, delivered a nationwide TV address the evening of Apr. 4, 1968. In his speech he lauded the slain Negro leader and appealed to "every citizen to reject the blind violence that has struck Dr. King, who lived by nonviolence."

The President, speaking from the White House, expressed shock and sorrow at "the brutal slaying" of King but said he hoped "that all Americans tonight will search their hearts as they ponder this most tragic incident." Mrs. Johnson and he had conveyed their sympathy to King's widow, Mrs. Coretta Scott King, he said, and he knew that "every American of goodwill joins me in mourning the death of this outstanding leader and in praying for peace and understanding throughout this land." "We can achieve nothing by lawlessness and divisiveness among the American people," Johnson continued. "It's only by joining together, and only by working together, can we continue to move toward equality and fulfillment for all of our people."

The President also announced the postponement of a trip to Hawaii, scheduled for that evening, where he had planned to confer with U.S. diplomats and military leaders on the Vietnamese war. The Hawaii conference was canceled altogether Apr. 5 so that Johnson could remain in Washington to deal with the violence, arson and looting that had erupted in Washington, Chicago and other major American cities. (By nightfall Apr. 5 Federal troops had been brought to Washington to restore order.)

Johnson spent most of Apr. 5 meeting with moderate black leaders, members of Congress and officials of the District of Columbia. Later he led his guests in a 12-car motorcade to the National Cathedral to attend a memorial service for King.

Among the leaders who conferred with Johnson that afternoon were: Vice Pres. Hubert H. Humphrey; Defense Secy. Clark Clifford; Senate Democratic leader Mike Mansfield (Mont.); House Speaker John W. McCormack (D., Mass.); Sen. Thomas H. Kuchel (R., Calif.); Reps. Carl Albert (D., Okla.) and William M. McCulloch (R., O.); Housing & Urban Development Secy. Robert C. Weaver; Supreme Court Justice Thurgood Marshall; Mrs. Dorothy I. Height, president of the National Council of Negro Women; Whitney M. Young Jr. of the National Urban League; Bayard Rustin of the A. Philip Randolph Institute; Gary (Ind.) Mayor Richard G. Hatcher; Washington Commissioner Walter E. Washington; the Rev. Leon Sullivan of the Opportunities Industrialization Center in Philadelphia; U.S. District Court Judge A. Leon Higginbotham Jr.; Roy Wilkins and Clarence Mitchell Jr. of the NAACP; Bishop George W. Baber of the American Methodist Episcopal Church; the Rev. Walter E. Fauntroy of the District of Columbia Council.

On his return to the White House Apr. 5, the President again went before the nation on TV to proclaim Sunday, Apr. 6, a national day of mourning for King and to announce that he had asked Congress, in adjournment over the weekend, to convene in joint session "at the earliest possible moment" to hear his proposals "for action—constructive action instead of destructive action—in this hour of national need." "The spirit of America weeps for a tragedy that denies the very meaning of our land," the President said. "It is the fiber and the fabric of the Republic that's being tested. If we are to have the America that we mean to have, all men of all races, all regions, all religions must stand their ground to deny violence its victory in this sorrowful time and in all times to come."

He believed "deeply," Johnson asserted, that "the dream of Dr. Martin Luther King Jr. has not died with him. Men who are white, men who are black, must and will now join together as never in the past to let all the forces of divisiveness know that America shall not be ruled by the bullet but only by the ballot of free and of just men." The work to remove "some of the stones of inaction and of indifference and of injustice" had begun, he said, "and we must move with urgency and with resolve and with new energy in the Congress and in the courts and in the White House and the statehouse and the city halls of the nation, wherever there is leadership—political leadership, leadership in the churches, in the homes, in the schools, in the institutions of higher learning—until we do overcome."

Johnson said he had not "understate[d] the case" when he spoke Mar. 31, 1968 "of the divisiveness that was tearing this nation apart." * "But together," he declared, "a nation united and a nation caring and a nation concerned and a nation that thinks more of the nation's interest than we do of any individual self-interest or political interest—that nation can and shall and will overcome." In his proclamation, the President referred to King as "a leader of his people" and "a teacher of all people." "The quest for freedom, to which he gave eloquent expression, continues," Johnson said. He urged Americans to "resolve before God to stand against divisiveness in our country and all its consequences."

The President ordered that the American flag be flown at half-staff at all federal facilities in the U.S. and abroad and in all U.S. territories and possessions until King's interment.

Nation Pauses in Tribute

King's death, like John Kennedy's in 1963, preempted the nation's attention for days. Memorial marches and rallies were held throughout the U.S.

Among the various institutions and activities affected by his death: many public school systems closed; public libraries and museums were shut; many businesses and the stock exchanges were closed; seaports from Maine to Texas shut down as longshoremen and seamen stopped work; the UN flag was flown at half-mast; the opening of the baseball season (scheduled for Apr. 8, 1968) was postponed; the Stanley Cup hockey playoffs and the playoffs in the American and National Basketball associations were postponed; Hollywood's Oscar

---

* In his Mar. 31 speech Johnson had cited the "divisive partisanship" in the nation as a reason for his withdrawal from the 1968 Presidential race.

award presentation ceremony was postponed, and the Presidential nomination campaign was temporarily suspended.

Most major Negro organizations and leaders paid high tribute to King and urged a continuance of his fight against discrimination in the nonviolent spirit. But many militant black leaders said King's death marked the death of the nonviolent movement and urged retaliation in kind.

Julius W. Hobson, an economist and chairman of ACT, a Washington civil rights group, said Apr. 4, 1968 that "the Martin Luther King concept of nonviolence died with him. It was a foreign ideology anyway—as foreign to this violent country as speaking Russian."

United Black Front Chairman Lincoln O. Lynch called on Negroes Apr. 4 "to abandon the unconditional nonviolent concept expounded by Dr. King and adopt a position that for every Martin Luther King who falls, 10 white racists will go down with him. There is no other way. White America understands no other language."

But Sen. Edward W. Brooke (R., Mass.), the Senate's only Negro, said Apr. 4 that "the sorrow which all Americans of good will feel at this terrible loss must bind us together, not rend us apart."

James Farmer, ex-national director of the Congress of Racial Equality (CORE), said Apr. 4 that "the only fitting memorial to this martyred leader is a monumental commitment—now, not a day later—to eliminate racism." CORE itself Apr. 6 called on "all black people to stop their normal activities ... [Apr. 9] in honor and memory of Dr. King, his principles, his contribution to all mankind, the supreme sacrifice that he made and the legacy that he gave the world." CORE National Director Floyd McKissick, however, had asserted Apr. 4 that King's philosophy of nonviolence had died with him. "White people are going to suffer as much as black people," McKissick said.

NAACP Executive Director Roy Wilkins warned Apr. 8 against retaliation. Despite the "talk about 'get whitey,' 'kill 10 whites for every Negro killed,'" he said, "the people who lose their lives are Negroes." He announced that the NAACP was mounting a nationwide drive against racial violence and stressing jobs for the unemployed and better community relations. King, he said, would have been "outraged" by the disorders following his assassination, and "millions of Negroes in this country" were opposed to violence.

Wilkins Apr. 8 criticized Black Power leader Stokely Carmichael. It was reported, he said, that Carmichael had responded in a reasonable manner on first hearing of King's death, but "the next day, miraculously, as if somebody had come to see him and talked to him, comes that talk about 'get your guns.'" "I am sorry, I don't know Mr. Carmichael and his connections well enough to guess whether he is his own man," Wilkins said. "Of course, I am concerned." (Wilkins Apr. 4 had expressed concern about "a racial collision." He warned that "too many officials in key states and local positions are interpreting 'riot control' and 'law and order' to mean a crackdown racially on Negro Americans.")

National Urban League Executive Director Whitney M. Young Jr. said in a TV interview Apr. 7 that "the only thing more tragic" than King's death "would be that the only response would be black anger and white sympathy." "What we need today is black determination and white action," he said. "We must have concrete, tangible action that will remove the iniquities in our society."

King's death became known to Sen. Robert F. Kennedy (D., N.Y.) as he was campaigning in the Midwest for the Democratic Presidential nomination. He said at a street-corner rally of Negroes in Indianapolis Apr. 4, shortly after the assassination:

"Those of you who are black can be filled with hatred, with bitterness and a desire for revenge.... I can only say that I feel in my own heart the same kind of feeling. I had a member of my family killed.... We can move toward further polarization. Or we can make an effort, as Martin Luther King did, to understand, to reconcile ourselves and to love." "Dr. King dedicated himself to justice and love between his fellow human beings.... It's up to those of us who are here ... to carry out that dream, to try and end the divisions that exist so deeply within our country and to remove the stain of bloodshed from our land." "I ask you now to return home to say a prayer for the family of Martin Luther King, that's true, but more important to say a prayer for our country ... and to say a prayer for understanding and ... compassion."

Services of "penitence and dedication" in memory of King were called for in a joint statement issued Apr. 5 by Dr. Arthur S. Flemming, president of the National Council of Churches, Rabbi Jacob Philip Rudin, president of the Synagogue Council of America, and the Most Rev. John F. Dearden, president of the National Conference of Catholic Bishops.

Several Southern leaders Apr. 6 praised King and his cause of non-violence. Atlanta Mayor Ivan Allen said King's death "takes from Atlanta one of its greatest citizens of all time." * The Fulton County (Atlanta) commissioners, in a joint statement, called King "the incomparable leader of a large segment of American citizenry" who "was capable of great vision." Louisiana Gov. John J. McKeithen called for "a rededication to the cause which he espoused during his lifetime—non-violence, with peace and good will to all men."

Foreign Reaction

The news of King's assassination and the widespread civil disorders that followed were received with shock in many countries around the world. The news was reported under banner headlines and caused the cancellation of many regularly-scheduled radio and TV programs. Government and religious leaders sent their condolences to Mrs. Coretta King and praised her husband as a man of peace who had sought to achieve racial harmony in the U.S. through non-violent means; they described his death as a loss to all mankind. Memorial services were held in a number of foreign capitals, and moments of silence were observed by various parliamentary bodies.

The *N.Y. Times* reported Apr. 6, 1968 that the assassination "evoked in Europe ... a reaction of intense horror at the deed and of fear for the stability of American society." Reporting on world reaction Apr. 7, the *Washington Post* said there was universal praise for King and the philosophy he had expounded but that certain countries, among them the Soviet Union, Communist China, India and West Germany, viewed the murder and subsequent rioting as "a sign of deep sickness in American society, if not outright disintegration."

---

* Mayor Allen, a civil rights advocate, had arranged a flight to Memphis for Mrs. Coretta King shortly after her husband was shot. He later broke the news of King's death to her at the Atlanta airport.

Belgian Premier Paul van den Boeynants warned Apr. 5 that the assassination represented "an escalation of racial violence of which the American nation will be the victim."

Members of all parties in the British House of Commons Apr. 5 introduced a resolution expressing "horror at the brutal and senseless murder" of King and pledging to wipe out racial discrimination in Britain. Opposition leader Edward Heath referred to King's death as "a great tragedy."

Most Europeans linked the assassination with that of Pres. Kennedy in 1963. The Spanish newspaper *Madrid* said Apr. 6: "John Kennedy and Luther King, who were friends and who worked together, were victims of bullets fired by the same assassin: hatred, nonunderstanding, fanaticism."

The Soviet government newspaper *Izvestia* headed its account of the assassination Apr. 6 with the words: "United States is a Nation of Violence and Racism." A lead editorial said that racists had feared King's planned "Poor People's" march on Washington later in April. It asserted that the shot had been "well aimed" and was "intended by the murderer as a warning to the Negro movement before the coming long hot summer." *Pravda,* the Soviet Communist Party newspaper, declared Apr. 6 that freedom in the U.S. "means to kill." The paper asserted: "Terrorist murders have become as ordinary an aspect of the American way of life as road accidents.... Violence and terror roam American streets."

Hsinhua, the Chinese Communist news agency, declared Apr. 6 that King's assassination had prompted a "large-scale Afro-American struggle against racial oppression." The agency cited the outbreak of violence in Washington and asserted that Pres. Johnson was "panic-stricken in the face of the violent storm of the black American struggle."

The assassination had a particularly heavy impact on African nations. Some African statesmen, among them Maj. Gen. Yakubu Gowon, head of the Nigerian federal military government, affirmed their belief that the philosophy of non-violence would prevail in achieving eventual racial harmony. But many Africans expressed the fear that King's murder had strengthened the hand of black extremists in America.

Pope Paul Apr. 7 devoted a portion of his Palm Sunday sermon in St. Peter's Basilica to King. The pope said: "And now, brothers and sons, we cannot omit to mention here also

the sad remembrance which weighs upon the conscience of the
world, that of the cowardly and atrocious killing of Martin
Luther King. We shall associate this memory with that of the
tragic story of the Passion of Christ.... May this execrable
crime take on the value of a sacrifice. May it not be hatred, or
vendetta, or a new abyss between the citizens of the same great
and noble country that are deepened and increased, but rather a
new common purpose of pardon, of peace, of reconciliation, in
equality of free and just right, overcoming the unjust
discriminations and present struggles."

The pope again referred to King's death in his annual
Easter message, delivered Apr. 14. Calling for a "clearer, more
authoritative and more effective affirmation of the rights of
man, which the civilized world is celebrating this year in a
special and solemn manner," the pope said: "After the
inauspicious and warning episode of the murder [King's] which
stirred the whole world, it would be most admirable if those
great collective egoisms, closed in upon themselves, such as are
racism, nationalism, class hatred and the dominion of privileged
peoples over the weaker ones, were made to open themselves up
to the courageous and generous adventure of universal love."

An estimated 2,000 delegates and observers present in
Tehran, Iran Apr. 22 for the beginning of a 3-week UN
International Conference on Human Rights stood for a minute
of silent tribute to the slain Negro leader.

Funeral & Burial

After the assassination Apr. 4, 1968, King's body lay in
state at the R. S. Lewis & Sons Funeral Home in Memphis. The
next day, Apr. 5, his body was flown to Atlanta on a plane
chartered by Sen. Robert F. Kennedy. The body was
accompanied by the widow, Mrs. Coretta King, by the Rev.
Ralph Abernathy and by other SCLC staff members.

King's body was put on public view at the Ebenezer
Baptist Church in Atlanta Apr. 6. Mrs. King, in a statement
made at the church, asked all who "loved and admired" her
husband to "join us in fulfilling his dream" of finding a
"creative rather than a destructive way" of solving the racial
crisis of the nation. "He knew that this was a sick society,
totally infested with racism and violence that questioned his

integrity, maligned his motives, and distorted his views," she said, "and he struggled with every ounce of his energy to save that society from itself."

Funeral services for King were held Apr. 9 at the Ebenezer Baptist Church. Among those attending: 70 U.S. Congress members (including Sens. Robert and Edward Kennedy), 3 governors, Supreme Court Justice Thurgood Marshall, Mrs. Jacqueline Kennedy, Black Power leader Stokely Carmichael, Republican Presidential candidate Richard M. Nixon, singer Harry Belafonte, basketball player Wilt Chamberlain, decathlon star Rafer Johnson, United Auto Workers Pres. Walter Reuther, ex-baseball star Jackie Robinson and Vice Pres. Hubert H. Humphrey, who represented Pres. Johnson.

In accordance with Mrs. King's request, the service included a tape-recording of her husband's last sermon, preached at the Ebenezer church Feb. 4, 1968:

"... If any of you are around when I have to meet my day, I don't want a long funeral. And if you get somebody to deliver the eulogy, tell him not to talk too long.... Tell him not to mention that I have a Nobel Peace Prize—that isn't important.... I'd like somebody to mention that day that Martin Luther King Jr. tried to give his life serving others. I'd like for somebody to say that day that Martin Luther King Jr. tried to love somebody.... I want you to be able to say that day that I did try to feed the hungry ..., that I did try in my life to clothe the naked ..., that I did try in my life to visit those who were in prison ..., that I tried to love and serve humanity. Yes, if you want to, say that I was a drum major. Say that I was a drum major for justice ..., for peace ..., for righteousness...."

After the service King's casket was placed on a faded green sharecropper's wagon and drawn by 2 Georgia mules for 4 miles to the campus of Morehouse College. Approximately 50,000-100,000 persons, including national leaders and King's disciples dressed in workmen's denim, joined the cortege.* At the college, Morehouse Pres. Emeritus Benjamin E. Mays, 72, eulogized King during a memorial service.

---

* At one point the cortege passed the Georgia capitol, where segregationist Gov. Lester Maddox had barricaded himself behind a heavy state police guard, whom he reportedly told: "If they [the mourners] start coming in here we're gonna stack 'em up." Earlier Maddox had refused to close the state's schools and had protested the lowering of the American flag to half-mast.

King's body was then driven to Atlanta's all-Negro South View Cemetery. After a graveside service, conducted by the Rev. Ralph Abernathy, King was buried in a white marble crypt bearing the epitaph "Free at last, free at last, thank God Almighty, I'm free at last."

TV and radio networks and stations again, as with Pres. Kennedy's funeral, canceled entertainment programs and commercial announcements to carry "live" coverage of King's funeral and burial.

(The National Academy of Television Arts & Sciences presented June 8, 1969 an "Emmy" award for outstanding achievement during the 1968-9 TV season to CBS executive producers Robert Wussler, Ernest Leiser, Don Hewitt and Burton Benjamin for their "Coverage of the Assassination of the Rev. Dr. Martin Luther King and Aftermath.")

Violence in 125 Cities

At least 125 cities in 28 states and the District of Columbia were hit by racial disturbances that swept the U.S. Apr. 4-11, 1968 in the wake of King's assassination. With the exception of the Southwest, Northwest and Northern Plains, no area of the country was exempt from the disorders. (Based on data gathered by the Civil Disturbance Information Unit of the Justice Department, Atty. Gen. Ramsey Clark announced Oct. 3, 1968 that Apr. 1968 was "the 2d worst month of rioting [in the U.S.] in recent years.")

Among the cities affected:

Alabama —Birmingham, Mobile, Tuscaloosa, Tuskeegee.

Arkansas—El Dorado, Fayetteville, Hot Springs, Malvern, North Little Rock, Paris, Pine Bluff.

California—Berkeley, East Palo Alto, Oakland, Pittsburg, Vallejo.

Colorado —Denver.

Connecticut —Hartford, New Haven.

Delaware —Wilmington.

Florida —Fort Pierce, Gainesville, Miami, Pensacola, Tallahassee, Tampa.

Georgia—Albany, Atlanta, Fort Valley, Macon, Savannah.

Illinois —Carbondale, Chicago, Joliet, Peoria, Rockford.

Iowa —Des Moines, Knoxville, Marshalltown.
Kansas —Topeka, Wichita.
Kentucky —Frankfurt.
Louisiana—New Orleans.
Maryland —Baltimore, Frederick, Hagerstown.
Massachusetts —Boston.
Michigan —Albion, Battle Creek, Detroit, Grand Rapids, Jackson, Kalamazoo, Lansing, Roseville, Royal Oak.
Minnesota —Minneapolis.
Mississippi—Clarksdale, Cleveland, Crystal Springs, Greenville, Greenwood, Holly Springs, Itta Bena, Jackson, Lorman, Meridian, Oxford.
Missouri —Jefferson City, Kansas City, St. Louis.
New Jersey —Bridgeton, Newark, Trenton.
New York —Buffalo, Greenburgh, Hamilton, Ithaca, Monticello, N.Y. City, Port Chester, Syracuse.
North Carolina —Charlotte, Durham, Goldsboro, Greensboro, High Point, Lexington, New Bern, Raleigh, Weldon, Wilmington, Wilson, Winston-Salem.
Ohio —Cincinnati, Dayton, Toledo, Youngstown.
Pennsylvania —Aliquippa, Braddock, Johnstown, Lancaster, Philadelphia, Pittsburgh, West Chester.
South Carolina —Hampton, Orangeburg.
Tennessee —Memphis, Nashville.
Virginia —Richmond, Suffolk.
Washington, D.C.
West Virginia —Wheeling.

These nationwide figures on the disorders were reported by the *N.Y. Times* Apr. 14, 1968:

Deaths —46 (confirmed by the Justice Department Apr. 23). All but 5 of those killed were Negroes, and 33 of the deaths occurred in Baltimore, Chicago, Kansas City, Mo. and Washington, D.C., the 4 hardest hit cities. (In contrast to the 1967 summer racial riots, the National Guardsmen and federal troops were not charged with guilt for any of the deaths.)

Injured —At least 2,600 persons, almost half of them in Washington, D.C. Most of the injured were Negroes.

Arrests —21,270. Most of the arrests were for looting.

Property damage —$45 million (a rough estimate provided by insurance companies). Most of the damage resulted from fires.

(The American Insurance Association estimated May 15 that insured losses incurred in the rioting totaled $67 million. Washington, D.C. was reported to have suffered the heaviest damage, $24 million; Chicago's damage was reported to total $13 million and Baltimore's $12 million. New York damage was estimated at $4.2 million.)

Troops involved—55,000, of whom 21,000 were federal troops and 34,000 were National Guardsmen. The federal troops were sent to Baltimore, Chicago and Washington. 22,000 additional federal troops were on ready-alert for possible deployment. (The Defense Department reported May 18 that the cost of using the federal troops totaled $5,375,400. The expenses covered the deployment of 35,890 regular soldiers and Marines and federalized National Guardsmen in Washington, Baltimore and Chicago, the moving and maintenance of 22,074 regular soldiers in stand-by position, the flying of troops thousands of miles, pay and allowances for National Guardsmen and upkeep.)

Details of some of the major disturbances:

Washington, D.C.—The nation's capital Apr. 4-7 experienced the worst outbreak of racial violence in its history. 10 persons were killed. 1,191 people were reported injured, including some policemen, firemen and military personnel. 7,650 persons were arrested. 1,130 fires were reported. And 13,600 federal troops were moved into the city before the disorders were quelled. (63% of Washington's 810,000 inhabitants were black.)

Looting and vandalism erupted in Washington late Apr. 4 after ex-Chairman Stokely Carmichael of the Student Nonviolent Coordinating Committee led about 50 youths down 14th Street to urge stores to close as a sign of respect for King. The group, shouting "Close the stores—Martin Luther King is dead," swelled to more than 400 persons about a mile north of the White House.

Within an hour Negroes began smashing store windows and looting, despite a plea by the Rev. Walter E. Fauntroy, vice chairman of the City Council, to Carmichael to disband his group and go home. But Carmichael reportedly refused to stop his march.

According to the *N.Y. Times,* Carmichael urged members of the crowd: "If you don't have a gun, go home." "When the white man comes he is coming to kill you. I don't want any black blood in the street. Go home and get you a gun and then come back because I got me a gun." But the *Washington Post* reported that Carmichael simply urged rioters to stop looting and "go home." "Not now, not now," he was quoted as shouting to looters.

Carmichael declared at a news conference the morning of Apr. 5: "When white America killed Dr. King last night she declared war" on black America. There was "no alternative to retribution." "Black people have to survive, and the only way they will survive is by getting guns."

Rioting in Washington Apr. 5 was generally held to 3 predominantly low-income Negro sections of the city—a 10-block strip along 14th Street N.W., a 10-block strip along 7th Street N.W. and a 12-block strip along H Street N.E. The downtown area near the Capitol and the White House suffered minor damage.

At 4:02 p.m. Apr. 5 Pres. Johnson signed a proclamation declaring that "a condition of domestic violence and disorder" existed. He issued an executive order mobilizing 4,000 regular Army and National Guard troops to supplement the city's 2,800-man police force. Police and troops were ordered to avoid excessive force. The troops were dispatched with the following orders: "I will, if possible, let civilian police make arrests, but I can, if necessary, take into temporary custody rioters, looters and others committing crimes. I will not load or fire my weapon except when authorized in advance by an officer under certain specific conditions, or when required to save my life." The President named ex-Deputy Defense Secy. Cyrus R. Vance as his special representative in the crisis.

Washington Commissioner (Mayor) Walter E. Washington Apr. 5 issued an emergency order setting a 5:30 p.m.-to-6:30 a.m. curfew on the city and halting the sale of firearms and liquor. By 11 p.m. the death toll had climbed to 6, of whom 3 persons had been shot as looters.

A new wave of looting and arson broke out Apr. 6, and the curfew was extended to 4 p.m. An additional 8,000 federal troops were moved into the city; more than 9,500 troops were put on street patrol, and 3,000 were held in reserve. Serious food shortages began to be reported and hundreds of persons were homeless.

Pres. Johnson made a helicopter tour of the city Apr. 6. Sen. Robert F. Kennedy and his wife, Ethel, toured 22 riot-torn blocks Apr. 7 with the Rev. Walter Fauntroy.

A return to normality was reported Apr. 8 after the death toll had reached 8, including 7 Negroes. The District of Columbia Redevelopment Land Agency made a preliminary estimate that damage to buildings totaled $13 million. City agencies, church groups and the Agriculture Department began distributing tons of food Apr. 8. Commissioner Washington said that 35 distribution centers had been established to supply nearly 185,000 riot victims with food.

2 more deaths were reported Apr. 9, and the total reached 10. (7 of the deaths were said to be unquestionably related to the rioting, the other 3 only possibly related.) Troops remained on duty Apr. 9, but the number of daytime patrols was decreased. Commissioner Washington Apr. 11 reduced the curfew hours to midnight to 4 a.m. and eased the liquor-sale restrictions.

A gradual withdrawal of troops from the city was begun Apr. 12 when 3,726 troops were ordered out by midnight. Commissioner Washington ended the curfew Apr. 12.

(The District of Columbia government reported May 1, 1968 that the April rioting had resulted in 9 deaths, 1,202 injuries and 6,306 arrests.)

Chicago —11 Negroes died in racial violence that swept Chicago Apr. 5-7. Federal troops and National Guardsmen were called to the city to quell the disorders, in which more than 500 persons were injured and nearly 3,000 arrested. 162 buildings were reported entirely destroyed by fire, and a score more were partially destroyed. Total property damage was estimated at $9 million. (1.3 million, or 16%, of Chicago's 8,282,000 inhabitants were Negroes.)

The disturbances began Apr. 5 when black youths, released from school early in memory of King, began roving downtown streets and smashing windows. They swept through the downtown Loop section and by nightfall had caused severe damage in the 2300 and 2400 blocks of West Madison Street. 4 deaths were reported: 2 looters were shot, one person died in a fire, and another person was shot to death. A fireman was wounded by a sniper.

6,000 National Guardsmen were mobilized the afternoon of Apr. 6 by Lt. Gov. Samuel H. Shapiro after he consulted with Gov. Otto Kerner, who was in Florida. Under the command of Brig. Gen. Richard T. Dunn, the Guardsmen joined the city's 10,500 policemen. They were instructed to shoot only in self-defense and then to shoot only at definite targets.

Shortly thereafter Mayor Richard J. Daley and Gen. Dunn made a tour of the riot area and declared the situation "under control." Later in the day, however, violence was renewed with increased vigor and spread from the West Side to the South Side and the Near North Side. 800 arrests and 125 major fires were reported during the day. By evening the mayor ordered a 7 p.m.-to-6 a.m. curfew for everyone under 21 years of age; he barred the sale of firearms and liquor. 1,500 additional Guardsmen were called into the city, and both Guardsmen and police were ordered to take more "aggressive action" against lawbreakers.

In the evening of Apr. 6, after 9 Negroes had been killed in the disorders, Shapiro asked Pres. Johnson for federal aid to quell the "serious domestic violence in or near the city of Chicago." The first of some 5,000 federal troops ordered to the city began arriving at 9:30 p.m. The President also sent Deputy Atty. Gen. Warren Christopher to Chicago as his special representative.

While troops took control in the North and West sides of the city Apr. 6, the situation on the South Side deteriorated. Firemen trying to put out fires were under constant attack from snipers. By nightfall thousands of Negroes were reported homeless. The Chicago Conference on Religion & Race set up "Operation Home" to find temporary quarters for the displaced. The Chicago Commission on Human Relations established a "rumor control center." 3 emergency bond courts were set up to speed the processing of arrest cases.

(18 Negroes who had been jailed for a week filed suit Apr. 12 on charges that the chief justice of the Cook County Circuit Court and other county officials were "suspending due process of law" by failing to act on their cases. The prisoners charged that they had been denied preliminary hearings and were unable to post the "excessive" bonds that had been "set without proper bond hearings." Following charges by the predominantly black Cook County Bar Association that there

was a "deplorable breakdown in judicial processes" in the handling of the arrests, the county magistrates held an extraordinary court session Apr. 14 and reduced bond for 207 prisoners. Bond had been set at from up to $1,000 for disorderly conduct to $120,000 for arson and conspiracy charges.)

Sporadic incidents of sniper fire, looting and arson were reported Apr. 7 as federal troops continued to patrol the city. Police reported 11 black deaths, 7 of them directly and 4 indirectly related to the rioting. Of the 7 directly-related deaths, all were of men, 6 shot, one stabbed. Of the 4 others, one was shot, one died of a skull fracture and 2 died in fires.

Shapiro said at a news conference Apr. 8 that the emergency had ended. Troops, National Guardsmen and police, however, continued to patrol the city. Members of 2 major Negro South Side gangs, the Blackstone Rangers and the East Side Disciples, agreed to suspend hostilities and aid patrols to prevent further outbreaks of violence and destruction. Although no violence was reported Apr. 8, the 7 p.m.-6 a.m. curfew remained in effect. 5 black militants were arrested Apr. 8 on charges of conspiracy to commit arson; they were held on $120,000 bond. Those arrested were Frederick (Doug) Andrews, 29, founder of the Garfield Organization (announced purpose: the improvement of economic conditions on the West Side); Edward Crawford, 46, president of the National Negro Rifle Association; Andrew Brown, 24, of the Garfield Organization; Curlee Reed, 19; Anthony Williams, 17.

Mayor Daley ended the curfew Apr. 10. The 5,000 federal troops left the city Apr. 12 after Daley and Gov. Kerner had asked Pres. Johnson to withdraw the troops and return the National Guardsmen to state control.

Daley announced at a news conference Apr. 15 that he would instruct policemen "to shoot to kill" arsonists and to "shoot to maim or cripple" looters in any future rioting. His orders, transmitted to police through Police Supt. James B. Conlisk, said: "Such force as is necessary including deadly force shall be used" to prevent the commission of such forcible felonies as arson, attempted arson, burglary and attempted burglary and "to prevent the escape of the perpetrators." Daley said he had thought those orders were in effect during the Apr. 5-7 violence but that he had discovered the morning of Apr. 15 that policemen had been instructed to use their own discretion as to whether to shoot. Daley said he thought that arson was "the most hideous crime." He declared: "If anyone doesn't think this was a conspiracy, I don't understand."

(Daley's "shoot to kill" order was met by sharp reaction from various federal and local government officials.

(In New York, Mayor John V. Lindsay said at a news conference Apr. 16: "We happen to think that protection of life ... is more important than protecting property or anything else.... We are not going to turn disorder into chaos through the unprincipled use of armed force. In short, we are not going to shoot children in New York City."

(At a news conference in Trenton Apr. 16, N.J. Gov. Richard J. Hughes scored the shooting of looters and arsonists. "My own judgment is that the sanctity of human life is such that an intelligent response by the police will result in arrests rather than shootings," Hughes declared.

(Following an address to the American Society of Newspaper Editors in Washington Apr. 17, in response to a question from the audience, Atty. Gen. Ramsey Clark repudiated Daley's instructions as "a very dangerous escalation of the problems we are so intent on solving." "I think that to resort to deadly force is contrary to the total experience of law enforcement in this country," Clark said. "I do not believe it [the use of deadly force] is permissible except in self-defense or when it is necessary to protect the lives of others.")

Mayor Daley, in a statement Apr. 17 to the Chicago City Council, revised his comment. He said: Arsonists and looters "should be restrained if possible by minimum force" but could not be given "permissive rights" for their criminal behavior. Residents of the West Side, where most of the violence occurred, "had one universal demand—protect us from the arsonists, from the looter, from the mob and its leaders." "We cannot resign ourselves to the proposition that civil protest must lead to death or devastation, to abandonment of the law that is fundamental for the preservation of the rights of the people and their freedom."

Baltimore —6 people died in the racial violence that erupted in Baltimore Apr. 6. The National Guard and federal troops were called in to quell the rioting. More than 700 persons were reported injured Apr. 6-9, more than 5,000 arrests were made, and the number of fires reported exceeded 1,000.

(378,000, or 41%, of Baltimore's 930,000 inhabitants were Negroes.)

Gov. Spiro T. Agnew declared a "state of emergency and crisis" in Baltimore Apr. 6 after black youths set at least 20 fires, smashed windows and looted stores in the predominantly Negro section of East Baltimore. Police temporarily gained control of the area when they sealed off a 5-block part of the commercial Gay Street section. But violence was renewed, and the governor called in 6,000 National Guardsmen and the state police at 10 p.m. to aid the city's 1,100-man police force. Guardsmen were armed with bayonets and tear gas and were instructed to carry their guns unloaded. Agnew banned the sale of liquor, firearms and gasoline in containers. Mayor Thomas D'Alesandro 3d, 38, imposed an 11 p.m.-6 a.m. curfew.

4 people were killed the night of Apr. 6: one Negro and one white were victims of a fire caused by a fire bomb, and 2 Negroes were shot to death in 2 separate tavern incidents. More than 300 persons were reported injured. The level of violence rose during the night, fell by morning and then increased steadily throughout Apr. 7. The curfew was reimposed at 4 p.m. Maj. Gen. George M. Gelston, Maryland adjutant general, kept the National Guardsmen under strict orders not to shoot unless fired on and to return fire only when given orders by an officer or when the source of attack could be definitely identified.

At nightfall Apr. 7 Agnew declared that he had "determined that federal reinforcements are necessary in the city." 2,995 federal troops were immediately dispatched to Baltimore, and Lt. Gen. Robert H. York, a paratroop officer, assumed over-all command from Gelston.

Despite the curfew, bands of youths roamed the city streets, looting and setting fires. Fires were reported scattered over a wide area of the city and not concentrated in particular areas, as in other cities. By morning violence subsided.

Pres. Johnson sent an additional 1,900 federal troops to Baltimore Apr. 8 to reinforce the 2,995 federal troops sent earlier, the 5,953 mobilized National Guardsmen and 1,500 state and local police on duty.

In sections east and west of the downtown business district, troops used tear gas Apr. 8 to dispel mobs who were reportedly bombarding police and firemen with rocks and bottles and interfering with efforts to control fires. Food and drug shortages were reported. As looting and arson spread late Apr. 8 the first sniper fire was reported.

The rioting's 6th fatality was reported early Apr. 9 when a Negro was found burned to death in an apartment over a grocery store that had been firebombed. Scattered incidents of looting and arson were reported Apr. 9.

At the urging of civil rights leaders, military and police officials agreed Apr. 9 to permit Negroes to patrol ghetto neighborhoods as "peacemakers" to try to bring an end to the vandalism. State Sen. Clarence Mitchell 3d, a Negro, had met with 150 slum residents that afternoon for a "peace rally" and to have them "pass the word" that the patrols would be out at night to ease the tension. After the 7 p.m. curfew took effect, 16 black "block leaders" under police and military escort toured the riot-torn areas, where they urged residents to obey the curfew and clear the streets.

Curfew restrictions were eased Apr. 10 while federal troops continued patrols. City workers were sent to East Baltimore to begin removing debris and cleaning the area. Agnew urged Pres. Johnson and Maryland Congress members to act to bring civil disorders under provisions of disaster relief laws.

About 80 elected and appointed Negro officials walked out of a meeting with Agnew Apr. 11 after he charged them with failing to help enough in preventing the riots. He also accused militant young Negroes of inciting the black community to violence. Before the governor finished his remarks someone yelled: "Let's have a black caucus.... It's an insult." They then walked out and held a meeting at a Negro parish church in west Baltimore. Agnew had also told the group: "It's no mere coincidence that a national disciple of violence, Mr. Stokely Carmichael, was observed meeting with local Black Power advocates and known criminals in Baltimore Apr. 3, 1968—3 days before the Baltimore riots began."

Agnew Apr. 12 asked Washington to withdraw the federal troops and defederalize the National Guard as soon as possible. 2,000 troops were removed immediately, and the remaining troops were removed Apr. 13. The National Guard was relieved of active duty Apr. 14 when Agnew lifted the state of emergency and lifted bans on gun and gasoline sales.

Kansas City —6 Negroes were shot and killed in racial violence in Kansas City, Mo. Apr. 9-11. 3,000 National Guardsmen were called to the city, and order was restored by Apr. 14. (100,000, or 20%, of Kansas City's 488,000 inhabitants were Negroes.)

The violence began Apr. 9 after police fired tear gas into a crowd of about 1,000 Negroes who had gathered at city hall to hear an address by Mayor Ilus W. Davis. The Negroes, mostly teenagers, had marched to the building to protest the city's decision to keep the schools open that day—the day of King's funeral—in contrast to the decision of neighboring Kansas City, Kan. to close its schools. The police said they had fired the tear gas after a Negro threw a bottle at them. The crowd then dispersed but began a rampage in the black East Side area; members of the mob smashed windows, set fires and looted stores. By the end of the night one Negro had been shot and killed by police while he was looting a liquor store; 57 persons were injured (7 by gunfire) and about 270 were arrested. About 75 fires were set, and windows were broken in some 200 business establishments. The city imposed a 9 p.m.-to-6 a.m. curfew, and 300-400 National Guardsmen were called in.

The most serious violence broke out Apr. 10. The first incident occurred in the morning outside predominantly black Lincoln High School, where students were milling about waiting for classes to begin. Police urged the students to go inside the building, but, when they apparently felt that the students were putting up resistance, they fired tear gas into the crowd. The students ran into the school, and the police followed and fired tear gas again inside the building. The school was evacuated, and most of the students went home. Despite the incident, the city remained relatively calm most of Apr. 10, and Mayor Davis announced in the afternoon that the curfew would be lifted that night.

About an hour later, however, crowds of Negroes began roaming through the East Side, and the situation quickly got out of hand. Rioters threw Molotov cocktails at police and National Guardsmen, set about 70 fires, looted stores and harassed police and firemen with sniper fire. 4 Negroes were shot and killed by unknown persons in a 4-block area of sniper fire along Prospect Street. 22 persons were injured, about half of them by gunfire, and about 150 persons were arrested, most of them for destruction of property and curfew violations. Police reported that their command post was under sporadic sniper fire, and the police academy was severely damaged by fire. Davis ordered all police to duty, reinstated the curfew, closed all taverns and liquor stores and banned the sale of guns, ammunition and gasoline in closed containers. The National Guard force was increased during the day to 3,000 men.

Although the violence fell off considerably Apr. 11, Davis declared a state of emergency and imposed a dusk-to-dawn curfew. One Negro was shot and killed by police in a gunfight; his death raised the 3-day toll to 6. Only 5 confirmed sniping incidents and minor arson were reported Apr. 12, and nobody was injured. Scattered sniping and firebombing continued Apr. 13, but the city moved the curfew back to 11 p.m.

Officials announced Apr. 14 that order had been restored and that about 2,500 of the National Guardsmen were being sent home. One battalion of military police and about 100 state troopers remained on duty in the city. Davis lifted the ban on gasoline sales but not on the sale of firearms and ammunition.

Boston—Massachusetts National Guardsmen were placed on standby alert in Boston Apr. 5-6 after sporadic rock throwing and looting in the Roxbury and Dorchester districts Apr. 4-6. 15,000 people, mostly whites, staged a 3-mile memorial march for King. They were joined by Negroes from Roxbury.

The United Front, a coalition of civil rights groups, presented a list of 21 demands to the city Apr. 8 at a rally attended by 10,000 Negroes in White Stadium in Roxbury. The demands included Negro control of ghetto police stations, Negro ownership of all ghetto businesses, the payment of $100 million by the city to the Roxbury section, where about half of the city's 85,000 Negroes lived, the employment of only Negroes in Roxbury schools and Negro control of social welfare and antipoverty programs. Boston Mayor Kevin H. White Apr. 9 rejected the demands.

Cincinnati—Ohio Gov. James A. Rhodes ordered 1,200 National Guardsmen to Cincinnati Apr. 8 to quell rioting that erupted following a memorial service for King in the predominantly Negro suburb of Avondale. 2 people were killed in the disorders. Mayor Eugene Ruehlman imposed a 7 p.m.-to-6 a.m. curfew and ordered all liquor stores and gasoline stations to close.

The disorders spread after James Smith, a Negro guard, accidentally shot and killed his wife while trying to ward off youthful looters from the English Jewelry Store. Rumors spread, however, that Mrs. Smith had been killed by a frightened policeman. Firebombing, looting and window smashing followed.

In suburban Mount Auburn black teenagers dragged Noel Wright, 30, a white graduate student and art instructor at the University of Cincinnati, and his wife from their car Apr. 8. They stabbed Wright to death, and 3 black girls beat Mrs. Wright.

About 200 persons were reported arrested, including 40 juveniles. Damage resulting from some 55 fires was estimated at about $150,000. The Avondale business association said damage from theft and vandalism was approximately $200,000.

400 National Guardsmen patrolled the city Apr. 9, and no disturbances were reported. The curfew restrictions were removed Apr. 10 and the Guard withdrawn Apr. 12.

Detroit—4,000 National Guardsmen and 400 state policemen were sent to Detroit Apr. 5 to help 4,200 city policemen quell racial violence. Mayor Jerome P. Cavanagh proclaimed a state of emergency Apr. 5 and ordered an 8 p.m.-to-5 a.m. curfew. 2 Negroes were killed by policemen in looting incidents. Gov. George Romney said one looter was killed "accidentally."

1,483 people were arrested Apr. 5-9; 802 of the arrests were for curfew violations. 12 persons were injured. 378 fires were reported.

Romney Apr. 10 reduced the curfew to 1 a.m.-5 a.m. He announced the end of the state of emergency Apr. 12 and said that the National Guard would be withdrawn gradually.

Nashville, Tenn.—Sporadic incidents of looting, firebombing and vandalism were reported in Nashville's Negro sections Apr. 5-9. About 4,000 National Guardsmen were sent into the city Apr. 5-6. 2,000 Guardsmen sealed off the campus of the predominantly black Tennessee A&I State University Apr. 6 after 2 students were wounded in violence Apr. 5, and 50 Guardsmen dispersed a crowd of about 200 students with tear gas. The city was placed under curfew, and liquor sales were banned. After calm was restored, the curfew and liquor ban were removed Apr. 14.

Newark, N.J.—Sporadic looting broke out in Newark Apr. 9 after dozens of fires were set in the city's predominantly Negro Central Ward. 15 persons were arrested; 6 persons were reported injured in the fires, and 600 persons were left homeless. 500 black youths patrolled the streets in the evening urging the community to "cool it." Mayor Hugh J. Addonizio Apr. 10 praised the Negroes and whites for cooperating in trying to keep the peace.

N.Y. City—The disorders in New York Apr. 4-5 were considered relatively minor. The police followed a policy of using large numbers of policemen rather than firearms to restore and maintain order, and many black leaders, including militants, urged Negroes to "cool it" and forego rioting.

Bands of black youths roved the streets of Harlem and Brooklyn's Bedford-Stuyvesant areas Apr. 4 after the announcement of King's death. Mayor John V. Lindsay made a walking tour of Harlem at 10:40 p.m. and urged crowds to go home. Several fires were reported, and store windows were smashed and their contents looted.

Scattered incidents of looting were reported throughout Apr. 5. The city's 28,788-man police force, on emergency alert, was instructed: "There will be no indiscriminate use of the gun. In these situations, a firecracker can get everybody to draw his weapon. You will not use your revolvers to pick off snipers. In case you see snipers, take cover, notify the command, and a special sniper team will be sent. We want looters arrested, but ... we don't want to hurt anyone." Police Apr. 5 reported 94 arrests, 30 persons injured, including 10 policemen, and 158 incidents of looting, arson and rock throwing.

Volunteer peace-keepers who fanned out through black ghetto neighborhoods in Harlem and Bedford-Stuyvesant Apr. 5 were credited with keeping violence to a minimum. Members of Harlem's CORE, Harlem Youth Unlimited, the Harlem-Cadet Corps and the Manhattan NAACP walked through ghetto areas, talked to the people and urged restraint. One peace-keeping group was led by Charles Kenyatta, leader of the paramilitary Harlem Mau Maus. Manhattan Borough Pres. Percy Sutton made a radio appeal for peace, and Mayor Lindsay appealed on TV and walked through Harlem and Bedford-Stuyvesant.

In the early evening Apr. 5 police arrested 28 Negro youths in the Times Square area after 50-100 youths smashed windows and looted stores there.

10,000 people marched through Harlem Apr. 7 and then met in Central Park to pay tribute to King. Among the leaders of the march were N.Y. Gov. Nelson A. Rockefeller and Charles Kenyatta, who walked arm-in-arm.

Lindsay Apr. 8 issued a proclamation declaring Apr. 9— the day of King's funeral—a day of mourning throughout the city.

Oakland, Calif. —Bobby James Hutton, 17, an officer of the militant Black Panther Party, was killed and 4 other persons were wounded during a 90-minute gun battle between Negroes and police in predominantly Negro West Oakland Apr. 6. 2 policemen and Eldridge Cleaver, 32, a Black Panther leader and author of *Soul On Ice,* were among those injured; 8 persons were arrested.

According to the police, the firing had erupted when policemen stopped to question occupants of 3 parked cars. As the patrolmen stepped from their car, they reportedly were shot at without warning. Then the civilian occupants of the cars fled to a nearby building. Police reinforcements arrived, traded gunfire with the men in the house and then used tear gas. The men in the house finally agreed to surrender. Hutton emerged first. One report indicated that someone had shouted that Hutton had a gun. Police Chief Charles Gain said Hutton bent over and began to run. "The officers could not see his hands clearly and, assuming he was still armed, then ordered him to halt," Gain said. "Upon failure to do so, they fired at him." Black Panther chairman Bobby George Seale, 31, asserted Apr. 7 that witnesses had "said that Hutton was shot when his hands were in the air." He added Apr. 12 that the police had ordered Hutton to run and then had shot him.

Pittsburgh —Violence swept through black areas of Pittsburgh Apr. 4-8. 5,200 National Guardsmen and 375 state policemen were called in to assist the 1,500-man city police force; all were ordered not to shoot looters. More than 1,100 persons were arrested, but hospitals reported treating fewer than 40 persons.

Scattered incidents of vandalism and firebombings were reported Apr. 5, but the disorders spread Apr. 6 from the predominantly Negro Hill district to the North Side, where black gangs set fires, smashed windows and stoned cars. Mayor Joseph M. Barr Apr. 6 ordered bars and liquor stores in the city closed, and Gov. Raymond P. Shafer ordered all liquor stores in the state closed. More than 90 persons were reported injured.

Shafer Apr. 7 declared a state of emergency, imposed a 7 p.m.-to-5 a.m. curfew and called in reinforcements. 2,200 National Guardsmen and 300 state policemen moved into the city immediately. Among the 24 persons reported injured Apr. 7 were 2 Guardsmen, 3 firemen and 4 policemen. About 1,000 people marched from the Hill to downtown Pittsburgh Apr. 7 in a tribute to King that was delayed while the marchers waited for sufficient police protection.

New violence was reported in the Homewood-Rushton district Apr. 8. The number of fires reported since Apr. 4 rose to 190.

1,000 additional National Guardsmen were moved into the city Apr. 9, although the city was generally reported calm. Barr lifted the curfew restrictions Apr. 10 and the National Guardsmen were withdrawn from the city Apr. 11-12.

Trenton, N. J. —Harlan M. Joseph, 19, a Negro member of the Mayor's Youth Council and divinity student at Lincoln University (Oxford, Pa.), was shot to death in Trenton Apr. 9 by Michael A. Castiello, a white policeman. The shooting took place during the 2d night of sporadic outbreaks of racial violence. State police were called in to aid city policemen, and Gov. Richard J. Hughes Apr. 10 placed National Guardsmen on standby alert. More than 235 persons were arrested Apr. 9-12, in most cases for violating a 9 p.m.-to-6 a.m. curfew imposed by Mayor Carmen J. Armenti Apr. 9. 30 persons were injured; dozens of stores were looted and/or damaged by fire.

According to police, Joseph was one of 5 black youths who had smashed the display windows of a haberdashery store across the street from City Hall and had stolen apparel. Police said Joseph was "a looter, and loot was recovered from his person." Detective Capt. Leon Foley said that Patrolman Castiello had fired a warning shot in the air and then had tried to wound one of the fleeing youths in the leg. "But his gun was jostled by the crowd just as he fired," Foley said, "and the bullet struck the Joseph kid in the back." Other witnesses said Joseph was trying to stop the looters and was not looting.

Hughes withdrew the Guard Apr. 12.

Wilmington, Del. —Rioting and other violence was quelled in Wilmington, Del. after Gov. Charles L. Terry Jr. called out the National Guard Apr. 9. Amidst much criticism, the governor later extended the Guard's tour of duty indefinitely to avoid similar outbreaks of violence. Defending his action Sept. 4, 1968, Terry asserted that the National Guard patrols had "stopped at least 2 riots" in the city that summer. His action, however, resulted in his defeat, Nov. 5, 1968 in election for a 2d term as governor. The newly-elected governor, Russell W. Peterson, withdrew the Guardsmen within 3 hours of his inauguration Jan. 21, 1969. He said that "the provocation of white soldiers policing black neighborhoods" had "helped breed fear and suspicion and hate" and had made the city a "national spectacle."

Among comments on the disorders:

Justice Department officials acknowledged Apr. 13 that methods of riot control in the disorders had been based on a "humanitarian" plan of restraint and a minimum use of gunfire. The policy, largely the work of Atty. Gen. Ramsey Clark and ex-Deputy Defense Secy. Cyrus R. Vance, called for the use of "overwhelming law enforcement manpower" coupled with military and police restraint. The heavy use of tear gas was substituted for gunfire. A department official said: "That old stuff about 'looters will be shot on sight' is for the history books and maybe the movies. It's for people who don't know how it is to be in a riot where, if you shoot, they shoot back and you've got a lot of dead cops and troops along with the dead citizens." "We have drawn back from all that the law allows because it is our duty to stop riots, not to kill rioters."

Pres. Johnson, in a letter to Defense Secy. Clark M. Clifford (made public Apr. 23), praised the "wise and restrained use of force" by federal troops and National Guardsmen in the rioting. The President noted that not one death had been caused by military forces. He said that the more than 26,500 Army troops and 47,000 National Guardsmen had "fulfilled with distinction an assignment that was regrettable but unavoidable."

Student Unrest

The murder of Martin Luther King also provoked demonstrations and disorders among students at various high schools and colleges across the nation.

In one incident about 300 black students barricaded themselves inside Boston University's Administration Building for more than 12 hours Apr. 24. The students, members of an Afro-American group, demanded the admission of more black students, financial aid for black students, the employment of more black faculty members and courses in Negro history. They also demanded that the university name the building housing the School of Theology in memory of Dr. King.

The Riot Data Clearinghouse of the Lemberg Center for the Study of Violence at Brandeis University in Waltham, Mass. said that 91 incidents of high-school disorders were reported in Apr. 1968, compared with 42 incidents for all of 1967. Among the disorders reported were Negro student demonstrations and boycotts in demands for educational reforms (including more emphasis on Negro culture studies) in high schools in White Plains, N.Y. (April and May), Camden, N.J. (May 9), Newark, N.J. (May 13-20), Yonkers, N.Y. (May 17) and Pittsburgh, Pa. (May 31-June 8). Fighting between white and Negro students was reported in Westbury, N.Y. and Newark, N.J.

SCLC Reorganized, Continues King's Campaigns

The Rev. Ralph David Abernathy was named Apr. 5, 1968 to succeed King as president of the Southern Christian Leadership Conference. SCLC's first activity under his leadership, Abernathy said, would be to carry out the march in support of the striking sanitation workers in Memphis that King had planned to lead.

Abernathy was officially elected SCLC president in Atlanta Apr. 9. Mrs. Coretta King and singer Harry Belafonte were elected to the 53-member board of directors. Abernathy pledged that SCLC would be "more militant than ever" while continuing to use non-violent methods.

Pres. Johnson had sent Labor Undersecy. James Reynolds to Memphis Apr. 5 to meet with representatives of the city and the sanitation workers union, the American Federation of

State, County & Municipal Employes (AFSCME), in hopes of breaking the deadlock of the 8-week-old strike that had culminated in King's death.

The U.S. District Court in Memphis Apr. 3 had enjoined King from leading his 2d protest march in Memphis Apr. 8, but after King's death, Bayard Rustin, executive director of the A. Philip Randolph Institute, the Rev. James Bevel and the Rev. James Lawson, chairman of the Congress on the March for Equality (COME), announced Apr. 5 that they planned to hold the march as a memorial tribute as well as a demonstration of support for the strike.

During the night of Apr. 4-5 more than 30 people were injured in rioting in Memphis. At least 3 major fires were reported and dozens of stores looted. There were several reports of sniper fire. The first death resulting from violence was reported Apr. 6. Gov. Buford Ellington (D., Tenn.) immediately ordered 4,000 National Guardsmen into the city, and Mayor Henry Loeb reinstated a 7 p.m.-to-5 a.m. curfew.

Loeb said Apr. 5 that "in view of the tragic circumstances," the city would withdraw its objections to the march. He said that in response to the demands of Gov. Ellington, he would meet with the strike mediators to "get this thing behind us and find a solution to our differences." He made little headway that day, however, in 2 meetings, one with 144 Negro and white clergymen and the other with 9 Negro schoolteachers. The clergymen led a memorial march Apr. 5 down 7 city blocks past the National Guardsmen. At a memorial service later they adopted a resolution asking the mayor to end "racial prejudice and arrogant paternalism" in Memphis.

The march King had planned was held Apr. 8 with Mrs. Coretta King taking her husband's place in the front rank ahead of an estimated 42,000 silent marchers, including thousands (estimated at 30% of the total) of whites. The march ended with a rally in front of City Hall, where Mrs. King urged the crowd to "carry on because this is the way he would have wanted it." But, she cried, "how many men must die before we can really have a free and true and peaceful society? How long will it take?"

A settlement of the 65-day strike was reached Apr. 16. The accord was ratified unanimously by the union's members and approved by the City Council with one dissenting vote. AFSCME Pres. Jerry Wurf said the agreement was "a good settlement that couldn't have been achieved without the coalescence of the union and the Negro community."

The Poor People's Campaign, planned by King in Aug. 1967, brought 9 caravans of poor people to Washington, D.C. beginning May 11, 1968. As proposed by King, the campaign called for massive lobbying by the nation's poor in Washington to pressure Congress and the Administration to enact legislation to reduce poverty. Plans were made for the encampment of thousands of participants in a canvas-and-plywood "Resurrection City, U.S.A." in the capital and for massive demonstrations. The caravans started from various parts of the country May 2-17. They held rallies and picked up additional participants along the way to Washington.

An opening phase of the Poor People's Campaign began Apr. 29 when SCLC Pres. Abernathy led a "delegation of 100" (ranging at times from 130 to 150 persons), representatives of Negroes, Puerto Ricans, Mexican-Americans, American Indians and Appalachian whites, in Washington conferences with Cabinet members and Congressional leaders to present a long list of legislative demands.

The National Park Service of the Interior Department May 10 issued a 37-day renewable permit to allow the campaign leaders to erect their plywood-and-canvas shantytown for 3,000 participants on a 16-acre West Potomac Park site, about 2½ miles from the Capitol and a mile from the White House.

Many Southern members of Congress had reacted adversely to the prospect of the encampment of the poor in the capital. But efforts to prevent or limit the campaign were largely abortive. The House Public Works Subcommittee on Public Buildings & Grounds held hearings May 6 on 75 bills designed to limit large-scale demonstrations on federal property, to limit the chances of violence and to set bond requirements to compensate for any possible damage.

The Defense Department announced May 11 that "selected troop units" had been alerted to help District of Columbia police in the event of violence. Pres. Johnson, at a news conference May 3, had announced that the government had made "extensive preparations" to meet "the possibilities of serious consequences flowing from the assemblage of large numbers over any protracted period of time in the seat of government, where there's much work to be done and very little time to do it."

The 2d phase of the campaign began May 12 when Mrs. King led a 12-block Mother's Day march of "welfare mothers" from 20 cities to the Cardozo High School Stadium in the center of Washington's Negro ghetto. (Mrs. King was accompanied by several white women, including Mrs. Harry Belafonte; Mrs. Robert F. Kennedy; Mrs. Joseph S. Clark, wife of the Democratic Senator from Pennsylvania; Mrs. Philip A. Hart, wife of the Democratic Senator from Michigan.)

Mrs. King declared at the rally, attended by 5,000 participants, that she would try to enlist the support of "black women, white women, brown women and red women—all the women of this nation—in a campaign of conscience." She stressed the need for non-violence but admitted that it was "not an easy way, particularly in this day when violence is almost fashionable, and in this society, where violence against poor people and minority groups is routine." But, she continued, "I must remind you that starving a child is violence. Suppressing a culture is violence. Neglecting school children is violence. Punishing a mother and her family is violence.... Ignoring medical needs is violence. Contempt for poverty is violence. Even the lack of will power to help humanity is a sick and sinister form of violence."

The erection of the prefabricated shelters was started May 13 when Abernathy, dressed in blue denims, drove a ceremonial nail at the dedication of "Resurrection City, U.S.A."

Abernathy said he would conduct a non-violent protest "to arouse the conscience of the nation." He vowed to "plague the pharaohs of this nation with plague after plague until they agree to give us meaningful jobs and a guaranteed annual income." Abernathy said: "Unlike the previous marches which have been held in Washington, this march will not last a day, or 2 days, or even a week. We will be here until the Congress of the United States decide that they are going to do something about the plight of the poor people by doing away with poverty, unemployment and underemployment in this country."

If necessary, "we will stay until Congress adjourns." "And then we're going to go where Congress goes, because we have decided that there will be no new business until we first take care of old business."

William A. Rutherford, executive director of SCLC, had said in an interview May 11 that the organization had obtained about 30% of $1 million required for the campaign through June 30. The anticipated expenses included costs of medical equipment, sewage systems, electrical wiring and phone lines, food, shelters, bedding and bathing facilities.

Abernathy May 17 asked the United Presbyterian Church's General Assembly, meeting in Minneapolis, Minn., to establish a $10 million Martin Luther King Poor People's Development Fund. The General Assembly May 20 pledged $100,000 toward the $10 million to be used to encourage development of low-cost housing, self-help industries and cooperatives and businesses.

As demonstrations got under way in Washington May 21, however, the campaign appeared to be confronted by increasing difficulties. Along with a lack of organization and disunity in the staff leadership, the problems of insufficient cooking, bathing and sanitation facilities were compounded by unusually heavy rainstorms, which forced many people out of the campsite.

The campaign ended in late June 1968. Bearing little fruit in terms of the dramatic goals asserted by its leaders, it did bring at least a promise of reform in a series of agreements negotiated with federal agencies. These included an expanded food distribution program, changes in welfare guidelines and eligibility requirements, and new provisions for participation of the poor in local operations of several government agencies.

The Interior Department permit for Resurrection City expired June 23. 124 residents were arrested June 24 after they refused to leave the campsite, and several hundred others, including Abernathy, were arrested for an illegal demonstration on the Capitol grounds. National Guardsmen were called in June 24 to curb violence that erupted following the closing of the camp.

Abernathy, released from jail July 13, announced July 16 that the Washington direct-action phase of the Poor People's Campaign was ended. He called on the 300 demonstrators remaining to go home and await assignments for protest "on a national level."

Abernathy said that even though Congress had "failed to move meaningfully against the problem of poverty," the campaign had made major gains. He asserted that poverty would never again be ignored in the U.S. and that national attention had been turned from the question of violence to the deeper issue of "the poverty and exploitation that breed violence."

SCLC held its 11th annual conference Aug. 14-18 in Memphis. The convention pledged that SCLC would remain a non-violent and biracial organization, but Abernathy warned Aug. 15 that it would no longer be a peacemaker in U.S. racial disputes. Despite rumors of dissatisfaction with Abernathy's leadership, the delegates unanimously elected him president of the organization Aug. 16.

SCLC board member Alfred Daniel Williams King, 38, younger brother of Martin Luther King, was found dead July 21, 1969 of accidental drowning in his swimming pool in Atlanta. The younger King, who had led integration movements in Birmingham, Ala. and Louisville, Ky., had assumed the co-pastorate of the Ebenezer Baptist Church (Atlanta) in 1968 after his brother's assassination.

SCLC officially ended its long period of mourning for Martin Luther King at the organization's 12th annual conference, held Aug. 14-16, 1969 in Charleston, S.C.

Search for Assassin

Aided by fingerprints found on the abandoned rifle left near the rooming house in Memphis and various other clues, local law enforcement agents and the FBI initiated one of the most extensive manhunts in police history for King's assassin.

Finally, a white Mustang automobile (similar to the one witnesses saw leave the Memphis rooming house immediately after King's murder), which had been abandoned in Atlanta, was traced Apr. 11, 1968 to an Eric Starvo Galt.

The FBI issued a federal fugitive warrant in Birmingham, Ala. Apr. 17. It charged Eric Starvo Galt, 36, with conspiracy in the assassination of King. The warrant said Galt had conspired with a man "whom he alleged to be his brother" to "injure, oppress, threaten or intimidate" King. A Tennessee warrant charging Galt with first-degree murder was issued in Memphis the same day by District Atty. Phil Danale. The FBI also released 2 photos of Galt. (An FBI report which apparently had been released by mistake in Miami Apr. 11 and was withdrawn that evening, had indicated that an Eric Starvo Galt, 37, was being sought for questioning in the slaying.)

The FBI announced Apr. 19 that Eric Starvo Galt was an alias of James Earl Ray, 40, of Illinois, who had escaped from the Missouri State Penitentiary Apr. 23, 1967 after serving 7 years of a 20-year sentence for armed robbery and auto theft. The FBI released several photos of Ray. His identity was announced after an extensive investigation of fingerprint records. Ray was reported also to have used the aliases of James McBride, James Walton, W.C. Herron and James O'Connor. Earlier aliases cited by the FBI had included John Willard and Harvey Lowmyer. Later reports included the name Paul Bridgman. The FBI placed Ray on its "10 Most Wanted" list Apr. 20.

Ray was indicted under the name of Eric Starvo Galt in Memphis Apr. 23 on charges of murder and conspiring to violate the civil rights of King. He was reindicted May 7 under his real name.

Ray Arrested in London

James Earl Ray was arrested by Scotland Yard detectives at Heathrow Airport in London, England June 8, 1968.*

Ray was apprehended when he went to the airport to board a plane for Brussels. His capture was the result of a coordinated effort by the FBI, the Royal Canadian Mounted Police and Scotland Yard, the British national police force. Arrested on charges of possessing a fraudulent Canadian passport and of carrying a revolver without a permit, Ray was taken to

---

*The news of Ray's arrest, announced in the U.S. by Atty. Gen. Ramsey Clark, came as funeral services were being held for Sen. Robert F. Kennedy, himself a victim of an assassin's bullets.

James Earl Ray

Wide World

London's Cannon Row police station and detained under conditions of maximum security. He was moved to Brixton Prison June 10 and to Wandworth Prison June 11.

Fred M. Vinson Jr., assistant U.S. Attorney General in charge of the Justice Department's Criminal Division, flew to London June 8 to "review on behalf of the U.S. the custody, protection and expeditious return to this country" of Ray.

Ray was arraigned on the London charges June 10 under the name Ramon George Sneyd (the name on his passport). The same day, at the request of the U.S. embassy, the Bow Street Magistrate's Court issued a provisional warrant for his extradition to the U.S. to stand trial for murder. The U.S. formally applied for Ray's extradition June 12. Chief Metropolitan Magistrate Frank Milton ruled in London June 18 that the charges on which Ray had been arrested would be set aside pending action on the extradition request.

After his arrest June 8, the FBI and Justice Department had released the following information:

● Ray had arrived in Birmingham, Ala. in the summer of 1967 and had established his new identity as Eric Starvo Galt. He bought a white 1966 Mustang auto and obtained a driver's license as Galt. During the fall and winter he made several trips to the West Coast, where he took dancing lessons and a course in bartending. He left Los Angeles for New Orleans Dec. 15, 1967 and returned Dec. 21. He was graduated from a bartending school in Hollywood Mar. 2, 1968.

● Ray, using the name John Willard, checked into the Memphis rooming house facing the Lorraine Motel, where King was staying, the afternoon of Apr. 4. He refused a room on the north side of the house but took one near the back with a view of the balcony outside King's room. One boarder reported that he saw Willard emerge from the bathroom with something wrapped in newspaper after the murder shot was fired.

● A Remington 30.06 pump rifle with a telescopic sight and a case containing binoculars were found lying on the sidewalk a few feet from the entrance of the rooming house. The gun, traced through its serial number by the FBI, had been bought in Birmingham, Ala. by Ray, using the name of Galt or Lowmyer.

● A white 1966 Mustang with an Alabama license plate was impounded by the FBI in Atlanta Apr. 11; the car, believed to be Ray's, had been parked near a housing project there since Apr. 5.

● Ray had entered Canada by auto Apr. 8; by Apr. 16 he had taken up residence in a Toronto rooming house. A Canadian passport in the name of Sneyd was issued to Ray Apr. 24 in Ottawa and was sent to him through the Kennedy Travel Bureau, Ltd. in Toronto. Ray reportedly flew from Toronto to London May 6 and on to Lisbon, Portugal May 7. He obtained a 2d passport from the Canadian embassy in Lisbon May 16, claiming that the original had been spoiled. He returned to London May 17 and apparently remained there until his arrest. (According to the first reports of his capture, Ray was seized when he arrived in London from Lisbon and tried to change planes for Brussels. FBI spokesmen issued a corrected version of the story June 11.)

Canadian police reported June 11 that 3 of the men whose names Ray used as aliases—Eric St. V. Galt, Paul Bridgman and Ramon George Sneyd—all lived in the same neighborhood in Toronto and all bore a marked resemblance to Ray in appearance, age, height and weight. The 3 men did not know each other. Ray had begun using the name of Eric Starvo Galt (apparently based on a misreading of the real Galt's signature) as early as Apr. 1967. He used the Bridgman name when he first went to Toronto and the name of Sneyd when he applied for a passport. A 4th alias used by Ray was that of another Toronto man—John Willard—who was described as not resembling Ray. None of the men reportedly knew Ray.

(Because of the ease with which Ray had obtained a Canadian passport during his flight from U.S. authorities, the Canadian government issued more restrictive passport requirements Jan. 22, 1969.)

Ray was extradited by a London court July 2, 1968 and returned to the U.S. July 19. At his arraignment July 22, he was charged with murder and carrying a dangerous weapon; he entered a plea of not guilty.

Ray's Background

James Earl Ray, an acknowledged racial bigot and

supporter of Alabama Gov. George Wallace, grew up in the Midwest during the Depression amidst extreme poverty, alcoholism and indolence.

Ray was born Mar. 10, 1928 in Alton, Ill. He was one of 8 children. His father was a laborer, often unemployed and frequently away from home. His mother, who bore the main responsibility for raising the children, was an alcoholic. The family moved twice during Ray's youth, to St. Louis, Mo. in 1929 and to Ewing, Mo. in 1932.

A constant truant, Ray left school in the 8th grade when he was 15. Shortly thereafter the family broke up, his mother and several of the other children moving to Adams and then Quincy, Ill. where the 3 younger children were placed in a Roman Catholic home in Alton. Ray was sent to his grandmother, who lived on a farm in Missouri. The 2 later moved to Alton. When he was 16, Ray took a job at a tannery in Hartford, Ill.; 2 years later he lost the job and enlisted in the Army. A private in the military police, he was sent to Germany, where he was eventually imprisoned in an Army stockade for drunkenness and resisting arrest. He was given a general discharge by the Army Dec. 23, 1948 because of "ineptness and lack of adaptability to military service."

Ray then returned to Alton, where he was arrested for the first time as a civilian—on a traffic-violation charge—in Jan. 1949. For the next few years he shifted back and forth between Chicago and California, working for short periods as a laborer. During this time he was arrested several times on charges ranging from burglary and vagrancy to armed robbery. For the latter offense he served 2 years in the Illinois State Prison in Pontiac. While awaiting trial for burglary in Edwardsville, Ill. in 1955, he was found guilty of forging a U.S. Post Office money order; he spent the next 3 years in the federal prison at Leavenworth, Kan. After his release he worked for a year at various laborer jobs; at this time he also began to use the first of his many aliases.

Ray was arrested in Oct. 1959 for armed robbery of a St. Louis supermarket and sentenced to a 20-year term at the Missouri State Penitentiary. 2 attempts to escape were unsuccessful, but in Apr. 1967 he succeeded by hiding in a large breadbox being sent from the prison bakery. He was later described by the Missouri warden, Harold Swenson, as "extremely dangerous, cold-blooded and ruthless."

Conspiracy Doubted

The possibility that King's murder was the work of a conspiracy had been discounted by Atty. Gen. Ramsey Clark in Memphis Apr. 5, 1968 immediately after the slaying. At an impromptu news conference Clark had said that there was no evidence of a "widespread plot—this appears to have been the act of a single individual." He reiterated Apr. 7: "We have evidence of one man on the run. There is no evidence that more were involved."

But as evidence accumulated, a widespread feeling grew that more than one person had been involved in the slaying and that Ray might have been a hired assassin. Among the indications of a conspiracy: a broadcast on the police radio band shortly after the slaying reporting that a white Mustang auto was being pursued in a direction opposite to that apparently taken by Ray; heavy spending by Ray under the alias of Galt in various parts of the country; the 4 aliases used by Ray in the U.S. and Canada; his extensive travels in the U.S., Canada and Europe.

Atty. Gen. Clark, interviewed on the ABC-TV program "Issues and Answers" June 9, 1968, the day after Ray's capture, asserted again that Ray had acted alone. "We have no evidence of any other involvement by any other person or people," he said. Asked whether he thought that someone had "bankrolled" Ray's travels to Europe and Canada, Clark said: "He is a person ... who lived a life of crime, who obtained funds, money, through crime, and I think we can reason that there is a very plausible possibility as to the source of his funds."

Trial Postponed

Ray's attorney, Arthur J. Hanes Sr., asked the Memphis Criminal Court Aug. 16, 1968 to dismiss its murder charge against Ray on the ground that "pervasive and widespread" publicity made it impossible for him to receive a fair trial. Judge W. Preston Battle rejected the request Sept. 6; he said that while excessive publicity could bring about a change in the site of the trial, it could not result in a dismissal of the charges.

At the same hearing, Battle also ruled that the defense could have access to most of the prosecution's evidence against Ray.

Ray dismissed Hanes as his attorney Nov. 10, 1968. Ray's new lawyer, chosen Nov. 12, was Percy Foreman, of Houston, Tex. In approving the change of defense lawyers, Judge Battle also delayed the trial, originally scheduled to begin Nov. 12, until Mar. 3, 1969. Battle ordered Hanes to turn over all his data on the case to Foreman. Hanes was also required to continue to observe strict publicity restrictions imposed on the case and to post a $1,000 bond to assure his return to Memphis to be sentenced for violating those rules. (Hanes, 2 Memphis newspaper reporters and a private detective had been cited for contempt of court Sept. 30 for public statements about the case.)

Foreman sought another delay in the trial Dec. 18 but was rebuffed by Judge Battle, who ordered the trial held as scheduled. Battle also ruled that Ray was a pauper and assigned the Memphis Public Defender's office to aid Foreman in his defense.

Ray Pleads Guilty, Gets 99-Year Term

Ray pleaded guilty in Memphis Mar. 10, 1969 to King's murder. He was sentenced the same day to serve 99 years in prison. Judge Battle ordered Ray sent to the Tennessee State Penitentiary in Nashville after brief court proceedings during which Ray indicated that he disagreed with the prosecution's theory that there had been no conspiracy.

The case was settled in Shelby County Courthouse during a short hearing at which prosecutor Phil M. Canale, 51, presented evidence against Ray to a 12-man jury. (Under Tennessee law, a jury must decide both on the verdict and on the sentence in capital cases.) Both Canale and Percy Foreman, Ray's attorney, told the court that there was no evidence of a conspiracy. During the hearing, however, Ray rose to say that he could "not accept" their statements. Ray asserted that he did not agree with "Canale's, Mr. [Ramsey] Clark's, and Mr. J. Edgar Hoover's [theories] about the conspiracy, [but] I don't want to add something on that I haven't agreed to in the past." Foreman then explained to the judge: "I think that what he said is that he doesn't agree that Ramsey Clark is right or that J. Edgar Hoover is right."

After Ray's outburst, Battle was careful to get an explicit statement from the defendant on his plea. He asked Ray: "Are you pleading guilty to murder in the first degree in this case because you killed Dr. Martin Luther King under such circumstances that it would make you legally guilty of murder in the first degree under the law as explained to you by your lawyer? Your answer is still yes?" Ray replied: "Yes, sir."

The 99-year sentence, an arrangement by the state and the defense agreed to in advance by the jury, allowed parole after completion of half the sentence. If Ray had pleaded not guilty and had been convicted of first degree murder, he could have received either a life sentence (and have been eligible for parole in 13 years), or he could have been sentenced to death.

Battle said that he believed the 99-year term a "just one to both defendant and the state." He added: "It has been established that the prosecution at this time is not in possession of enough evidence to indict anyone as a co-conspirator in this case. Of course, this is not conclusive evidence that there was no conspiracy."

Canale told newsmen after the hearing that there were a number of unexplained incidents in the case that might make the idea of a conspiracy conceivable. But he said that the unanswered questions might have been related to other illegal activities that Ray had been involved in before King's murder. He mentioned specifically that Ray had smuggled narcotics from Canada and jewelry either into or from Mexico.

The Justice Department said Mar. 10 that "the investigation into the conspiracy allegation is still open." But the *N.Y. Times* reported Mar. 11 that federal officials had no evidence that Ray had been hired or that he had planned the murder with another person.

Mrs. Coretta King said in Atlanta Mar. 10 that she believed the assassination was the result of a conspiracy and that "all concerned people must press the state of Tennessee and the U.S. government to continue until all who are responsible for this crime have been apprehended."

(The Rev. James L. Bevel, an SCLC official and longtime associate of King's, had claimed in Philadelphia Jan. 19, 1969 that Ray was innocent and that he had "evidence that would free him." Bevel Jan. 15 had sent a telegram to Ray, offering to defend him in his trial. In the telegram Bevel said he had been present at the Memphis motel where King was shot, and "of course, I know you are not guilty." Beverly Sterner, Bevel's administrative assistant, said Jan. 19 that the offer to defend Ray was not meant merely as a symbolic gesture to shift the blame for the murder from Ray personally and place it on white racism in general. "This is a serious offer" and Bevel would present his evidence in court, she said. But after Bevel requested permission to associate himself with Ray's defense, Judge Battle ruled Jan. 24 that Bevel could not help defend Ray. Battle said Tennessee law prohibited Bevel from practicing law without a license.

(The Rev. Ralph Abernathy, who succeeded King as head of SCLC, at first supported Bevel's statements about Ray's innocence. Abernathy said in Atlanta Jan. 23 that Bevel was "speaking to the real issue—namely that it is not who killed Dr. King but what killed him." But Abernathy conceded Jan. 28 that he did not believe Bevel had evidence of Ray's innocence.)

Ray's Appeals Denied

Criminal Court Judge Arthur C. Faquin Jr. May 26, 1969 denied a request by Ray for a new trial. Faquin ruled that Ray had given up his right to appeal Mar. 10 when he had pleaded guilty. The judge told Ray's lawyers that they could seek a new trial in higher courts. Ray was ordered to continue serving his 99-year sentence.

Faquin, 44, had been appointed to the case Apr. 3 following the death Mar. 31 of Ray's trial judge, W. Preston Battle, 60. Ray had retained 3 new lawyers to present the appeal: J. B. Stoner, 44, of Savannah, Ga., a former Ku Klux Klan organizer and the 1964 Vice Presidential candidate of the segregationist National States Rights Party; Robert J. Hill Jr., of Chattanooga, Tenn.; Richard J. Ryan, of Memphis.

Ray's attorneys based his appeal on legal technicalities concerning the validity of Ray's guilty plea. The prosecution argued that there could be no appeal for a "new" trial since Ray had been sentenced after a guilty-plea hearing and technically there had been no trial.

Ray's attorneys declined Faquin's offer to open the hearing to charges made by Ray that he had been "pressured" into a guilty plea to serve the financial interests of his 2 former defense attorneys, Percy Foreman and Arthur Hanes, and free-lance writer William Bradford Huie. Huie had purchased rights to Ray's life story, and Ray had used the money to hire defense lawyers. Huie, Foreman and Hanes had written a series of articles for *Look* magazine. Movie and book rights were also involved in the suit.

(Huie had written 2 articles, published in the Nov. 12, 1968 and Nov. 26, 1968 issues of *Look,* in which he detailed Ray's activities prior to and after King's assassination. Based on his own investigation, Huie concluded that Ray had not acted alone but was part of a larger conspiracy to kill King.

(In a 3d article, published in the Apr. 15, 1969 issue of *Look,* Huie reversed himself and claimed that Ray had not been a member of a conspiracy, but had killed King mainly to gain status. He based his opinion on these factors: [1] His confidence that Ray's complicated activities and trip to Canada after the assassination were within his capabilities; [2] Ray's pride in having committed the murder and escaping unaided; [3] Ray's involved efforts to trace King's whereabouts and plans prior to Apr. 4, 1968; [4] the conclusion that the shot that killed King could have been fired by an unexperienced marksman because of the short distance and angle required to hit the target; [5] the feeling that Ray's experiences in the Missouri Penitentiary had transformed him from a "stupid bungler" into a "crafty criminal"; [6] Ray's ability to support himself and finance his travels after the slaying through robberies and narcotics smuggling; [7] the conviction that it was a misconception that Ray was not a racist and that he could only have been motivated by money; [8] the determination, based on psychiatric examinations taken at Fulton, Mo. State Hospital in 1966, that Ray was capable of committing murder.

(Huie said he had found no evidence of a conspiracy linking King's murder and the assassination of Pres. John Kennedy in 1963.

(Articles by Hanes and Foreman also appeared in the Apr. 15, 1969 issue of *Look.* Hanes said he believed that Ray was a member of a conspiracy. He reported that he had never heard Ray express hate or resentment in any discussions about race or politics. Foreman, conversely, believed that Ray had acted alone, motivated primarily by a deep need to win recognition and make the remainder of his life exciting.)

In a petition filed in Federal District Court Apr. 11, 1969, Ray had requested that his contracts with Huie and Foreman be voided. Ray charged that Foreman "never intended for him to have a fair trial and testify in his own behalf as this would then make the facts and testimony public property and no one would or could have exclusive [story] rights in the matter." Similar charges had been made in Ray's Apr. 7 motion for a new trial.

(Hanes and Huie had been among 7 persons found in contempt of court by Judge Battle for violating pretrial publicity bans. Faquin May 23, 1969 reversed Battle's findings and dismissed all of the contempt citations arising out of Ray's trial.)

The Tennessee Supreme Court Jan. 8, 1970 refused to consider a plea for a new trial for Ray. The court said that once a defendant "pleads guilty and fully understands what he is doing, ... there can be no legal ground for granting of a new trial."

Prison Conditions Improved

Tennessee Gov. Buford Ellington dismissed State Commissioner of Correction Harry S. Avery May 29, 1969, charging improper conduct in the handling of Ray. The action followed Avery's refusal of the governor's request that he resign after an investigation into reports that Avery was contemplating writing a book about the Ray case.

U.S. District Court Judge William E. Miller Dec. 29, 1969 ordered Tennessee State Prison officials to provide "recreation, work and exercise" for Ray. Ray had sought an injunction against continued maximum security confinement, contending that his health was being impaired and his rights violated. Miller approved a plan Jan. 12, 1970.

It was reported Mar. 26, 1970 that Ray had been transferred from the state penitentiary in Nashville, Tenn. to the small, maximum security Brushy Mountain Prison near Petros, Tenn.

KING HONORED

Awards & Memorials

Among the many awards and memorials honoring Martin L. King Jr. posthumously:

● Indian Education Min. Triguna Sen announced in New Delhi, India May 27, 1968 that King had been chosen winner of the 1966 Jawaharlal Nehru Award for International Understanding.

Indian Pres. Zakir Hussain presented the 100,000-rupee ($13,000) award to Mrs. Coretta King in New Delhi Jan. 24, 1969. The citation accompanying the prize, read by Indian Vice Pres. V. V. Giri, said that the award had been conferred in "gratitude to a man who, like Mahatma Gandhi, laid down his life to show all mankind a sane way to the promised land of justice and equality." Indian Prime Min. Indira Gandhi said that the Nehru award was the "highest tribute our nation can bestow on work for understanding and brotherhood among men."

In accepting the honor, Mrs. King said: "In a profound way Martin Luther King continues the struggle for peace and understanding between men and nations more powerfully in death than in life ... for his spirit has been loosened upon a violent and loveless world."

● The first Dr. Martin Luther King Jr. International Freedom Games for sports were held May 18, 1969 in Villanova, Pa.

● Negroes and whites across the nation Jan. 15, 1970 quietly celebrated King's 41st birthday. Several governors, including Nelson A. Rockefeller of New York, Frank Licht of Rhode Island and Kenneth M. Curtis of Maine, declared Martin Luther King Days in their states.

(After a meeting with Pres.-elect Richard M. Nixon and 5 Negro leaders Jan. 13, 1969, SCLC Pres. Ralph Abernathy had reported that Nixon had requested a memo on Abernathy's proposal to declare Jan. 15, King's birthday, a legal holiday as an "act of redemption" for Nixon's failure to designate a Negro to his cabinet. But the day was never so honored.)

In some cities, including Baltimore, New York, Harrisburg, Pa., Philadelphia, Kansas City, Mo. and Poughkeepsie, N.Y., public schools were closed. In Illinois the state legislature designated a "commemorative holiday," and although Illinois schools remained open, part of the school day was devoted to the study of King's work. The same classroom routine was followed in San Francisco.

Memorial church services were held across the nation.

In Atlanta, 400 persons heard Atlanta Mayor Sam Massell eulogize King. Following the service, Mrs. Coretta King dedicated the city's new Martin Luther King Jr. Memorial Center, which included King's home, the Ebenezer Baptist Church and the crypt where King was buried.

Plans for the center were later expanded to include a memorial park at the gravesite, a library-documentation project to collect and document King's papers and other materials related to his work, the Institute of the Black World to help define and determine the role of black scholarship in U.S. thought and values and an institute for non-violent social change. Due, however, to a lack of interest both on the part of public donors and the federal government, which was to assist in the center's funding, the project soon developed financial problems. As a result many of the project's personnel were dismissed. (Mrs. Coretta King was picketed by former center workers, all Negroes, Aug. 4, 1970 during a news conference in which she announced changes in the center's management.)

● *King: A Film Record ... Montgomery to Memphis,* a documentary depicting King's civil rights campaigns, was released Mar. 24, 1970 for a special single night showing in U.S. and foreign motion picture theaters. The film, produced by Ely Landau, contained much new footage and was narrated by prominent personalities, including actress Joanne Woodward and singer Harry Belafonte. An estimated 700,000 persons attended the screening; it raised approximately $3.5 million for the continuance of King's civil rights and antipoverty campaigns.

● The Rev. Ted Cuveston, president of the Memphis chapter of Inner-City Communications, announced Nov. 25, 1970 that his group had been granted permission to launch a statewide campaign to raise money for the purchase and renovation of the Lorraine Motel, where King had been shot. Cuveston said the motel would be converted into a home for the city's needy elderly as a living memorial to the slain civil rights leader.

Post-Assassination Books

Among books published about King after his assassination:

● *Martin Luther King, Jr. His Life, Martyrdom and Meaning for the World,* by William Robert Miller, published Oct. 1968 by Weybright and Talley. A biography of King with emphasis on his civil rights campaigns.
● *My Life With Martin Luther King Jr.,* by Coretta Scott King, published Sept. 25, 1969 by Holt, Rinehart & Winston. The memoirs of King's widow.
● *King: A Critical Biography,* by David L. Lewis, published Jan. 15, 1970 by Praeger. A Negro historian assesses King's career.
● *He Slew the Dreamer. My Search, with James Earl Ray, for the Truth About the Murder of Martin Luther King,* by William Bradford Huie, published May 25, 1970 by Delacorte Press. The author discusses the life and motives of King's assassin.
● *The King God Didn't Save. Reflections on the Life and Death of Martin Luther King Jr.,* by John A. Williams, published Aug. 17, 1970 by Coward-McCann. Negro journalist theorizes that King was killed by a "white power" conspiracy.

Anniversary of Death Marked

The first anniversary of King's death was marked by a recurrence of the disturbances that had followed his assassination. Demonstrators rallied in major cities across the nation Apr. 4-6, 1969 to commemorate the anniversary, and, in many cases, to protest the war in Vietnam. Violence broke out in some cities but was quickly brought under control.

Among the developments reported:

Atlanta —A 45-hour vigil in commemoration of King's death began Apr. 4 in Atlanta and culminated in a march for peace by some 2,000 persons Apr. 6. The demonstrations were sponsored by SCLC and the Southwide Mobilization Against the War in Vietnam & for Self-Determination. The vigil took place on the grounds of the Georgia Capitol and in front of the Central Presbyterian Church across the street. It was the first such demonstration that Gov. Lester G. Maddox had allowed on state property. The Rev. Ralph Abernathy, leader of SCLC, and National Mobilization leader David Dellinger were among those who addressed the crowd following the march.

Chicago —Gov. Richard Ogilvie ordered the 4,800-member Illinois National Guard to duty Apr. 3 at the request of Chicago Mayor Richard J. Daley as disturbances in the city's Negro neighborhoods resulted in the arrest of more than 200 persons. Police were able to control the disturbances, caused mostly by Negro youths, before the troops arrived.

Ogilvie said that Daley had requested the troops "to head off any worse trouble by activating the Guard early." Daley imposed a dusk-to-dawn curfew for persons under 21 years of age, prohibited the sale of firearms and ammunition and the sale of flammable material in portable containers, closed taverns in troubled areas and cancelled all days off for policemen for the rest of the week.

The disturbances had apparently begun near high schools in the city, in some cases after memorial services for King. The violence was limited mostly to rock and bottle throwing, although some looting was reported. Passing motorists were harrassed, and windows were broken. Some 90 persons were reported injured, including 4 policemen, but only 2 were hospitalized.

Police controlling the disorders were restrained; they fired only once, into the air, to break up a crowd menacing police cars. A reporter at police headquarters said that youths arrested appeared to be unhurt and were reminded of their rights. A Chicago SCLC leader, the Rev. Calvin Morris, complained Apr. 4, however, that the Guard was not needed and might have caused more violence.

The Guard was demobilized and restrictions were lifted Apr. 5 following a peaceful march of more than 10,000 demonstrators protesting the war in Vietnam.

Memphis —Scattered violence and looting was brought quickly under control by Memphis policemen Apr. 4 while some 10,000 persons gathered in tribute to King. Sen. Edward M. Kennedy (D., Mass.) and the Rev. Abernathy addressed the crowd following a march that led past the Lorraine Motel, where King had been shot.

Mayor Henry Loeb imposed a dawn-to-dusk curfew after Negro youths ran through the city streets breaking windows and looting stores as the parade of marchers passed. Cut off from the violence by the police, the demonstrators waited quietly while the disorder was quelled. Riot police and National Guardsmen were on hand but were kept out of sight while traffic officers wearing regular equipment controlled the crowd.

Kennedy, in an unscheduled appearance, addressed the crowd at the end of the march. He urged the U.S. to resolve "that yesterday's grief and today's crises will be tomorrow's opportunity." Abernathy spoke after Kennedy and promised to continue King's fight against poverty.

Loeb lifted the curfew Apr. 6. Some 76 persons had been arrested during the 3 days, 31 of them for violating the curfew.

Montgomery, Ala. —Abernathy spoke at a King memorial in Montgomery Apr. 5 after more than 1,000 marchers paraded through the rain. Abernathy recalled the work he and King had done together in the city. SCLC official Hosea Williams hailed Abernathy afterwards as "the only man" who could lead the organization.

N.Y. City—More than 20,000 demonstrators marched through the rain in New York Apr. 5 in a demand for U.S. withdrawal from Vietnam. Among the demonstrators were dozens of servicemen, dressed in civilian clothes, who marched in protest against the war. Although there was heckling by counter-demonstrators, including members of the Young Americans for Freedom, the parade was orderly.

Selma, Ala. —About 2,000 Negroes, joined by dozens of whites, marched through Selma Apr. 4 in memory of King. They stopped to pray at the site where Alabama troopers had beaten back civil rights demonstrators with clubs and tear gas Mar. 7, 1965 during the Selma-Montgomery voter-registration drive. The march had begun at the Tabernacle Baptist Church after a meeting led by the church's pastor, the Rev. Louis L. Anderson, president of the Dallas County Progressive Movement for Human Rights. Cleve Strong, sitting in a mule-drawn farm wagon, led the marchers through streets lined with silent troopers, deputies and policemen.

Washington, D.C.—Despite pressure on Washington merchants and on the City Council to observe Apr. 4 as a holiday to commemorate King's death, the city's downtown stores remained open. Most small shops in areas affected by the Apr. 1968 rioting, however, were closed. After pressure by some 150 citizens, the council Apr. 1 had adopted a motion to ask Commissioner (Mayor) Walter E. Washington and the city's business community to undertake appropriate observances "to the extent possible" on the anniversary of King's assassination. About 1,000-1,500 National Guardsmen had been alerted to prepare for possible violence. Several fires "of a suspicious nature" and scattered incidents of window breaking had been reported Apr. 3.

Elsewhere—Other demonstrations in memory of King were held Apr. 4, in Nashville, Tenn., where 300 persons marched past the penitentiary in which James Earl Ray, King's assassin, was serving his sentence; in Asheville, N.C., where several hundred Negroes began a 250-mile march to Raleigh, N.C. to dramatize SCLC goals; and in Cincinnati, O., where 1,000 persons participated in a march through the rain. 2,000 people, led by the Rev. James E. Groppi, marched through Milwaukee, Wis. in King's honor Apr. 5, and 3,000 persons gathered in Little Rock, Ark. Apr. 6 for a memorial service that included an address by Arkansas Gov. Winthrop Rockefeller.

1963 Charges Vs. King Dropped

The U.S. Supreme Court Mar. 10, 1969 posthumously cleared King of charges of parading without a permit in Birmingham, Ala. in 1963.

In a test appeal brought by the Rev. Fred L. Shuttlesworth, one of King's former aides, the court ruled unanimously that a group of Negroes led by King and Shuttlesworth were within their rights in their Good Friday march through Birmingham in 1963 although they had not obtained a city permit.

The court ruled that the city's police commissioner, Eugene (Bull) Connor, had made it clear that anti-segregation marches would not be allowed; therefore, the court said, the demonstrators could march without applying for a permit since they could be reasonably sure permission would be denied. Justice Potter Stewart stressed that if the marchers had gone to court for a permit, Easter weekend would have passed without a demonstration.

FBI Wiretaps

An FBI agent disclosed June 4, 1969 that the bureau had maintained phone surveillance on King until his death. During a special hearing ordered for boxer Cassius Clay in Houston, Tex., the agent, Robert Nicols, gave details of the King wiretapping.

(The hearing, conducted by Appeals Court Judge Joe Ingraham, was ordered by the U.S. Supreme Court after the Justice Department disclosed that the FBI had tapped phone conversations involving Clay. The court ordered the hearing to determine whether illegal wiretap evidence had contributed to Clay's 1967 draft evasion conviction.)

Nicols testified that King's phone had been monitored at a time when King had criticized the FBI for assigning Southern rather than Northern agents to protect civil rights workers.

Testimony at the hearing June 6 indicated that the FBI had continued to maintain phone surveillance on King and Black Muslim leader Elijah Muhammad after Lyndon Johnson, then President, had ordered an end to all wiretaps except those authorized by the Attorney General for national security purposes. Nicols testified that he had supervised the wiretap of King's phone until May 1965.

Clyde Tolson, associate director of the FBI, told the *Washington Star* June 19 that the phone surveillance on King had been authorized in writing by Robert F. Kennedy when he was Attorney General. Tolson said the wiretapping did not violate Johnson's order restricting such surveillance to national security investigations. Tolson asserted that the wiretap was "within the provisions laid down by the then President of the United States." He said that the wiretap was related to internal security and therefore was legal.

FBI Director J. Edgar Hoover told the *Star* June 19 that the King wiretap had been proposed by Atty. Gen. Kennedy in June 1963. He said Kennedy had authorized it in writing in Oct. 1963. Hoover said Kennedy had first proposed the wiretap after expressing concern at the activities of King's followers. Ex-Atty. Gen. Nicholas deB. Katzenbach June 19 confirmed Hoover's statement that Kennedy had authorized the King wiretap but denied Hoover's claim that Kennedy had initiated the idea.

Ramsey Clark, attorney general under Johnson, said June 20 that Hoover had repeatedly asked him to authorize a tap on King's phone but that he had refused the director's requests. Clark said Hoover had asked him for permission to resume the King wiretap 2 days before King was slain. Clark said he had again denied the request.

Pres. Nixon said June 19 that he had personally investigated the wiretap controversy and had found that the FBI had not violated any government restrictions when it monitored King's phone. Speaking at a press conference, the President said Kennedy had authorized the King wiretap: "I found that the wiretapping had always been approved by the Attorney General."

THE ASSASSINATION
OF
ROBERT F. KENNEDY

Robert Francis Kennedy   Wide World Photo

ROBERT FRANCIS KENNEDY (1925-68)

Robert Francis Kennedy was born Nov. 20, 1925 in Brookline, Mass. He was the 3d son and 7th of 9 children of Joseph P. and Rose Kennedy. For most of his early life "Bobby" Kennedy was overshadowed by his 2 older brothers, Joseph Kennedy Jr., who was killed in 1944 during a bombing mission over Germany, and John F. Kennedy, who later became President. Small in frame and lacking somewhat in academic achievement, he was, according to his father, the Kennedy that strove hardest. He succeeded primarily by his intelligence, energy and drive.

"Bobby" Kennedy was graduated from Milton Academy in Massachusetts, then entered Harvard University. Shortly after his brother Joseph's death in 1944, he left Harvard during his sophomore year to join the Navy as a seaman. He was later commissioned a lieutenant. By personally appealing to Navy Secy. James V. Forrestal, he was assigned to a new 2,200-ton destroyer named Joseph P. Kennedy Jr. *(in honor of his brother), which was launched in 1945. He served on the ship for the rest of his military service.*

After his discharge from the Navy in 1946, Kennedy returned to Harvard, where he played end on the school's football team. He graduated in 1948 with a BA degree. Before entering the University of Virginia Law School later that year, he went to Palestine to serve as a war correspondent for the Boston Post. *He received a law degree from the University of Virginia in 1951 and shortly thereafter was admitted to the Massachusetts bar. Before settling down, however, he went on a trip around the world. Among his honorary degrees: LL.Ds from Assumption College (1957), Mt. St. Mary's College (1958), Tufts University (1958), Fordham University (1961), Nihon University (1962), Manhattan College (1962).*

Kennedy entered government service in 1951 as an attorney with the Criminal Division of the U.S. Department of Justice. Most of his work dealt with the prosecution of graft and income-tax cases. He resigned in 1952 to manage his brother John's successful Senate election campaign.

179

The late Sen. Joseph R. McCarthy (R., Wis.) hired Kennedy in Jan. 1953 as one of 15 assistant counsels to serve under Chief Counsel Roy Cohn on McCarthy's Permanent Subcommittee on Investigations. Kennedy resigned July 31, 1953 after a walkout by the Democratic members of the subcommittee, who objected to McCarthy's investigative methods. But Kennedy was rehired Feb. 17, 1954 as the subcommittee's Democratic counsel. During several of the intervening months between the 2 posts, he served as an assistant counsel with the Hoover Commission on Organization of the Executive Branch of the Government. He was chosen one of the "10 most outstanding men" of 1954 by the U.S. Junior Chamber of Commerce.

In late summer of 1955 Kennedy took a leave of absence from the subcommittee to join Supreme Court Justice William O. Douglas on a 6-week tour of 5 Soviet Republics in Central Asia. On his return, he spoke at an alumni gathering at Notre Dame University Dec. 11, 1955 and urged a UN investigation of Soviet "colonialism" in the area he had toured. In Mar. 1956 he assailed the support of Western colonialism in Indochina and elsewhere as "the fatal error in United States foreign policy."

When the Democrats took control of the Senate in 1955 Kennedy became the investigation subcommittee's chief counsel and staff director under the chairmanship of Sen. John L. McClellan (D., Ark.). A year later, in 1956, Kennedy served as special assistant to Democratic Presidential candidate Adlai Stevenson's campaign manager. He was appointed chief counsel and head of an investigative staff of 65 persons of the Select Senate Committee on Improper Activities in the Labor or Management Field, commonly known as the Senate Rackets Committee, in 1957.

Under the direction of McClellan, the committee undertook as "top priority" the investigation of the Teamsters Union and its president, Dave Beck. The subsequent hearings, often televised, gained national prominence for Robert Kennedy and his brother John, a member of the committee. Beck, later sentenced to a 15-year prison term for stealing union funds, was replaced as Teamsters president by James Hoffa. Hoffa, too, was investigated. The frequent angry exchanges between Kennedy and Hoffa resulted in a loss of labor support for Kennedy in his political career and earned him the tag of "a ruthless little monster" by Hoffa and other union officials. Kennedy was chosen the first recipient of the Outstanding Investigator of the Year award from the Society of Professional Investigators in Nov. 1957. He left the committee in 1959.

Kennedy emerged as a leading political figure in 1960 after he successfully managed his brother's Presidential campaign. Appointed U.S. Attorney General, he became the President's chief adviser and confidant, counseling him on such matters as foreign policy, national security, domestic policy and political management. Among his actions as Attorney General were the extension of civil rights, the ending of racial discrimination in bus terminals, the prosecution of voting and school segregation cases, the disposition of controversial anti-trust rulings and the further investigation of labor racketeering.

Greatly affected by the assassination of his brother Nov. 22, 1963, Kennedy nevertheless remained in the post of Attorney General after Lyndon B. Johnson became President. Johnson-Kennedy relations became strained, however, and Kennedy resigned Sept. 3, 1964 after it became apparent that Johnson would not choose him for his Vice Presidential running mate in 1964.

Kennedy Sept. 1, 1964 had overcome "carpetbagger" charges to become the Democratic nominee for U.S. Senator from New York. He was elected Nov. 3, 1964. As Senator he worked hardest in the areas of antipoverty action, medicare, education and the improvement of the plight of Negroes, Puerto Ricans, American Indians and Mexican-Americans. He sharply criticized the escalation of the Vietnamese war, urging a halt in the bombing of North Vietnam and the inclusion of the Viet Cong in a coalition government.

In the fall of 1967 Kennedy was urged by supporters to oppose Johnson for the 1968 Democratic Presidential nomination. He delayed his decision, however, until after Sen. Eugene McCarthy (D., Minn.), another Democratic anti-war contender, had made a strong showing Mar. 12, 1968 in the New Hampshire primary. 4 days later Kennedy, citing his opposition to Johnson's Vietnam and domestic policies, announced his candidacy. His late entry into the race was viewed by critics as an example of his "opportunism." He won 5 of the 6 primaries he entered and received write-in votes in 3 others.

Kennedy married Ethel Skakel June 17, 1950 in Greenwich, Conn. They had 11 children—Kathleen Hartington (born July 4, 1951), Joseph Patrick, Robert Francis, David Anthony, Mary Courtney, Michael L., Mary Kerry, Christopher, Matthew Maxwell, Douglas Harriman and Rory Elizabeth (born Dec. 12, 1968, 6 months after her father's death).

Kennedy's books included: The Enemy Within *(1960), a narrative of his work on the Senate Rackets Committee;* Just Friends and Brave Enemies *(1962), a report on his round-the-world trip;* The Pursuit of Justice *(1964), a collection of 12 speeches he delivered as Attorney General;* To Seek a Newer World *(1967),an adaptation of speeches and other notes on major issues;* Thirteen Days. A Memoir of the Cuban Missile Crisis *(1969), an account of top-level events and personal insights during the 13 days of the 1962 Soviet-U.S. Cuban missile confrontation.*

ASSASSINATION & AFTERMATH

Kennedy Shot in Los Angeles

The assassination of Sen. Robert Francis Kennedy (D., N.Y.) took place in Los Angeles in June 1968 in the midst of his campaign for the Democratic Presidential nomination. The assassin was a young Jordanian who had been born in the Arab section of Jerusalem but who had been a resident of the U.S. for nearly half his life.

Kennedy, 42, had entered the 1968 Presidential campaign Mar. 16, 1968 in an effort to unseat incumbent Pres. Lyndon B. Johnson, whose Vietnam policies he strongly opposed. When Johnson later dropped out of the race, the Democratic nomination centered around 3 men—Kennedy, Sen. Eugene McCarthy (D., Minn.), another peace candidate, and Vice Pres. Hubert H. Humphrey, who generally backed the Johnson Administration policies.

Kennedy entered 6 primaries; he won 5 but lost what political experts considered one of the most important ones, the Oregon primary. Describing the defeat as a "setback I could ill afford," Kennedy May 29 indicated that his candidacy would be put to a final test in the June 4 California primary. "I will abide by the results of that test," he told newsmen in Los Angeles May 29. The South Dakota primary was also to be held June 4.

While awaiting the results of the California primary June 4, Kennedy was informed that he had won the South Dakota contest with 50% of the popular vote. He hailed the victory as a confirmation "that the people of the nation want a change from the policies" of the Johnson Administration. A few hours later it became evident that he had also won the primary in California.*

At about midnight June 4, Kennedy and his wife, Ethel, left their suite in Los Angeles' Ambassador Hotel to go downstairs to the Embassy Ballroom for a victory rally. There,

---

* Final figures showed that Kennedy had received 46% of the total Democratic vote in California, McCarthy 42% and a 3d slate of delegates 12%. His victory was attributed to a heavy vote for him from minority groups—Negroes and Mexican-Americans—and from labor.

in a speech before a crowd of campaign workers and a nationwide TV audience, Kennedy, after thanking his supporters, said "I think we can end the divisions within the United States. What I think is quite clear is that we can work together.... We are a great country, a selfless ... and a compassionate country.... So my thanks to all of you, and on to Chicago [for the Illinois primary], and let's win."

Then, rather than go through the crowded ballroom to a nearby press room, where he was scheduled to hold a short news conference, Kennedy decided to take a short-cut through a back passageway. Followed by his wife and several staff members, he parted the gold curtains behind the speaker's platform and exited through a double door that led into a serving pantry.

As the Senator shook hands with the kitchen workers, at about 12:16 a.m. PDT June 5, a short, swarthy man, standing about 5 feet away, suddenly opened fire with a .22-caliber pistol. 8 shots were fired, and Kennedy fell to the floor, hit in the back of the head by one bullet and in the back of the right armpit by 2 others. 5 other persons were wounded, none fatally, by the shots.

Bleeding heavily, Kennedy reportedly expressed concern for others as he lay on the floor. He said "Oh no, no, don't" or "Don't lift me, don't lift me" when placed on a stretcher at about 12:30 a.m. Those were his last words. Accompanied by his wife and campaign aide Fred Dutton, Kennedy was rushed by ambulance first to Central Receiving Hospital, where Dr. Vasilius F. Bazilauskas reported later that Kennedy arrived almost dead—comatose, in deep shock, not breathing, with little blood pressure and "practically pulseless."

After external heart massage, adrenalin and use of a heart-lung machine, Kennedy revived slightly. He was then taken to the better equipped Good Samaritan Hospital, where a team of surgeons worked for almost 4 hours to remove bullet fragments from his brain. The fatal bullet had entered the cerebellum (the part of the brain responsible for coordination) after penetrating the mastoid bone behind the right ear. The surgical team was headed by Dr. Henry M. Cuneo of the University of Southern California. Assistants included Dr. Nat D. Reid of USC and Dr. Maxwell M. Andler of UCLA.

After surgery, Kennedy's condition was described first as "very critical," then as "extremely critical" and "extremely critical as to life." Kennedy press secretary Frank Mankiewicz announced a minute before 2:00 a.m. June 6 that Kennedy had died at 1:44 a.m., about 25 hours after he had been shot.

A preliminary autopsy was done June 6 by Los Angeles County Medical Examiner Thomas T. Noguchi and a team that included Col. Pierre Finck of the Armed Forces Institute of Pathology, who had assisted in the autopsy of Pres. John F. Kennedy. Their report, issued later that day, revealed "extensive injury" to the brain, penetration by bullet fragments of the cerebrum (the "thinking" part of the brain) and damage to the cerebellar artery. The coroners removed from the back of the lower neck a bullet that had not been considered a major problem during the brain operation.

(The others wounded in the Kennedy attack, all of whom recovered, were: Paul Schrade, 43, a regional director of the United Auto Workers and Kennedy campaigner, who underwent surgery for removal of a bullet from his skull; William Weisel, 30, an ABC newsman, who had a bullet removed from his abdomen; Ira Goldstein, 19, of Encino, Calif., an employe of Continental News Service, struck in the hip; Mrs. Elizabeth Evans, 43, of Sangus, Los Angeles County, injured in the scalp; Irwin Stroll, 17, a campaign worker, struck in the calf.)

Assassin Seized

The assassin was seized with a revolver in his hand moments after Kennedy was shot.

Roosevelt Grier, 287-pound defensive tackle for the Los Angeles Rams football team, wrested the gun—a snubnose .22-caliber Iver Johnson Cadet model—from the gunman while Kennedy lay on the floor bleeding. Rafer Johnson, decathlon champion of the 1960 Olympic Games, and William Barry, a Kennedy bodyguard, recovered the revolver when it fell to the ground. Johnson, Grier and a teammate of Grier's, 260-pound Deacon Jones, had been accompanying Kennedy throughout his California campaign to protect him and clear paths for him through the crowds.

Sirhan Bishara Sirhan   Wide World

Grier also saved the assassin from assault by the angry crowd gathered around him in the pantry until Los Angeles policemen arrived. They carried the prisoner out by his arms and legs.

The then-unidentified suspect, refusing to give police any information about himself, was arraigned at 7 a.m. June 5, 1968 in municipal court as "John Doe." He was charged, in a complaint by District Atty. Evelle Younger, with 6 counts of assault with intent to murder. He was represented by chief public defender Richard S. Buckley. A. L. Wirin, chief counsel in Los Angeles for the American Civil Liberties Union, also conferred with the defendant, who was kept in the medical ward of Central Jail because he had sustained a broken left index finger and a sprained ankle during the struggle in the hotel.

Los Angeles Mayor Samuel W. Yorty announced at a news conference at police headquarters later June 5 that the suspect had been identified as Sirhan Bishara Sirhan, 24, a Jordanian citizen, who had been born in Palestinian Jerusalem of Arab parentage but who had been a resident of the Los Angeles area since 1957. He had been admitted to the U.S. as a permanent resident Jan. 12, 1957.

Yorty said the identification had been established through a brother, Adel Sirhan, after police had traced by computer the ownership of the fatal revolver to another brother, Munir Bishara Slamaeh Sirhan (also known as Joe Sirhan). The identification was confirmed by fingerprints that had been filed in Sacramento when Sirhan Sirhan, while a student at Muir High School in Pasadena, had applied for a job as an exercise boy for horses at Hollywood Park Race Track.

Yorty revealed later June 5 that 2 notebooks had been discovered in the defendant's home and that one of them contained "a direct reference to the necessity to assassinate Sen. Kennedy before June 5 [the first anniversary of the 1967 Israeli-Arab war]." Yorty said the suspect had in his possession a schedule of Kennedy's speaking engagements for June, 4 $100 bills and a clipping of an article on Kennedy (identified as written by Washington columnist David Lawrence and purporting to indicate that Kennedy was a dove on the Vietnam war issue but a hawk on the Israeli-Arab situation).

Yorty said the notebook entries indicated that the suspect had left-wing sympathies. At a news conference June 6, Yorty said Sirhan had "clearly expressed his Communist sympathy in his writings," and authorities "have learned his car was seen outside meetings where Communist organizations or Communist-front organizations were in session." "From that circumstance," he said, "we probably can deduce he was in contact with Communists."

The Yorty comments drew public criticism from State Atty. Gen. Thomas Lynch and the Civil Liberties Union on the ground that the release of such information might affect the legality of evidence and the course of the trial.

After Kennedy's death, Sirhan was indicted June 7 by a Los Angeles County grand jury on a charge of first-degree murder. He was also indicted on 5 counts of assault with intent to kill the 5 other persons injured. The grand jury transcript, released June 13, revealed testimony that: (a) Kennedy was struck by 3 bullets rather than 2, as originally reported—the fatal one in the head, a 2d bullet in back of the right armpit and a 3d about a half inch lower; (b) Sirhan was seen at a suburban rifle range only 12 hours before the murder practice-shooting "very rapidly" with a revolver.

After the indictments were handed down, Superior Court Judge Arthur Alarcon shifted court to the jail to have the defendant state his plea. But Sirhan entered no plea. His counsel, Deputy Public Defender Wilbur Littlefield, asked, and was granted, a delay for psychiatric examination of Sirhan. The ACLU representative, Wirin, attended the indictment proceedings as an "official observer" at Alarcon's request. At the jail, Wirin requested, as "a friend of the court," a conference of all parties concerned on naming private counsel for Sirhan.

Sirhan was held in strict isolation under heavy guard. Law enforcement officials were ordered by Alarcon to prevent the release of information that could be prejudicial to an impartial trial. Reporters attending the proceedings were searched. Cameras were barred.

(King Hussein of Jordan June 6 sent Pres. Johnson a message expressing his shock at the assassination. In Amman June 9 he told a *N.Y. Times* interviewer that an intensive investigation by "all our security organizations" had uncovered no evidence that Sirhan was part of a conspiracy or had had any connection with Jordan since "he left here as a child." A statement from the Jordanian embassy in Washington June 5 had expressed deep regret "that the suspect appears to be someone of Jordanian origin." It condemned "this criminal act committed against an outstanding American leader and public servant." Condemnation of the assassination was also expressed in a message written in the book of condolences at the U.S. embassy in Amman June 8 by Jordanian Premier Bahjat al-Talhouni.)

Sirhan's Background

Sirhan Bishara Sirhan (the name means "wanderer" in Arabic) was a tempestuous Christian Arab with strong anti-Jewish feelings that had been heightened by Israel's victory in the 1967 Middle East war.

Sirhan was born Mar. 19, 1944 in Jerusalem, the 4th of 5 sons of Bishara Salameh Ghatas and Mary Bishara Sirhan. His father, a violent man who often beat his children, was the senior Arab officer in charge of the city's waterworks under the British mandate rule. His mother was a religious zealot. At the time of Sirhan's birth, the family, although Greek Orthodox, lived in the Armenian sector of the Old City in a small house that they rented from a nearby Armenian convent.

Sirhan attended a local school run by the Lutheran Evangelical Church of the Savior. While his academic record was good, he was reportedly nervous and withdrawn and had expectations of future grandeur. With the advent of the 1948 Arab-Israeli war, the family moved repeatedly, although they always remained within the Arab sector of Jerusalem. After the British left Palestine, Sirhan's father worked as a plumber for the Jordanian authorities until 1957. Then, due to domestic strife, the parents and 5 of their 6 children went to the U.S. under a limited refugee-admission program sponsored by the UN Relief & Welfare Agency and the World Council of Churches. Shortly thereafter the parents separated, and Sirhan's father returned to Jordan.

Mrs. Sirhan took the children to Pasadena, Calif., where Sirhan entered the 10th grade at John Muir High School in 1959. He did well enough in school to get admitted to Pasadena

City College in 1964. He dropped out in 1966. During his late teens he became quarrelsome, hostile to authority and very anti-Jewish. His desire to become a jockey was thwarted because of his lack of qualifications, and he took a job as exercise boy for horses at the Hollywood Park Race Track. In Sept. 1966 he was thrown by a horse, suffering head and back injuries. After the fall his mother detected a change in his personality, and a doctor who treated him for a year after the accident described Sirhan as "a fairly explosive personality." Most of his rages were aimed at Israel and the Jews.

Later Sirhan worked as a $2-an-hour clerk in the Pasadena Organic Health Food Store. He quit in Mar. 1968 after the store's owner criticized him for mixing up a delivery order.

Woman Linked to Suspect

The Los Angeles grand jury that indicted Sirhan for the murder of Kennedy June 7, 1968 heard testimony the same day that an unidentified woman had been seen talking with the assassin seconds before the shots were fired. The testimony was given by Vincent T. Di Pierro, 19, son of the banquet manager of the Ambassador Hotel, where the murder occurred.

According to the official transcript of the testimony, released June 13, young Di Pierro, working that night as a waiter, had walked next to Kennedy just prior to the shooting and had noticed the girl, dressed in a polka-dot dress, standing next to Sirhan. Di Pierro told the jury: "Together, they were both smiling.... In fact, the minute the first 2 shots were fired, he still had a very sick-looking smile on his face." His testimony reinforced a report by a local Democratic leader, Sandra Serrano, that she had seen a woman in a polka-dot dress run out of the hotel just after the shooting exclaiming: "We shot him! We shot him!"

Cathy Fulmer, a young woman who had been at the Ambassador Hotel the night of the shooting wearing a polka-dot scarf later voluntarily surrendered to police. After explaining that she had just been a frightened spectator who might have screamed "They shot him, they shot him," authorities released her.

President Mourns

As a wave of sorrow, shame and indignation engulfed the nation, Pres. Johnson, grieved and dismayed, pleaded with Americans June 5, 1968 to "put an end to violence and to the preaching of violence." On hearing of the attack on Sen. Kennedy, the President had said there were "no words equal to the horror of this tragedy." He ordered Secret Service protection for all the announced Presidential candidates of major parties. (Authorizing legislation for such protection was passed immediately by Congress June 6 and signed by the President a few hours later.)

Johnson deplored the brutal interruption of Robert Kennedy's "brilliant career." He extolled the Senator as "a young leader of uncommon energy and dedication who has served his country tirelessly and well and whose voice and examples ... touched millions throughout the entire world."

After Kennedy's death June 6, Johnson proclaimed June 9 a day of national mourning and directed that the U.S. flag be flown half-staff on all federal property. "During his life, he knew far more than his share of personal tragedy," he said. "Yet he never abandoned his faith in America. He never lost his confidence in the spiritual strength of ordinary men and women. He believed in the capacity of the young for excellence—and in the right of the old and poor to a life of dignity. Our public life is diminished by his loss."

In a TV broadcast June 6, the President read a June 5 statement in which he had called on Congress, "in the name of sanity, in the name of safety—and in the name of an aroused nation—to give America the gun control law it needs." He said "the terrible toll inflicted on our people by firearms—750,000 Americans dead since the turn of the century"—was "far more than have died at the hands of all of our enemies in all of the wars that we have fought."

(About 12 hours after Kennedy's death Congress June 6 passed and sent to Pres. Johnson an omnibus anticrime bill that included a provision barring the interstate shipment and out-of-state purchase of handguns. Although he said he considered the bill as only a "halfway measure" that "leaves the deadly commerce in lethal shotguns and rifles without effective control," the President signed it June 19.

(The Administration June 10 sent Congress its proposals to ban the mail-order sale of rifles, shotguns and ammunition, the over-the-counter sale of such firearms to out-of-state residents and the sale of rifles and shotguns to minors. A watered-down version of the proposals, which excluded all registration and licensing provisions, was passed by the Senate Oct. 9, 1968 and by the House Oct. 10. The President signed it Oct. 22.)

Pleas Vs. Violence

Following the assassination of Robert Kennedy, many prominent Americans made public pleas against the increasing violence in American life. Among the statements made:

● Sen. Eugene J. McCarthy (D., Minn.), who had canceled his campaign activities after the shooting, said June 5 in Beverly Hills and later in Los Angeles, where he visited the hospital to which Kennedy had been taken: "It is not enough, in my judgment, to say that this is the act of one deranged man, if that is the case." "The nation, I think, bears too great a burden of guilt, really, for the kind of neglect which has allowed ... violence to grow here in our land." "We've got to give more rational attention, rational control to the problems of America."

● Arthur M. Schlesinger Jr., historian and close friend of the Kennedy family, June 5 (at commencement exercises at N.Y. City University)—The shooting of Robert Kennedy raised the question: "What sort of people are we, we Americans?" The answer: "We are today the most frightening people on this planet.... The atrocities we commit trouble so little our official self-righteousness, our invincible conviction of our moral infallibility." Americans must realize "that the evil is in us, that it springs from some dark, intolerable tension in our history and our institutions." "It is almost as if a primal curse had been fixed on our nation, perhaps when we first began the practice of killing and enslaving those whom we deemed our inferiors because their skin was another color." "We must uncover the roots of hatred and violence and, through self-knowledge, move toward self-control."

● Gov. Ronald Reagan (R., Calif.) June 5—"This nation can no longer tolerate the spirit of permissiveness that pervades our courts and other institutions." The attitude "that says a man can choose the laws he must obey, that he can take the law into his own hands for a cause, that crime does not necessarily mean punishment ... has been spurred by demagogic and irresponsible words of so-called leaders in and out of public office, and it has been helped along by some in places of authority who are fearful of the wrong but timid about standing for what is right. In so doing they have thrown our nation into chaos and confusion and have bred a climate that permits this ultimate tragedy." "This is not a sick society but it is a society that is sick of what has been going on in this nation."

● Terence J. Cooke, Roman Catholic archbishop of New York, June 6—"It is impossible for our country to survive if we are subjected to the type of violence we've been subjected to over the past few months." But the country "has much to hope for" if its people would unite in the spirit of hope and optimism exemplified by Kennedy. "I don't despair about America at all." "I have great faith as Robert Kennedy did. I don't think he would have wanted his followers to despair."

● Gov. Nelson A. Rockefeller (R., N.Y.) June 6—"I don't think the whole American society needs to feel guilty. Let's not be frustrated by guilt. Let's not be frustrated by hate. Let's move forward in love." Public officials and political candidates must "not be intimidated" by the assassination. If they could no longer mingle with the crowds, "then we've lost one of the greatest resources and strengths of this great land of ours— freedom of movement, freedom of expression, freedom of the individual to go and be with the people. This is essential for a democracy. I have faith in this country. I have faith in people. And I have no fear."

● Milton S. Eisenhower, former president of Johns Hopkins University, June 8 (in a Kent [O.] State University commencement speech)—"Apathy is being replaced by mass protest," which "too often ... becomes the unruly mob which senselessly defies laws and rules and contemptuously destroys values essential to a civilized, orderly society and stimulates the individual of disordered mind or passion to murder." "It is but a short step from licentiousness and persistent violence to anarchy, and the ... almost inevitable cure for anarchy is dictatorship, of the right or the left." "As never before in our history, we now need citizens who can reason objectively,

critically and creatively within a moral framework; we need ...
a new breed of Americans who will devote as much time and
energy to being wise, democratic citizens as they do to being
good physicians, engineers or businessmen."

Foreign Reaction

Among the international reactions to the assassination of
Robert Kennedy:

June 5—Pope Paul VI, informing a throng of worshipers
in front of St. Peter's Basilica that Kennedy had been shot,
called for a "common proposal to ban the methods of violence,
of dissent, of battle and of crime." "We deplore this new
manifestation of violence and terror," the pope said.

An article in *Izvestia,* the Soviet government newspaper,
declared: "A cancer of violence is eating away at the organism
of capitalist society. Violence is innate to imperialism.... For
Washington, international law has been transformed into the
law of the mailed fist. For Washington, democratic freedom
has been transformed into freedom to murder anyone with
different opinions. American society, acting abroad like an
international gendarme, is degenerating more and more into a
gangster within its own borders."

Le Soir, Belgium's largest newspaper, asserted that it was
difficult not to believe that a "sinister conspiracy has been
mounted systematically against the most liberal elements of the
U.S. by a kind of mafia using paid killers and having resort to
powerful protection."

The British Broadcasting Corp. delivered this morning
prayer: "We pray for the American people that they may come
to their senses."

June 6—The UN flag flew at half-staff in front of the UN
building in New York. Normally such a tribute was paid only
when chiefs of state or high UN dignitaries died.

UN Secy. Gen. U Thant said: "I admired his courage, his
energy, his clearness of mind, his wit and warmth. He was
passionately interested in the great aims for which we strive in
the United Nations. His death is an incalculable loss to the
world community."

Queen Elizabeth of Britain declared: "I am shocked and distressed by the tragic death" of Kennedy. British Prime Min. Harold Wilson expressed his countrymen's feelings of "horror and sorrow" at this "sad time."

French Pres. Charles de Gaulle said: "The drama which has just dismayed the U.S. and bereaved the Kennedy family deeply saddens all Frenchmen."

Canadian Prime Minister Pierre Elliott Trudeau declared: "He worked for the underprivileged and for those who were in distress. His death is a blow to all of us, but we will try to continue working for the values for which he stood."

Indian Prime Min. Indira Gandhi said: "A man of great energy and high idealism has been struck down in the prime of life and on the threshold of a bright new phase in his career. Memories of Pres. Kennedy and Martin Luther King are poignantly fresh in our minds. Each such violent act strikes a blow at the very foundations of democracy and civilization."

Yugoslav Pres. Tito said: "The tragic death of Sen. Kennedy represents an irreparable loss for the American people and peace in the world."

June 7—The UN General Assembly observed a moment of silence in tribute to Kennedy after a short eulogy delivered by Assembly Pres. Corneliu Manescu of Rumania.

The Chinese Communist radio reported Robert Kennedy's death for the first time and asserted that the assassination was "another proof that U.S. imperialism's political and economic crises have been deepened."

Swedish Premier Tage Erlander said: "Robert Kennedy realized more clearly than most the tension at the bottom of the difficulties in the U.S. Therefore, he worked to even out the differences between rich and poor, white and colored. Millions of people outside his own country believed in him. Robert Kennedy is dead, but we must never cease to believe in the ideals he fought for."

Mourning & Burial

Robert Kennedy's body was flown by Presidential jet plane to New York June 6, 1968. Passengers who accompanied the body included his widow, Ethel, pregnant with their 11th child; his 3 oldest children (Kathleen, Joseph and Robert Jr.); his brother, Edward; his sisters, Patricia (Mrs. Pat Lawford) and Jean (Mrs. Stephen Smith); his sister-in-law, Mrs. Jacqueline Kennedy, widow of the assassinated President; Mrs. Coretta Scott King, widow of the murdered civil rights leader; Charles Evers, brother of the assassinated Negro leader Medgar Evers of Mississippi.

The body was brought to St. Patrick's Cathedral, where it lay in state from 5:30 a.m. June 7 until 5 a.m. June 8. Thousands of persons quietly queued up to enter the cathedral and pass the closed coffin, flanked on each side by 3 persons standing vigil (more than 600 persons participated in the vigil). The queue stretched for more than a mile, and those in it endured a wait of up to 7 hours. Police estimated that 151,000 persons filed past the bier in 23½ hours.

A pontifical requiem mass, celebrated in the liberalized spirit of the Vatican's Ecumenical Council, was held for Kennedy at St. Patrick's June 8. 2,300 persons attended, including Pres. Johnson and the 4 major Presidential candidates: Vice Pres. Hubert Humphrey, Sen. Eugene J. McCarthy, Gov. Nelson A. Rockefeller, and ex-Vice Pres. Richard M. Nixon. The mass was presided over by Richard Cardinal Cushing of Boston and Angelo Cardinal Dell'Acqua, vicar general of Rome, who represented Pope Paul VI; Archbishop Terence J. Cooke of New York was the principal concelebrant and deliverer of the eulogy.

The main eulogy was delivered by Sen. Edward M. Kennedy, who, in a strong but at times quivering voice, said: "My brother need not be idealized or enlarged in death beyond what he was in life. He should be remembered simply as a good and decent man, who saw wrong and tried to right it, saw suffering and tried to heal it, saw war and tried to stop it. Those of us who loved him and who take him to his rest today pray that what he was to us, and what he wished for others, will some day come to pass for all the world. As he said many times, in many parts of this nation, to those he touched and who sought to touch him: 'Some men see things as they are and say, why. I dream things that never were and say, why not.'"

The mass included, for the first time, music from a symphony—the Adagietto movement from Mahler's *Fifth Symphony,* played by members of the N.Y. Philharmonic under the direction of conductor Leonard Bernstein. It ended with the singing of 2 Protestant works, *The Battle Hymn of the Republic,* sung by a popular vocalist, Andy Williams, and the Hallelujah Chorus from Handel's *Messiah.*

After the mass, the body was brought by motorcade to New York's Pennsylvania Station, where it was put aboard a 21-car funeral train to be taken to Washington. The rail trip, delayed by crowds (a crowd of 5,000 in Baltimore sang *The Battle Hymn of the Republic* as the train slowly passed), took 8 hours, 6 minutes and arrived in the capital 4½ hours late. This was the greatest such demonstration since Pres. Franklin D. Roosevelt's body was borne from Warm Springs, Ga. to Washington in 1945. (As the train passed Elizabeth, N.J., a man and a woman in the crowd spilling over onto other tracks were killed by a New York-bound express train. In Trenton, a youth watching from a boxcar was critically burned by a live wire.)

The burial service, led by Archbishop Philip Hannan, took place under floodlights late June 8 at Arlington National Cemetery near the grave of John F. Kennedy. Pres. and Mrs. Johnson, who had met the train on its arrival in Washington, attended the interment service, which ended at 10:45 p.m.

The events of the 4-day period were covered fully by most TV and radio networks and stations.

On the day of national mourning, June 9, private services were conducted at the White House by the Rev. Billy Graham; and thousands of people visited the graves of the 2 Kennedy brothers.

Political Developments

The death of Robert Kennedy brought the Presidential campaign to a temporary but complete standstill.

Theodore C. Sorensen, a key aide of Robert Kennedy's, predicted June 13, 1968 that most of the Presidential delegates who had backed Kennedy would remain uncommitted until the Democratic convention. He indicated that the Kennedy organization would not support either Vice Pres. Hubert Humphrey or Sen. Eugene J. McCarthy unless they moved more "in the direction" of these Kennedy positions: "a more intensive and genuine search for a negotiated settlement in Vietnam"; a commitment to a policy of "no more Vietnams" and recognition that the U.S. was not the world's policeman; commitments to an end of racial bias and violence; an emphasis on "jobs instead of handouts."

Close associates of Sen. Edward Kennedy's had reported June 11 that he would not replace his late brother as a Presidential campaigner or accept a Vice Presidential nomination, reportedly offered informally by Humphrey associates.

Major changes in U.S. election procedures were proposed by Senate Democratic leader Mike Mansfield (Mont.) in a Senate speech June 11. Mansfield, who said he was "mighty disturbed" by recent events, suggested that the current election system be changed to provide for: uniform nationwide primaries, followed soon afterwards by the general election; direct election of the President and Vice President; limitation of the Presidency to a single, 6-year term; restriction of Presidential candidates to TV and radio appearances and of the President to public appearances only under "circumstances and occasions for which there can be provided total protection."

Gov. Nelson A. Rockefeller Sept. 10, 1968 appointed Rep. Charles E. Goodell (R.), 42, of Jamestown, N.Y. to the Senate seat left vacant by Kennedy's death. The appointment extended to the end of 1970. Rockefeller's decision, however, aroused the ire of New York Democratic Senate nominee Paul O'Dwyer (opposing Sen. Jacob K. Javits), who charged that the appointment had "robbed the state's voters of the type of representation they chose at the polls." Goodell was sworn in as the youngest Republican Senator Sept. 12. The U.S. Supreme Court Jan. 20, 1969 unanimously upheld a lower court ruling that allowed Goodell to fill the Senate seat until Dec. 1, 1970. The court, in effect, thus held that Gov. Rockefeller had acted constitutionally in appointing Goodell to the 27-month term rather than calling a special election.

Family Thanks Country for Sympathy

The Kennedy family thanked the American people June 15, 1968 for their expressions of sympathy on the death of Robert Kennedy. The family's thoughts were expressed by the late Senator's mother, Mrs. Rose Kennedy, 77, and his brother, Sen. Edward Kennedy, in a brief TV message taped on the front lawn of the Hyannis Port, Mass. home of ex-Amb. Joseph P. Kennedy, the late Senator's father. Amb. Kennedy, 79, who had suffered a stroke in 1961, sat in a wheelchair beside them.

Edward Kennedy said he hoped that "the countless thousands" who had sent messages of condolence "could realize the strength and the hope that they" gave the family "during these last several days." He said that those involved in his brother's Presidential campaign would have to decide their future courses "in a private way."

Mrs. Kennedy pledged the family to "carry on the principles for which Bobby stood . . ., not with vain regrets and mourning, but by acting now to remove the starvation of the people in this country and working now for the great masses of inarticulate people for whom he felt so deeply and for whom he worked so long, during the night as well as the day."

(Mrs. Ethel Kennedy, 40, gave birth by caesarean section to her 11th child, an 8-pound, 4-ounce girl, in Washington, D.C. Dec. 12, 1968. The baby was named Rory Elizabeth Katherine.)

Books & Memorials

Among books published about Robert F. Kennedy after his assassination:

● *The Unfinished Odyssey of Robert F. Kennedy,* by David Halberstam, published Jan. 29, 1969 by Random House. Background of Kennedy's 1968 Presidential primary campaign.

● *85 Days. The Last Campaign of Robert Kennedy,* by Jules Witcover, published Jan. 31, 1969 by G. P. Putnam's Sons. A chronological history of Kennedy's 1968 primary campaign.

● *Robert Kennedy: A Memoir,* by Jack Newfield, published June 10, 1969 by Dutton. A personal chronicle of the late Senator, from Sept. 1966 until his death, based on conversations, anecdotes and observations.

● *The Kennedy Legacy,* by Theodore C. Sorensen, published in Sept. 1969 by Macmillan. The author, a close friend of the Kennedys, discusses the careers of John, Robert and Edward Kennedy.

● *On His Own. Robert F. Kennedy 1964-1968,* by William Vanden Heuvel and Milton Gwirtzman, published Apr. 10, 1970 by Doubleday. 2 of Kennedy's political associates shed light on his personality and career.

● *American Journey. The Times of Robert Kennedy,* by Jean Stein and George Plimpton, published Nov. 25, 1970 by Harcourt Brace Jovanovich. More than 200 different interviews with people who knew Kennedy.

Among the many memorials honoring Robert F. Kennedy posthumously:

● A memorial film on Sen. Kennedy was shown Aug. 29, 1968 during a stormy session on the last day of the Democratic National Convention in Chicago. Shown to delegates in the city's International Amphitheatre on closed circuit TV, it featured an appearance by Sen. Edward Kennedy. The convention unruliness, which had stemmed from certain delegations' disapproval of the party's Vietnamese war plank and their objection to police action against antiwar demonstrators outside the hall, turned into general chaos after the picture was shown. The film evoked an ovation that generated endless refrains of *The Battle Hymn of the Republic* and a counter-demonstration from a gallery section packed with Chicago Mayor Richard J. Daley supporters. The singing did not subside until Alderman Ralph Metcalfe of Chicago, a Negro, took the podium and began a tribute to the late Rev. Dr. Martin Luther King Jr.

● The Kennedy family Oct. 29, 1968 announced plans for a $10 million foundation as a memorial to Robert Kennedy. The foundation was to act as a "catalyst" in solving some of the nation's problems.

Mrs. Ethel Kennedy issued a statement expressing the hope that the foundation would "carry forward the ideals" of her late husband. Her statement said: "He wanted to encourage the young people and to help the disadvantaged and discriminated against both here and abroad, and he wanted to promote peace in the world." "These will be the goals of the memorial."

Sen. Edward M. Kennedy announced that Robert S. McNamara, ex-Defense Secretary and current World Bank president, would be chairman of the foundation's executive committee; Thomas J. Watson Jr., chairman of the board of IBM, was named finance chairman, and Frederick G. Dutton, ex-Assistant State Secretary, was named organizing director.

● D.C. Stadium in Washington was renamed the Robert F. Kennedy Memorial Stadium in time for the opening of the baseball season Apr. 7, 1969.

● *Robert Kennedy Remembered,* a 1968 short subject film on the life of the late Senator, was awarded an "Oscar" by the American Academy of Motion Picture Arts & Sciences Apr. 14, 1969.

● The first anniversary of Robert Kennedy's death was marked June 6, 1969 with a brief ceremony at the late Senator's grave in Arlington National Cemetery in Virginia.

● The federal government Nov. 4, 1970 awarded a contract for the construction of a permanent grave site for Robert Kennedy at Arlington National Cemetery. The cost of the construction was estimated at $747,000, with the government paying $181,000 and the Kennedy family $566,000. The project, designed by architect I. M. Pei of New York, was to include a granite plaza and a reflecting pool adjacent to the grave of John F. Kennedy.

Pre-Trial Developments

The selection of Los Angeles attorney Russell E. Parsons, 73, as defense counsel for Sirhan was announced in Los Angeles June 19, 1968 by A. L. Wirin, chief local counsel for the American Civil Liberties Union. Wirin, who had conferred with Sirhan June 5-10, said "the ACLU's interest in the case" had ended since Sirhan had obtained "the counsel of his choice." An additional lawyer was simultaneously selected by Sirhan, also from a list Wirin had supplied, but his identity was withheld temporarily. Parsons said he was serving "without fee and as a public service."

Wirin had revealed June 11 that Sirhan had rejected offers of free legal defense from prominent criminal lawyers Melvin Belli of San Francisco and F. Lee Bailey of Boston.

(Reports from Amman, Jordan said 4 Jordanian lawyers had been chosen by the Jordanian Bar Association to take part in Sirhan's defense but had dropped the project after meeting June 19 with Premier Bahjat al-Talhouni.)

(Pasadena, Calif. police revealed July 3 that an apparent attempt had been made on the life of Sirhan's eldest brother as he was driving on the Pasadena freeway early that morning. Saidallah Sirhan, 36, reported that 7 men in 2 cars had boxed him in and fired 2 shots; he was unhurt. Police found 2 bullets in his car.)

The Los Angeles County District Attorney's office confirmed July 15 that it would seek the death penalty against Sirhan.

Sirhan, arraigned in Los Angeles Aug. 2, pleaded not guilty to a charge of first-degree murder.

It was announced Sept. 19 that Superior Court Judge Herbert Van Walker, 69, had been chosen to preside over the Sirhan trial. In a rebuff to Sirhan's defense Oct. 22, Judge Walker held that evidence seized in a search of Sirhan's room June 5 could not be suppressed. The defense had argued that the search violated constitutional guarantees, but Walker held that the police had "reasonable authority" to enter the house without a search warrant because Sirhan's brother, Adel Sirhan, had given his consent.

Sirhan's trial, originally scheduled for Nov. 1, was postponed Oct. 14 until Dec. 9 on a motion by the defense. The trial was again postponed Dec. 5 to allow attorney Grant B. Cooper, 65, who had joined the defense team Dec. 3, to study the case. It was reset for Jan. 7, 1969. A New York lawyer, Emile Zola Berman, 65, became the 3d member of the defense team Dec. 18.

The U.S. Supreme Court Dec. 16 let stand a June 7 order banning publicity in the Sirhan trial. The original ruling, issued by the Los Angeles Superior Court, forbade lawyers, police witnesses and court officials involved in the case from discussing evidence outside the courtroom.

Trial Opens

Sirhan's trial opened in Los Angeles Jan. 7, 1969 with Judge Walker presiding. To insure against any repetition of the events of Nov. 1963, when John F. Kennedy's suspected assassin was slain before he could be brought to trial, extreme security precautions were taken to protect Sirhan. For 7 months he had been kept under constant guard in a 6-by-8 foot windowless cell in the Hall of Justice, 5 floors above the courtroom where his trial opened. Steel plates covered the courtroom's windows, and everyone admitted to the trial was searched.

3 deputy district attorneys, Lynn D. (Buck) Compton, 46, John E. Howard and David N. Fitts, appeared to present the case for the prosecution. Sirhan's defense attorneys were Grant B. Cooper, former president of the local bar association, Russell E. Parsons and Emile Zola Berman.

During the opening 3 days of Sirhan's trial, the defense introduced motions to quash the indictment on the ground that the grand jury that had returned it was unrepresentative, to set aside on a similar ground the petit jury panel from which jurors would be chosen for the trial and to select one jury to decide Sirhan's guilt or innocence and a separate jury to determine punishment. Judge Walker Jan. 7 denied the motion on separate juries. Walker Jan. 8 denied a defense request for a 30-

day continuance of the trial to prepare evidence to support the
other motions.

Sirhan Found Guilty

Sirhan was convicted of first-degree murder Apr. 17, 1969
for the assassination of Robert Kennedy. The jury decided Apr.
23 that the penalty should be death in the gas chamber. (During
the trial Sirhan Mar. 19 had marked his 25th birthday.)

The jurors in the trial had heard 61 witnesses for the
prosecution and 29 for the defense. After convicting Sirhan,
they then sat during a separate sentencing trial, prescribed by
California law, at which they made their decision to sentence
the convicted man to death.

The defense and prosecution lawyers had questioned 60
potential jurors before agreeing on a panel of 8 men and 4
women Jan. 24. Although Sirhan had pleaded not guilty to the
charge of first-degree murder at his arraignment, defense
attorney Grant B. Cooper had stated while questioning the first
prospective juror Jan. 13: "There will be no denial of the fact
that our client, Sirhan Sirhan, fired the shot that killed Sen.
Kennedy." His statement was the first courtroom indication of
the argument that the defense advanced throughout the trial.
The defense attempted to prove diminished "responsibility" or
"capability" in that their client had not been capable of
"mature" consideration when the act was committed. In
California, a successful argument of diminished capacity could
win a conviction for a lesser degree of murder. For a first-
degree murder conviction, the prosecution had to prove "malice
aforethought."

Judge Walker Jan. 17 upheld a prosecution challenge to the
seating of a juror, Mrs. Alvina N. Alvidrez, for "cause" because
she had said that she could never condemn Sirhan or anyone
else to death. Walker had originally seated Mrs. Alvidrez Jan.
15 in view of the U.S. Supreme Court's 1968 Witherspoon
decision that jurors generally opposed to the death penalty
could not be excluded automatically from a capital case. Over
defense objections, Walker reversed his ruling Jan. 17. He
based his new decision on a re-reading of recent California
precedents.

Sirhan and his mother, Mrs. Mary Sirhan, 56, took the witness stand for the first time Feb. 4 to testify in unsuccessful support of a defense motion that the indictment be set aside on the ground that it was handed down by an improperly constituted grand jury. Cooper argued that the grand jury did not represent a broad cross-section of the community since poor people, like Sirhan and his family, had been excluded. Testimony about the Sirhan family's economic situation failed to convince the judge that the argument was valid.

It was reported Feb. 13 that lawyers for the defense and prosecution had met with Walker Feb. 10 to discuss the possibility of Sirhan's changing his plea to guilty of first-degree murder in exchange for the prosecution's agreement to a life-imprisonment sentence. Such an agreement was allowed under California law with the consent of the presiding judge. Walker, however, was reported to have opposed the move; he was quoted as saying: "We don't want another Dallas," apparently alluding to the persistent rumors of conspiracy surrounding the death of Pres. Kennedy after suspected assassin Lee Harvey Oswald had been killed before the case could be brought to trial.

(Chief Deputy District Atty. Lynn D. Compton told reporters Mar. 1 that the prosecution "won't press for the death penalty." He acknowledged that to demand the gas chamber would be "somewhat awkward" in light of the abortive agreement with the defense to settle for a life sentence.)

In the opening statement for the state Feb. 13, David N. Fitts, a deputy district attorney, outlined the prosecution's version of events leading to the death of Kennedy in an attempt to show that Sirhan had practiced and plotted his actions for days in anticipation of the shooting. Emile Zola Berman, delivering the opening defense statement Feb. 14, said: "At the actual moment of shooting ... [Sirhan] was out of contact with reality, in a trance."

After introducing testimony to prove that Sirhan actually shot Kennedy and to show that he had planned the act in advance, the prosecution Feb. 25 offered in evidence papers from 3 notebooks found by police in the bedroom of Sirhan's home in Pasadena, Calif. Over the objections of the defense, which argued that the notebooks had been obtained illegally (since the police had not had a warrant to search Sirhan's home), Walker admitted the papers in evidence. On a page of the notebooks, dated May 18, 1968, 19 days before Kennedy was slain, were the words: "My determination to eliminate R.F.K. is becoming more of an unshakeable obsession." Further down on the page was the repeated message: "R.F.K. must die, ... Robert F. Kennedy must be assassinated before 5 June 1968." (June 5 was the first anniversary of the 1967 Arab-Israeli war.) One page also said: "Ambassador Goldberg [Arthur Goldberg, then U.S. ambassador to the U.N.] must die die die die die."

While the jury was out of the courtroom during the argument over whether to admit the notebooks as evidence, Sirhan Feb. 25 exploded in protest against the disclosure of his secret writings. According to a court transcript of a conference in the judge's chambers, Sirhan demanded that his attorneys change his plea to guilty rather than let the trial continue. Walker warned the defense counsel at a meeting in his chambers Feb. 26 that he would order Sirhan bound and gagged if he kept jumping out of his seat, shouting, or stirring up "any more commotion" in court. "He just gets worse and worse," the judge complained. But Sirhan was quiet as the jury inspected his notebooks Feb. 26.

During the first day of the defense's case Feb. 28, Sirhan once more interrupted his trial to demand that he be allowed to "plead guilty to all counts as charged." Walker denied the request and warned the defendant that if he could not control his outbursts, he would "be put in chains."

Sirhan took the stand for 4 days Mar. 3-6. He admitted that he had killed Kennedy but stated that he could not remember writing death threats in his notebooks. In his Mar. 4 testimony, Sirhan said he had decided to kill Kennedy after he saw him, on TV, joining Israelis in a celebration of Israel's independence. Through testimony from psychologists and psychiatrists, the defense tried to prove that Sirhan was not responsible for his actions on the day of the shooting. The prosecution Mar. 17 attempted to discredit the testimony of one of the defense psychologists, Dr. Martin M. Schorr, by pointing out striking similarities in the wording of Schorr's report on Sirhan and sections of a book entitled *Casebook of a Crime Psychiatrist* by Dr. James A. Brussel. Schorr Mar. 18 admitted using some of Brussel's language to make his own report "more exciting and vivid," but he denied that he had used the book to form conclusions about Sirhan.

The final doctor to testify for the defense was Dr. Bernard L. Diamond, a psychiatrist at the University of California at Berkeley. Diamond said Mar. 24 that, under hypnosis, Sirhan had re-enacted the slaying of Kennedy. Diamond said that he had concluded that Sirhan had acted "in a blind rage." He stated that the shooting was a "reflex action, an outgrowth not only of chronic psychosis but a very abnormal state that began when he became confused and vague by all the lights and mirrors" outside the hotel pantry where the shooting occurred.

After the defense rested its case Mar. 27, the prosecution called other doctors to rebut the defense contention that Sirhan had killed Kennedy while in a trance. The prosecution's main rebuttal witness, Dr. Seymour Pollack, a psychiatrist at the University of Southern California, said Mar. 28 that Sirhan had been "motivated by political reasons" and that he had "no significant paranoid features, no significant deviations." Pollack, however, told the court Apr. 3 that his confidential report on Sirhan to the district attorney stated that the defendant was a "psychotic" and that his mental illness "should be considered a mitigating circumstance" in sentencing.

During the closing arguments for the defense, attorneys Berman, Cooper and Parsons argued that Sirhan was too ill mentally to have premeditated Kennedy's murder in a responsible manner but conceded that their client deserved to spend the rest of his life in prison.

The jurors retired to consider their verdict Apr. 14. They pronounced Sirhan guilty as charged Apr. 17 after nearly 17 hours of deliberation. Sirhan was also convicted on 5 counts of assault with intent to kill for the wounding of 5 persons who had been standing near Kennedy the night of the shooting.

Before the jury retired a 2d time to deliberate on Sirhan's sentence, John E. Howard, a deputy district attorney, called Apr. 21 for the death penalty. He said that Sirhan "will regard permission to live as a triumph." After commenting on the danger of assassinations in the U.S., he called Sirhan a "cold-blooded, political assassin" who "has no special claim to further preservation." In opposing the death penalty, Parsons asked the jury: "Do we execute sick people in California? ... Do we follow Hitler, who struck down the lame ... and the sick?"

After nearly 12 hours of deliberation, the jury Apr. 23 condemned Sirhan to death in the gas chamber. One of the jurors, George A. Stitzel, 57, said afterwards that the panel's original vote was 5 for death, 3 for life and 4 undecided. He said that the jury had finally reached agreement on the 5th ballot. Stitzel, a pressroom foreman for the *Los Angeles Times,* said: "One item that was very important [to the decision] was the idea that we should stand behind our laws."

Under California law, Judge Walker had the power to reduce the sentence to life imprisonment if he felt the death penalty unwarranted. (No one had been executed in California since Apr. 12, 1967, when Aaron Mitchell was put to death for killing a policeman. At the time of the trial, the last man to be executed in the U.S. was Luis Jose Monge, who had been put to death in Colorado May 31, 1967 for the murder of his wife and 3 children.)

Los Angeles County Supervisor Kenneth Hahn reported Apr. 21 that Sirhan's trial had cost $900,000 and was the most expensive U.S. trial on record.

Sirhan Sentenced to Gas Chamber

Judge Herbert Walker May 21, 1969 sentenced Sirhan to death in the gas chamber. Despite a plea for clemency for Sirhan from Edward M. Kennedy, brother of the slain Senator, Walker refused to reverse the death sentence pronounced by the jurors Apr. 23. Walker also rejected defense motions for a new trial. (The sentencing, originally scheduled for May 14, had been delayed a week on request of the defense.)

Walker said that he had considered Edward Kennedy's message, read in court by defense attorney Grant Cooper, but that it was "the feeling of this court that the jury was right ... and I have no reason to change my opinion now." Kennedy's letter, handwritten May 18 and addressed to Los Angeles District Atty. Evelle Younger, said the Kennedy family had felt that any comment would have been inappropriate while the case was before the jury. But Kennedy wrote that he then considered it proper to tell the family's feelings.

Kennedy recalled his brother's pleas for "love and wisdom and compassion" at the time of the death of Martin Luther

King, and he wrote that his brother "would not have wanted his death to be a cause for the taking of another life."

Sirhan was transferred to San Quentin (Calif.) prison May 23, 1969 and was locked in a cell on death row. It was ordered that cells on either side of Sirhan were to remain empty for reasons of security.

Demands for Sirhan's release from prison were reportedly made Sept. 7, 1970 by Arab guerrillas who had hijacked 3 commercial jet airliners bound for New York from Europe and diverted them to the Middle East. Reports indicated that the guerrillas were willing to free the hijacked passengers, held in Jordan, for Sirhan's release. But the Popular Front for the Liberation of Palestine (PFLP), the Arab commando group responsible for the plane seizures, officially denied making such a demand. Sirhan's mother, Mrs. Mary Sirhan, sought to fly to Jordan from New York Sept. 8 in an attempt to seek the release of the detained passengers. But her departure was thwarted when the U.S. Immigration & Naturalization Service canceled the passports of her 2 accompanying lawyers, Luke McKissack and Mike McCowan. (McKissack was one of 2 attorneys retained by Sirhan Sirhan to file an appeal for a new trial.)

Sirhan's attorneys Nov. 12, 1970 filed a 740-page brief with the California Supreme Court appealing their client's death sentence. Among the 18 issues raised in the appeal were the refusal of Judge Herbert Walker to allow Sirhan to plead guilty in exchange for a life sentence and the alleged infringement on Sirhan's rights when police entered his home to seize his notebooks.

(In Apr. 1970 the attorneys had unsuccessfully attempted to obtain an injunction against the publication of the book *R.F.K. Must Die! A History of the Robert Kennedy Assassination and Its Aftermath,* by Robert Blair Kaiser, a former investigative member of Sirhan's defense team. Published Oct. 14, 1970 by Dutton, the book attempted to explain why Sirhan killed Kennedy. It contained excerpts from psychiatric interviews with Sirhan and portions of the author's own intimate journal on the defense, prosecution and Sirhan's personal behavior. The lawers contended that the book would prejudice Sirhan's right to a fair hearing if he were granted a new trial.)

VIOLENCE
IN THE
UNITED STATES

THE COMMISSION ON VIOLENCE

Panel on Violence Created

Pres. Lyndon B. Johnson announced shortly after Robert Kennedy's assassination that he was creating a special commission of distinguished citizens to study violence in the U.S. with a view to finding out "how we can stop it."

In a TV broadcast the evening of June 5, 1968, Johnson announced his creation of the National Commission on the Causes & Prevention of Violence to "examine this tragic phenomenon" of violence in the nation's life. It would be "wrong" to "conclude from this act [Sen. Kennedy's shooting] that our country is sick" and had lost "its common decency," he said. But the murders of John and Robert Kennedy and of Martin Luther King Jr. gave "ample warning that in a climate of extremism, of disrespect for law, of contempt for the rights of others, violence may bring down the very best among us." "Let us, for God's sake, resolve to live under the law," he urged. "Let the Congress pass laws to bring the insane traffic in guns to a halt.... Let us purge the hostility from our hearts, and let us practice moderation with our tongues. Let us begin in the aftermath of this great tragedy to find a way to reverence life, to protect it, to extend its promise to all of our people, this nation and the people who have suffered grievously from violence and assassination...."

Johnson appointed the following persons to the commission: Dr. Milton S. Eisenhower, ex-president of Johns Hopkins University, as chairman; Judge A. Leon Higginbotham Jr. of the U.S. District Court for the Eastern District of Pennsylvania, as vice chairman; Archbishop Terence J. Cooke of New York; attorney Albert E. Jenner Jr. of Chicago; Mrs. Patricia Roberts Harris, Howard University law professor and ex-ambassador to Luxembourg; the philosopher-longshoreman-author Eric Hoffer; Sens. Philip A. Hart (D., Mich.) and Roman L. Hruska (R., Neb.); Reps. Hale Boggs (D., La.) and William M. McCulloch (R., O.). The President June 21 added 3 more members to the commission: Ernest W. McFarland, chief judge of the Arizona Supreme Court; Leon Jaworski, a Houston, Tex. lawyer and close friend of the President; the psychiatrist W. Walter Menninger of the Menninger Clinic in Topeka, Kan.

Johnson met at the White House June 10 with his newly appointed commission and, in a televised statement, posed the principal questions the panel would attempt to answer. The President charged the commission "to undertake a penetrating search for the causes and prevention of violence—a search into our national life, our past as well as our present, our traditions as well as our institutions, our culture, our customs and our laws."

One of every 5 U.S. Presidents since 1865 had been assassinated (Abraham Lincoln, James A. Garfield, William McKinley and John F. Kennedy) and attempts had been made on the lives of 3 others (Theodore Roosevelt, Franklin D. Roosevelt and Harry S. Truman), Johnson said. He noted that guns were involved in more than 6,500 murders each year in the U.S. "This compares with 30 in England, 99 in Canada, 68 in West Germany and 37 in Japan." The President said that the commission must weigh whether American society could "any longer tolerate the widespread possession of deadly firearms by private citizens."

Among the questions Johnson put to the panel:

"Does the democratic process, which stresses exchanges of ideas, permit less physical contact with masses of people, as a matter of security against the deranged individual and obsessed fanatic?"

"Is there something in the environment of American society or the structure of our institutions that causes disrespect for the law, contempt for the rights of others and incidents of violence?"

"Has permissiveness toward extreme behavior in our society encouraged an increase of violence?"

"Are the seeds of violence nurtured through the public's airwaves, the screens of neighborhood theaters, the news media and other forms of communications that reach the family and our young?"

"What is the relationship between mass disruption of public order and individual acts of violence?"

The commission's major findings were issued after Johnson had left office and had been succeeded as President by Richard M. Nixon.

Panel Begins Probes

The commission announced Sept. 5, 1968 that it planned to investigate the disorders in Chicago that accompanied the Democratic National Convention in Aug. 1968. The commission's chairman, Dr. Milton Eisenhower, said the Chicago disorders were "a case of serious and mass violence in numerous respects." The commission planned to "devote first attention to ... events in Chicago and other recent events such as the outbreak of shooting in Cleveland." (11 persons had been killed during an outbreak of sniper fire between black nationalists and police in Cleveland July 23-26, 1968.)

The commission began its hearings Sept. 18. At its opening session the panel heard conflicting testimony about the Chicago disorders from Atty. Gen. Ramsey Clark and FBI Director J. Edgar Hoover. Clark warned of the dangers of police violence while Hoover said that the Chicago police had had "no alternative but to use force." 2 other commission study teams were formed to investigate the Cleveland slayings and the riot deaths that occurred in Miami, Fla. during the Republican National Convention Aug. 7-8, 1968.

The commission Oct. 23, 1968 took testimony from Thomas E. Hayden, 28, a founder of the Students for a Democratic Society (SDS), who gave his views on U.S. student protests. Hayden said that young people, encouraged by the election of John F. Kennedy in 1960, by the creation of the Peace Corps and by the national sympathy for the civil rights struggle, had later become disillusioned by government failures to satisfy needs in the ghetto and particularly by U.S. "aggression" in Vietnam.

The panel also heard testimony on student disorders from Dr. Kingman Brewster, president of Yale University, Henry Mayer, a leader of the 1966 demonstrations at the Berkeley campus of the University of California, and Samuel W. Brown Jr., coordinator of the youths who worked for the 1968 Presidential nomination of Sen. Eugene J. McCarthy. Brewster told the committee that "the urge to violence rises in proportion to the frustration of peaceful change."

The commission had reported Oct. 9, 1968 that 45.6 million firearms had been produced in the U.S. or imported between 1951 and June 30, 1968. The largest increase was in handguns (pistols and revolvers). The production and importation of handguns rose from 380,462 in 1951 to 973,823 in 1965; it totaled 1.1 million in 1966 and 1.6 million in 1967. The total number of weapons manufactured or imported rose from 2.4 million in 1951 to 2.9 million in 1965, 4.1 million in 1966 and 4.7 million in 1967. In the first 6 months of 1968, 3 million weapons had been manufactured in the U.S. or imported.

First Reports

The first reports published by the Commission on Violence were studies on the 1968 Chicago Democratic and Miami Republican convention disorders, the July 1968 riot in Cleveland, the Jan. 20, 1969 counterinaugural protests in Washington, the history of violence in America and police-demonstrator confrontations in the U.S. The reports, contracted by the commission with study groups or individual researchers, were released by the panel without comment or evaluation.

Among the findings and other developments involving these early reports:

Chicago convention report —The special panel set up by the commission to investigate the Chicago Democratic National Convention disorders issued its report Dec. 1, 1968. Known as the "Walker Report" after its chairman, Daniel Walker, 46, president of the Chicago Crime Commission and a vice president and general counsel of Marcor, Inc., the parent firm of Montgomery Ward & Co., the report sharply criticized members of the Chicago police force for excessive brutality in their handling of the demonstrations. The 233-page report, entitled "Rights in Conflict," charged that the actions of some of the police during the Chicago disorders had amounted to a "police riot" that far outweighed the demonstrations as a source of the violence that swept the convention city.

The report's summary charged that some Chicago policemen had responded to provocation by demonstrators with "unrestrained and indiscriminate police violence ... often inflicted upon persons who had broken no law, disobeyed no order, made no threat." It concluded that the loss of control and discipline of some of the police under "exceedingly provocative" circumstances "can perhaps be understood, but not condoned." The special panel's investigators said that the police had been conditioned to expect that violence "against demonstrators, as against rioters, would be condoned by city officials." Mayor Richard J. Daley's controversial "shoot-to-kill" order to the police during the riots that followed the death of Martin Luther King Jr. was cited as an example of the attitude displayed by Chicago officials. The report included a section describing police assaults on newsmen covering the convention. Investigators found that of the 300 newsmen covering the parks and streets of Chicago during convention week, 63 reporters and photographers had been physically attacked by police. The behavior of both the demonstrators and police was said to have been substantially influenced by the presence of the news media.

The report was the work of a 212-member study team set up by Walker, who, acting at the request of the national commission, assembled the team from among members of the Chicago Crime Commission, backed with lawyers and investigators lent for the project by Chicago banks and law firms. The panel's staff began work Sept. 27. It heard 1,410 eyewitness statements, reviewed 2,012 other statements provided by the FBI, and studied film, photos and news accounts before completing the study Nov. 18.

Miami convention report—A 2d panel, set up by the commission to investigate the disorders during the Republican National Convention in Miami, issued its report Feb. 11, 1969. Its findings were dissimilar from those of the Walker panel. According to the Miami report, the disturbances in Miami "originated spontaneously and almost entirely out of the accumulated deprivations, discriminations and frustrations of the [Miami] black community" and "involved no articulated political or ideological issues such as the Presidential campaign, Vietnam or the draft." Furthermore, the panel said, the Miami rioters were not "consciously seeking publicity as were those in Chicago."

The report held that "by almost any standard, the Miami disturbances were minor except to those involved." Although 4 people were killed in the riot, the report said that relatively few people were involved, that damage to property and persons was "less than in many other recent civil disturbances" and that the peak period of violence was short. The report praised the preparation and police cooperation in Miami Beach but said that "we do not intend ... to make invidious comparisons with police works in Chicago or elsewhere." According to the study, however, ex-Police Chief Walter Headley's call for tough suppression of looting had been a contributing cause of the disorders. But the report also said that a strong, organized display of force could have stemmed the rioting at almost any point.

The report was the result of a 3-month study by a 12-man staff headed by 2 Miami lawyers, Louis J. Hector and Paul L. E. Helliwell.

(A similar report, dealing primarily with U.S. civil disorders, was issued Feb. 27, 1969 by a study group made up of members of the Urban Coalition and Urban America. The 90-page report, entitled "One Year Later," warned that the nation was "a year closer to 2 societies—black and white, increasingly separate and scarcely less unequal." It recalled the Mar. 1, 1968 findings of the President's National Advisory [Kerner] Commission on Civil Disorders that stated that America was "moving toward 2 societies, one black, one white—separate and unequal." 2 former members of the Kerner Commission, N.Y. Mayor John V. Lindsay and Sen. Fred R. Harris [D., Okla.], and the commission's staff director, Washington lawyer David Ginsburg, served on the review board for the new study.

(The study noted an increased division between blacks and whites in the "perceptions and experiences of American society." It said that the deepening concern of some white Americans over ghetto problems, which had grown with the publication of the Kerner report and the death of Martin Luther King Jr., had been "counter-balanced—perhaps overbalanced—by a deepening of aversion and resistance on the part of others." As a reason for this growing aversion and "outright resistance to slum-ghetto needs and demands," the report cited an increasing concern for law and order that followed the assassination of Robert F. Kennedy and was highlighted during the Presidential campaign. The report warned that the mood of Negroes, standing somewhere "in the spectrum between militancy and submission," was "not moving in the direction of patience." It said that although there was some change in ghetto conditions, it was not enough. The situation, it declared, had led to an increase in number but a decline in intensity of civil disorders "due primarily to more sophisticated response by police and the military." The report warned that "the nation in its neglect may be sowing the seeds of unprecedented future disorders and division.")

Cleveland riot report —A study of the July 1968 Cleveland rioting, released May 29, 1969 by the Commission on Violence, said that the violence on the city's East Side might "have marked the beginning of a new pattern" in urban disorder. The 68-page report was written by Louis H. Masotti, associate professor of political science at Case Western Reserve in Cleveland, and Jerome R. Corsi, a Harvard graduate student.

As opposed to other recent urban riots, which the authors said had begun as attacks against property in ghettos, the researchers found that the Cleveland riot "began as person-oriented violence, blacks and whites shooting at each other, snipers against cops." They said a small group of Negro extremists had attacked white policemen as "symbols of the white society." Although they could not determine whether the police or the black nationalists had fired the first shots, the authors contended that the armed nationalists were immediately responsible for the violence and had provoked the police into firing.

The report criticized Cleveland newspapers for writing stories that allegedly increased racial tension.

Inaugural protests —A study of protests staged in Washington during the Jan. 20, 1969 Presidential inauguration was released May 31, 1969. It said that protesters and police had been generally restrained and well-behaved primarily because of the close cooperation among protest leaders and government officials. The entire episode proved, the study panel stated, that large-scale demonstrations could be organized and controlled, even with the presence of "numbers of unruly participants."

The report was prepared under the direction of Joseph R. Sahid, a co-director of the commission's law and law-enforcement study group.

Tradition of violence seen —A group of scholars appointed by the Commission on Violence said June 5, 1969 that in America the "grievances and satisfactions of violence have so reinforced one another that we have become a rather bloody-minded people in both action and reaction." The 350,000-word report, "Violence in America: Historical and Comparative Perspectives," had been prepared under the direction of Dr. Hugh Davis Graham, associate professor of history at Johns Hopkins University, and Dr. Ted Robert Gurr, assistant professor of politics at Princeton University.

The scholars examined labor violence in the U.S. to analyze the effects of governmental use of force for social control and the success of collective violence "as an instrument for accomplishing group objectives." They said that the effectiveness of governmental force depended on its legitimacy and consistency and on the success of "remedial action" for the causes of discontent. They reported that peaceful protest had been more effective than violence in achieving objectives.

Although the study cited 19th-century periods in which there was "greater relative turbulence" in America, it said that the 1960s "rank as one of our most violent eras." It asserted that the scope and magnitude of antiwar protest, urban unrest, black violence, university disorders and political assassinations were "essentially unprecedented in our history." The scholars said that the U.S. was "among the half-dozen most tumultuous nations in the world" in the post-1948 era, but they added: "Paradoxically, we have been both a tumultuous people and a relatively stable republic."

The report's general conclusion, written by Graham and Gurr, declared that Americans had always been a violent people but that they "have been given to a kind of historical amnesia that masks much of their turbulent past." Americans had magnified the usual "process of selective recollection," in some degree common to all nations, "owing to our historic vision of ourselves as a latter-day chosen people, a new Jerusalem." The researchers said that the "myth of the melting pot has obscured the great degree to which Americans have historically identified with their national citizenship through their myriad subnational affiliations" and that the U.S. thus functioned "less as a nation of individuals than of groups." They asserted that this national characteristic "has meant inevitable group competition, friction and conflict."

Police militancy —A report released by the Commission on Violence June 10, 1969 said that the militancy and political activism of police in America threatened to undermine public confidence in the nation's legal system. Police militancy, it said, "seems to have exceeded reasonable bounds" and to have contributed to "police violence" against demonstrators.

The 276-page report, entitled "The Politics of Protest: Violent Aspects of Protest and Confrontations," was prepared under the direction of Jerome H. Skolnick, 38, a member of the Center for the Study of Law & Society at the University of California at Berkeley. The study group collected material from widely diversified sources and conducted field research for about 5 months.

According to the study, police in the U.S. had developed into "a self-conscious, independent political power," which sometimes "rivals even duly elected officials in influence." The researchers blamed FBI Director J. Edgar Hoover for much of the alleged police misconception about protesters. The report said Hoover had encouraged the view that mass protest was the result of conspiracy, often directed by Communist agitators. As a result, police were often unable to distinguish "dissent" from "subversion." "No government institution appears so deficient in its understanding of the constructive role of dissent in a constitutional democracy as the police," the report said.

The panel warned that the nation had a choice between commitment to social reform or the emergence of a police state, "a society of garrison cities where order is enforced without due process of law and without the consent of the governed."

The researchers found that U.S. policemen were "overworked, undertrained, underpaid and undereducated." They recommended that the federal government review its role "in the development of the current police view of protest and protesters."

Panel Issues Recommendations

The National Commission on Violence June 9, 1969 issued the first of many recommendations on various subjects related to violence in the U.S. Among the proposals and statements it made in its various reports:

Campus unrest —The commission warned June 9, 1969 that new legislation intended to punish students or colleges for campus disorders is "likely to spread, not reduce, the difficulty."

A 3,600-word statement on campus unrest was released at a Washington news conference by Commission Chairman Milton Eisenhower. According to a *Washington Post* report June 9, although the commission had not reached unanimous agreement on all points in the report, no commission member had dissociated himself from the statement.

The statement explained that the campus situation was so threatening and the need for "calm appraisal" so essential, "that this commission feels compelled to speak now rather than to remain silent until publication of its final report next fall," in order that "constructive thought and action" might take place before the start of the next academic year.

The statement dealt with the multiple causes of student discontent and the methods of a "small but determined minority" bent on the "destruction of existing institutions" or convinced that "violence and disruption may be the only effective way of achieving societal and university reform." It condemned as a "misconception" the belief of some college officials that "civil law should not apply to internal campus affairs." The panel asserted that college administrations were loath to apply sanctions of expulsion or suspension because of "exposure of dismissed students to the draft and what students call the 'death sentence' of Vietnam."

The commission urged colleges to seek a "broad consensus" on permissible methods of dissent and manners of dealing with disruption that exceeds legitimate bounds. Specifically, the panel suggested that campuses should agree on and adopt student conduct codes and discipline procedures and should review such policies where they already exist. The commission said that universities should prepare contingency plans to deal with unrest and should address themselves to campus government reform. It held that professors should assume the responsibility to "deal appropriately and effectively" with issues raised in student demands. It emphasized the importance of improved "communications both on the campus and with alumni and the general public."

While recognizing that American citizens "are justifiably angry" at rebellious students, the commission deplored the public's support of legislation that would withhold financial aid from students engaged in disruption and from colleges that failed to deal effectively with unrest. It said that the result of such legislation "may be to radicalize a much larger number by convincing them that existing governmental institutions are as inhumane as the revolutionaries claim." The panel encouraged legislation that would help universities "deal more effectively with the tactics of obstruction." It suggested that local trespass laws might be reviewed and made effective against "forcible interference with the First Amendment rights of others."

The commission June 24, 1969 reiterated its concern over the possible consequences of political interference on the nation's campuses. It did so in a 2d report, issued after it investigated events that had led to a student strike and violence at San Francisco State College in January and February 1969. The 172-page report warned that universities across the country would become "screened and guarded camps" if state legislatures enacted politically popular measures intended to suppress disorders.

The study, written under the direction of William H. Orrick Jr., a San Francisco attorney, held that the violence at San Francisco State "mirrors the turmoil, the sharply divergent outlook and economic and social imbalances which bitterly divide the American people today." It acknowledged that "instances of police overreaction" had occurred at the college, but it said that this was inevitable in view of the many student-police confrontations there.

James Brann, one of the authors of the study, issued an independent statement June 24 complaining that the panel had found that police overreaction had intensified the violence but that this had been deleted from the final report. The study was later defended by Orrick, who explained that its purpose was to focus on the causes and prevention of campus conflicts and not to evaluate police behavior.

Firearms—The commission July 28, 1969 urged the nationwide confiscation of handguns owned by private citizens as a step toward curbing violence in America. In a statement adopted by 9 of the 13 commission members, the panel recommended legislation to set up federal minimum standards of firearm control that would restrict ownership of handguns to those who could demonstrate reasonable need for them.

The commission said that after extensive study it had found that the "availability of guns contributes substantially to violence in American society." The panel emphasized that handguns rather than long firearms were associated with crime and that firearms "generally facilitate rather than cause violence." The commission reported a sharp increase in ownership of firearms over the past 5 years and estimated that 90 million firearms were in private hands in the U.S. About half of the nation's households had at least one gun. The panel attributed increased gun sales to a rising fear of violence and to the "exhortations of extremist groups, both black and white." The commission cited statistics to show that violent crimes were committed increasingly by persons using handguns. It warned that guns in the home were dangerous and rarely could effectively protect a household.

The panel said the nation lacked an effective firearms policy because of "our culture's casual attitude toward firearms and its heritage of the armed, self-reliant citizen." But, the commission predicted, a national policy aimed at "reducing the availability of the handgun" would reduce firearms violence. It recommended that states receive the initial opportunity to develop effective firearms legislation in conformity with minimum national standards but that federal handgun licensing apply in states that failed to enact appropriate state laws within 4 years.

The panel said federal regulations should not include normal household protection as a sufficient reason for handgun ownership. It said that citizens required to give up previously lawful guns should be compensated by the federal government. The panel said that this cost could amount to $500 million. Recommended long-gun regulations included a system of identification for long-gun owners but not registration of the guns.

TV violence—The commission July 5, 1969 released a preliminary statistical study of TV violence based on a comparison of a sample week of viewing in early October in 1967 and 1968. The study, prepared by a research team from the University of Pennsylvania's Annenberg School of Communications, concluded that there was "no evidence of over-all decline in the prevalence of violence from 1967 to 1968." The study also found that TV's "good guys" and "bad guys" were equally likely to commit acts of violence.

In a formal statement released Sept. 24, 1969, the commission said that violence on TV "encourages violent forms of behavior and fosters moral and social values about violence in daily life which are unacceptable in a civilized society." "Violence is rarely presented as illegal or socially unacceptable," the statement said. "Indeed, as often as not, it is portrayed as a legitimate means for attaining desired ends. Moreover, the painful consequences of violence are underplayed and de-emphasized by the 'sanitized' way in which much of it is presented."

The panel found that on the average a TV set in an American home was in use about 40 hours a week, that low-income families were its heaviest viewers and that "children and adolescents spend ... from $\frac{1}{4}$ to as much as $\frac{1}{2}$ of their waking day before a television screen." Because so many young Americans, especially among the poor, "believed in the true-to-life nature of television content," the commission warned, TV violence could contribute to "a distorted, pathological view of society." "We believe," the panel said, "it is reasonable to conclude that a constant diet of violent behavior on television has an adverse effect on human character and attitudes."

While acknowledging the TV networks' efforts to decrease violence in their programming, the panel offered the following recommendations to the industry:

(1) "The broadcasting of children's cartoons containing serious, non-comic violence should be abandoned." (2) "The amount of time devoted to the broadcast of crime, Western and action-adventure programs containing violent episodes should be reduced" and "restricted to late viewing hours when fewer very young children are watching television." (3) "More effective efforts should be made to alter the basic context in which violence is presented in television drama." (4) The industry should become more involved in "research on the effects of violent television programs," and its policies should be more responsive to the findings of social and psychological research.

Justice system reform—The commission Nov. 1, 1969 called for an overhaul of U.S. justice machinery, and it urged reforms to meet the legal needs of the nation's poor. The panel charged that the country's system of justice—including law enforcement, the judicial process and correction procedures—

was fragmented and had no unity of purpose. The commission suggested that deficiencies in U.S. legal and government institutions contributed to alienation and lawlessness among poorer citizens "who feel they have gained the least from the social order and from the actions of government."

The major recommendation of the commission was that the U.S. double the total federal, state and local budgets (currently about $5 billion a year) for the administration of justice and the prevention of crime. The panel said the federal government would have to lead in increasing fund commitments, and it urged local governments to join in programs to match federal appropriations.

To coordinate police work, trials and rehabilitation efforts, the commission recommended that metropolitan areas create central justice agencies. The panel said that "some catalyst is needed" and a "full-time criminal justice office is basic to the formation of a criminal justice system." The commission also suggested the creation of citizens' groups to fight crime and to act as grievance committees to investigate complaints against police officers and other public officials.

In recommendations on the legal needs of the poor, the commission said that the "independence of all government-supported legal services to the poor should be safeguarded against governmental intrusion into the selection of the types of cases government-financed lawyers can bring on behalf of their indigent clients." The commission called for adequate state and federal payments to encourage private lawyers to assist the poor in criminal and civil cases.

Urban crime—The commission warned Nov. 23, 1969 that the fear of violent crime "is gnawing at the vitals of urban America." In an 8,000-word report, the panel predicted that in a few more years, "lacking effective public action," cities would be divided into "fortified" high-rise residential compounds and ghetto neighborhoods, which would be "places of terror."

At a news conference in Washington Nov. 23, commission Chairman Milton Eisenhower said the report—"Violent Crime: Homicide, Assault, Rape and Robbery"—was "by all odds the most important" of the reports released by the panel. Statistics in it were based on a study of 10,000 arrest records in 17 cities—Atlanta, Boston, Chicago, Cleveland, Dallas, Denver, Detroit, Los Angeles, Miami, Minneapolis, New Orleans, New York,

Philadelphia, St. Louis, San Francisco, Seattle and
Washington.

According to the report, the rate of criminal homicide in
the U.S. had increased 36%, between 1960 and 1968, the rate of
forcible rape 65%, the rate of aggravated assault 67% and the
rate of robbery 119%. The panel said the U.S. had the highest
reported rate of violent crime of any of the modern, stable
nations in the world. "The 26 cities with 500,000 or more
residents and containing about 17% of our total population
contribute about 45% of the total reported major violent
crimes," it reported.

Violence was concentrated among youths between the ages
of 15 and 20; between 1958 and 1967 arrest rates of the 10-14-
year-old group for assault and robbery had increased 200-
300%. The panel found that violent crime in cities was
committed "primarily by individuals at the lower end of the
occupational scale" and that urban arrest rates for violent
crime were disproportionately high for urban Negroes.

The commission urged that if other obligations prevented
an immediate, full-scale war on urban problems, "we should
now legally make the essential commitments and then carry
them out as quickly as funds can be made available." The panel
indorsed a 10-point urban policy advocated by the White House
aide Daniel Patrick Moynihan, presidential assistant for Urban
Affairs, to lessen poverty and social isolation among central-
city minority groups. The commission also recommended
increased use of interracial police foot patrols, improved police-
community relations, a controlled drug program for narcotics
addicts and restrictive licensing of handguns.

Reforms for youth —In "Challenge to Youth," a report
issued Nov. 25, 1969, the commission called for draft reforms
and a constitutional amendment to lower the minimum voting
age to 18. It also recommended that state and federal laws be
relaxed to make use and incidental possession of marijuana no
more than a misdemeanor.

Milton Eisenhower, introducing the 12-page report at a
Washington news conference, said many youths turned to
violence because of frustration at not being able to influence
policy through voting. He estimated that 75% to 80% of young
Americans opposed the war in Vietnam but said that only "a
very small minority have refused to serve." He credited "a lot

of good common sense" to the statement that those "old enough to carry out the foreign policy of this country by offering their lives in war are also old enough to decide if we are to have a war."

The panel praised Congress for approving Pres. Richard M. Nixon's plan for a draft lottery but called for reforms to assure due process in the operations of local draft boards and to provide one seat on every board for a member under 30 years of age. It said that for persons under 21, "the anachronistic voting age limitations [in all but 4 states] tend to alienate them from systematic political processes" and drive them towards sometimes violent alternatives. The commission contended that harsh marijuana penalties had "become a principal source of frustration and alienation among the young."

Group violence—The commission said Dec. 3, 1969 that unless ways were found to make group violence "both unnecessary and unrewarding" as a political tactic, the danger existed in America that "extreme, unlawful tactics will replace legal processes as the usual way of pressing demands." The panel, in its 16-page statement, also said that the "widely held belief that protesting groups usually behave violently is not supported by fact."

The panel contended that group violence occurred when "expectations about rights and status are continually frustrated," when "peaceful efforts to press these claims yield inadequate results" or when "the claims of groups who feel disadvantaged are viewed as threats by other groups occupying a higher status in society."

To lessen the danger of group violence, the commission recommended legislation that would empower federal courts to grant injunctions, sought by private citizens or the Attorney General, against threatened interference with freedom of speech, press or assembly. Such injunctions might be used against campus disrupters or against police or local officials who refused to grant demonstration permits. The panel also urged local police departments to improve preparations for handling large-scale protests.

Civil disobedience—The commission Dec. 8, 1969 issued a statement condemning massive civil disobedience including nonviolent action. By a bare 7-6 majority, the panel said even nonviolent civil disobedience could lead to "nationwide disobedience of many laws and thus anarchy." 6 members of the panel, including Chairman Eisenhower, dissented from the majority statement although they indorsed a longer staff report condemning "violent or coercive" tactics of civil disobedience.

The majority said that since segregationist governors, civil rights leaders and striking teachers had ignored court orders in recent years, "it was not surprising that college students destroyed scientific equipment and research data, interfered with the rights of others ... and in several instances temporarily closed their colleges." As an alternative to massive civil disobedience, the majority urged that the constitutionality of laws should be tested by individuals or small groups. They said the majority of dissenters should abide by a questionable law until it was invalidated by the courts.

Several of the dissenters on the commission, including the panel's 2 black members—Judge A. Leon Higginbotham Jr. and Mrs. Patricia Roberts Harris, a law professor—wrote separate dissents. Mrs. Harris said that civil disobedience, when there was a willing acceptance of the penalty, "can represent the highest loyalty and respect for a democratic society. Such respect and self-sacrifice may well prevent, rather than cause, violence." Higginbotham said that if the majority's doctrine of waiting for court decisions had been adhered to in the 1960s, "probably not one present major civil rights statute would have been enacted."

Another dissenter, Terence Cardinal Cooke, archbishop of New York, said peaceful civil disobedience was justified only as a last resort and when a civil law "is conscientiously regarded as being clearly in conflict with a higher law—namely our Constitution, the natural law or divine law." Other dissenters were Sen. Philip A. Hart and Dr. W. Walter Menninger.

Final report —In its final report, issued Dec. 12, 1969, the Commission on Violence called on the nation to commit at least $20 billion a year to solving social problems. Basing its statements on estimates of the Council of Economic Advisers, the panel said that the nation could divert $19 billion from defense to domestic spending after the conclusion of the Vietnamese war and that regular growth in the nation's economy could produce additional revenue.

Calling for a reordering of national priorities, the commission contended that "our most serious challenges to date have been external—the kind this strong and resourceful country could unite against." But, it continued, "while serious external dangers remain, the graver threats today are internal: haphazard urbanization, racial discrimination, disfiguring of the environment, the dislocation of human identity and motivation created by an affluent society—all resulting in a rising tide of individual violence."

Commission Chairman Milton Eisenhower said he had presented the final 338-page report, entitled "To Establish Justice, To Insure Domestic Tranquility," which included 9 statements and recommendations previously issued by the commission, to Pres. Nixon. Eisenhower announced that "the President authorized me to say he is gravely concerned about the problems we studied ... and that he will study with care every part of this report."

During its 18 months, the commission had spent $1.6 million and at one point employed a staff of 100 persons.

Media council urged—The establishment of a "center for media study" that would judge the performance of the press and broadcasters was recommended in a task force report released by the commission without comment Jan. 12, 1970. In its 614-page report—"Mass Media and Violence"—the task force said the news media could reduce the potential for violence in America by "functioning as a faithful conduit for intergroup communication, providing a true market place of ideas ... and reducing the incentive to confrontation that sometime erupts in violence." The independent council on mass media was one of the panel's recommendations to make the media more responsive to the public.

The task force proposed that the center study the performance of the news media and make recommendations independently of the government, although the President would make initial appointments to the council. The panel noted that such a body had first been advocated 20 years previously by the Commission on Freedom of the Press, headed by Dr. Robert M. Hutchins.

The task force also criticized the Federal Communications Commission (FCC) for becoming, along with other regulatory agencies, "not guardians of public interest ... but service agencies for the industries involved." The panel urged the Justice Department and the FCC to use their power over mergers and licenses to avoid "greater concentration of media ownership." The task force also suggested that the FCC clarify its fairness doctrine so that it would not have "a dampening effect on willingness of many broadcast news organizations to treat controversial subjects."

Statement on Assassination

The Commission on Violence Nov. 2, 1969 released its study of assassination patterns in the U.S. and abroad. In it the commission warned that conditions that might lead to an increased risk of conspiratorial assassination appeared to be developing in the U.S. The commission recommended basic changes in Presidential campaign practices, including increased Secret Service protection, the avoidance of massive outdoor political rallies and more reliance on TV for national exposure.

The "Official Commission Statement on Assassination":

I

This commission was established in the dark hours following the assassination of Sen. Robert F. Kennedy as he campaigned for the presidential nomination of his party. Just 2 months earlier, one of America's great spiritual and moral leaders, the Rev. Martin Luther King, had been slain by an assassin's bullet. Not quite 5 years before these terrible murders, Pres. John F. Kennedy had been assassinated in the prime of his life.

As we Americans mourned the loss of these 3 young and vital men, we could not help but wonder if the slayings were grotesque symptoms of some awful disease infecting the nation. Had assassination become part of our political life? What did these assassinations signify for America and its future?

Assassination is only one of many topics within this commission's purview, but an especially important one. Eight American Presidents—nearly one in 4—have been the targets of assassins' bullets, and 4 died as a result.

Violence has been a recurring theme in American life, rising to a crescendo whenever social movements—agrarian reform, abolition, reconstruction, organized labor—have challenged the established order. Though Presidential assassinations have not been typical of these periods of great stress, such periods have often produced assassinations of other prominent persons. Consistently they have subjected political leaders to vilification and threats to their safety.

The 1960s afford a grim example. The present decade, though by no means the worst in American history, has witnessed disturbingly high levels of assassination and political violence. No clear explanation emerges from a consideration of the men who have been slain; no ideological pattern fits murders as diverse as those of George Lincoln Rockwell and Medgar Evers or Pres. Kennedy and Dr. King.

In comparison to the other nations of the world, the level of assassination in the United States is high. It is still high when the comparison is limited to other countries with large populations or other Western democracies.

Probably no other form of domestic violence—save civil war—causes more anguish and universal dismay among citizens than the murder of a respected national leader. Assassination, especially when the victim is a President, strikes at the heart of the democratic process. It enables one man to nullify the will of the people in a single, savage act. It touches the lives of all the people of the nation.

The reaction to the slaying of a President lives in the public memory and is recorded in national surveys. Americans were shocked by the killing of Pres. Kennedy. Most described themselves as "at a loss" or "sad" or "hopeless" Many adult Americans wept, were dazed and numb or felt very nervous; others had trouble sleeping and eating. Many were ashamed of their country and felt a burden of collective guilt for the assassination. Some escaped the feeling by insisting that the act had been committed by a foreign agent.

The other side of the public reaction was an outpouring of rage and vindictiveness against the assassin. Only one out of 3 Americans felt Lee Harvey Oswald deserved a trial; one in 5 was pleased that Oswald had been murdered. (Vindictiveness attended earlier presidential assassinations: John Wilkes Booth, for example, probably shot himself, but a Union sergeant claimed to have killed him as an agent of God and was widely acclaimed for the alleged killing. Garfield's assassin, Charles Guiteau, though not killed, was shot at twice—also with widespread approval. The trial of Leon Czolgosz for the assassination of McKinley took less than $8\frac{1}{2}$ hours, including the time spent impaneling the jury.)

Deeply affected by Pres. Kennedy's assassination, many chose conspiracy as the only possible explanation of the dreadful and otherwise senseless act. Although 3 out of 4 persons believed Oswald was the assassin, 62% believed others were involved. When asked who or what was to blame, apart from the man who pulled the trigger, only 20% could specify a group: 15% said Communists or leftists, and 5% said right-wingers or segregationists.

Suspicions of conspiracy are rooted in the history of American presidential assassinations. When a deranged house painter tried to kill Andrew Jackson in 1835, rumor spread that the man was an agent of a Whig conspiracy against Jackson. Charles Guiteau's sister and others argued that Pres. Garfield was killed by a member of the conservative faction of the Republican party. When Giuseppe Zangara shot at Pres.-elect Roosevelt in 1933 but killed the mayor of Chicago instead, some claimed the killing was not a mistake but the intent of a gangland conspiracy. Technically a conspiracy existed in the murder of Abraham Lincoln, though the conspirators were a motley few with no backing from powerful groups; still the suspicion survives in folklore that Booth and his crew were associated with prominent government officials. Suspicions about Oswald as conspirator may survive as long, despite the exhaustive investigation and contrary findings of the Warren Commission.

Considering the high visibility, the substantial power, and the symbolic (as well as actual) importance of the American presidency, it is not surprising that Presidents are prime victims of assassination, or that conspiracy theories attend the event. The presidency is the fulcrum of power, the focus of hopes, and the center of controversy in American politics. What better target for those who wish to punish a nation, strike out at a symbol of great power, or simply draw the attention of the world and history to themselves? John Wilkes Booth remarked that the person who pulled down the Colossus of Rhodes would be famous throughout history.

II

The evidence from American history is overwhelming: no Presidential assassination, with the exception of an abortive attempt on the life of Pres. Truman, has been demonstrated to have sprung from a decision of an organized group whose goal was to change the policy or the structure of the United States government. With that single exception, no United States Presidential assassin has ever been linked to such a group, either as a policy maker or as a member or hireling carrying out its directives.

The occasions on which American Presidents have been assassination targets have in common this absence of an organized conspiracy. But they have little else in common. The type of President, his party affiliation, his public policies, the length of time he was in office, his personal characteristics, his political strength—all of these provide no clue to the likelihood of his assassination. The men who have been targets differ greatly. For example, Lincoln was the President of a divided nation during a civil war, Garfield a compromise candidate of a faction-torn party and McKinley a popular President of a relatively unified and stable society.

To the extent that a pattern exists at all, it exists in the personalities of those who have been Presidential assassins. In the biographies of these lonely, demented men we may discern common elements that help to explain their actions. From those common elements we may begin to draw a picture of the archetypal assassin.

Richard Lawrence, the house painter who attempted to kill Pres. Jackson in 1835, was a man of grand delusions. At times he claimed to be Richard III of England; he believed the U.S. owed him large sums of money and, further, that Jackson was responsible for blocking his claim. As later assassins would do, Lawrence focused his mind on a particular political issue. Jackson had vetoed the bill to recharter the Bank of the United States; if Jackson were killed, Lawrence believed, the bank would be rechartered and all working men would benefit.

Other assassins were self-appointed saviors. John Wilkes Booth apparently believed that Lincoln had achieved the presidency through voting fraud and intended to make himself king. Booth claimed that he had acted as an agent of God in killing the President. Charles Guiteau thought it was his God-appointed task to kill James A. Garfield. After killing Pres. McKinley, Leon Czolgosz claimed that he had removed "an enemy of the good working people." John Schrank, who attempted to kill Theodore Roosevelt, saw McKinley's ghost in a dream and heard it accuse Roosevelt of the McKinley assassination; Schrank also regarded himself as an agent of God. Giuseppe Zangara apparently believed himself a savior of the poor; he bore no personal malice toward Franklin D. Roosevelt, but attempted to kill him just because he was the chief of state (though he had not yet taken office).

Alone among assassins, Oscar Collazo and Griselio Torresola were members of a recognized political movement. Both were ardent Puerto Rican nationalists, and their attempt to storm Blair House, the temporary residence of Pres. Truman, appears to have been part of a plot to dramatize the cause of an independent Puerto Rico. Yet the plot was inept, not only because Blair House was well secured, but because Truman was an inappropriate target. As President he had initiated important steps toward self-determination for Puerto Rico. After the attempted assassination, Puerto Ricans quickly denounced Collazo and Torresola.

Presidential assassins typically have been white, male and slightly built. Nearly all were loners and had difficulty making friends of either sex and especially in forming lasting normal relationships with women. Lawrence, Schrank, and Zangara were foreign-born; the parents of all but Guiteau and Oswald were foreign-born. Normal family relationships were absent or disrupted. Booth was an illegitimate child; Guiteau's mother died when he was 7; Czolgosz lost his mother when he was 12; Schrank's father died when Schrank was a child; Zangara's mother died when he was 2. Oswald's father died before he was born and his mother's subsequent marriage lasted only 3 years. All of the assassins were unable to work steadily during a period of one to 3 years before the assassination. All of the assassins tended to link themselves to a cause or a movement and to relate their crime to some political issue or philosophy. All but Oswald used a handgun. At great risk to themselves, nearly all chose the occasion of an appearance of the President amid crowds for the assassination attempt.

Thus it might have been hypothesized in 1968 that the next assassin to strike at a President—or Presidential candidate, as it turned out—would have most of the following attributes:

From a broken home, with the father absent or unresponsive to the child;

Withdrawn, a loner, no girl friends, either unmarried or a failure at marriage;

Unable to work steadily in the last year or so before the assassination;

White, male, foreign-born or with parents foreign-born, short, slight build;

A zealot for a political, religious, or other cause, but not a member of an organized movement;

Assassinates in the name of a specific issue which is related to the principles of philosophy of his cause;

Chooses a handgun as his weapon;

Selects a moment when the President is appearing amid crowds.

We do not know with any degree of certainty why these characteristics appear in the Presidential assassin. (Certainly the personal attributes can be found in many valuable, trustworthy citizens.) Nor do we know why the assassin politicizes his private miseries or why he chooses to express himself through such a terrible crime. Perhaps he comes to blame his own failures on others. Maybe because he does not live in a true community of men and has no rewarding relationships with others he relates instead to an abstraction: "the poor" or "mankind." Once his own inner misery becomes identified with the misery of those whom he champions, he places the blame for both on the nation's foremost political figure. Incapable of sustained devotion toward a long-range goal, the assassin is capable of short bursts of frenzied activity which are doomed to failure. Each failure seems to reinforce the self-loathing and need to accomplish—in one burst of directed energy—something of great worth to end his misery and assert his value as a human being.

III

Deranged, self-appointed saviors have been the murderers of American Presidents. They have also been responsible for many of the assassinations of other national leaders and public officials. This commission's Task Force on Assassination studied 81 assaults, fatal and nonfatal, on American Presidents, members of Congress, governors, mayors and other officeholders. In case after case, their study reveals, the attacks were prompted by fanatic allegiance to a political cause or revenge for some petty slight or imagined evil. Only in the years immediately following the Civil War were assassinations typically undertaken by organized groups to alter or terrorize government.

While non-conspiratorial assassination has been the American pattern, it surely has not been typical for the rest of the world. Throughout most of the world assassination has been used as an instrument of calculated political change, as a means of seizing power or terrorizing a government until it falls. Thus, for example, assassinations were a major part of the strategy of mass revolution in Russia and Eastern Europe beginning late in the 19th Century. In Latin America assassinations have been committed less by fanatics or unstable persons than by daring political adventurers bent on seizing power for themselves or their supporters. And in the Middle East, assassination continues to be used as a deliberate political weapon by one political group against another. Where conspiratorial assassination is common, many besides the chief of state are apt to be targets.

Because assassination typically serves a political function, it is possible to predict with a fair degree of accuracy, using characteristics that are crudely measurable, what countries will experience high rates of assassination at particular moments in their history. For example, high rates of assassination tend to occur in countries experiencing political instability, in countries undergoing rapid economic development, under regimes that are coercive but not wholly totalitarian, in nations with high rates of homicide but low suicide rates.

By several of these measurements, the United States should be a nation with a low rate of murders of political figures—contrary to the actuality of its high rate. Thus, for example, almost alone among the nations with the highest level of economic development and greatest degree of political freedom the United States has a high assassination rate. Countries with high suicide rates tend to have low assassination rates; the United States is among a handful of exceptions.

During only one period of its history did the United States experience the turmoil and instability classically associated with high assassination rates: in the Reconstruction era immediately following the Civil War. During that decade, America experienced close to half of all the assassinations in its history. In the defeated South, still occupied by Union troops, many officeholders were not regarded as "legitimate" incumbents by the population. Many white Southerners resented the continuing presence of the military, the systematic disenfranchisement of former Confederates, and the new political power of former slaves and Northern "carpetbaggers." Some took violent action: 2 governors of Louisiana and a host of other state and local political figures became victims of assassination plots.

A century later the assassination rate in the United States is only a small fraction of the rate during Reconstruction, but still it is comparatively high and remains to be accounted for. A number of explanations have been offered: our frontier culture, the ready availability of guns, tensions among diverse groups, a low standard of political decorum.

It may be that persistent low-level turbulence and non-conspiratorial assassination are associated, just as conspiratorial assassination usually occurs amid other intense forms of political violence. Consistent with its principles of freedom, the United States tolerates a fair amount of political tumult—not enough to inspire political assassination, but perhaps sufficient to provide the conditions under which the twisted mind of the assassin decides that an imagined evil must be set right through violence. Dissidents in the United States have often been very vocal and very abusive; they sometimes have heaped scorn on a President, even vilified him. Americans demonstrate boisterously, stage emotion-charged strikes and sit-ins, hurl stones and filth and foul language at authorities who, in turn, have not always been restrained and fair in their use of power. Though an assassin is mentally deranged, the violent rhetoric of our politics and our constant flirtation with actual violence may be factors that bring him at least halfway to his distorted perception of what actions are right and legitimate.

Although the United States has differed significantly from the rest of the world in the kind of assassination it has experienced, there are indications that the future may bring more similarities than distinctions. Many of the conditions associated with conspiratorial assassination in other countries appear to be developing in this country:

Political violence in the United States today is probably more intense than it has been since the turn of the century. If civil strife continues to become more violent, political assassinations may well occur.

There is much talk today of revolution and urban guerrilla warfare by extremists, and there have been outbreaks of violence with aspects of guerrilla warfare, as in the Cleveland shoot-out of July 1968. If extremists carry out their threats, we can expect political assassinations.

Even if the rhetoric of revolution and vilification of governmental authority is never translated into deed, the constant excoriation of America's institutions and leaders may destroy their legitimacy in the eyes of other segments of society. The assassinations during the Reconstruction era arose in just such a context.

Throughout the tragic history of race relations in this country, Negroes have been victims of white terrorist murderers. To this recurring threat is added a new one: plots and murders from within the radical wing of the black protest movement. The increasing number of Negroes holding public office and positions of political prominence will thus be running risks of assassination from 2 opposing extremist groups. From whichever direction, such attacks would appropriately be regarded as political assassinations.

Racial tensions have been at a high level in this country during the 1960s. If violent racial confrontations increase, the level of political violence in the United States could approach that of countries in which political assassinations typically occur.

Finally, the United States may in the next few years undergo even more rapid socio-economic change than it has in the recent past. Rapid change is another characteristic that correlates with high levels of conspiratorial assassination.

Present trends warn of an escalating risk of assassination, not only for Presidents, but for other officeholders at every level of government, as well as leaders of civil rights and political-interest groups. Accordingly, this commission suggests:

1. That the Secret Service be empowered to extend its protective services to that limited number of federal officeholders and candidates for office whose lives are deemed imperiled as a result of threat, vilification, deep controversy, or other hazardous circumstances. A Joint Resolution of the 90th Congress, in June of 1968, authorized the Secret Service to protect "major" presidential and vice presidential candidates, the eligibility of persons to be determined by the Secretary of the Treasury after consultation with a special advisory committee consisting of the congressional leadership. Specifically, we recommend that the secretary and the special advisory committee be empowered to designate, without publicity, a limited number of persons (federal officeholders or candidates) as temporary assassination risks and to assign them Secret Service protection wherever and whenever needed.

2. That state and local governments carefully review the adequacy of the protection accorded to candidates and officeholders, especially governors and mayors, and that the protection be strengthened where it is deficient. The responsibility for protection should be clearly delineated, and new avenues of cooperation should be opened between those with state or local protective responsibilities and the Secret Service and the Federal Bureau of Investigation, to include a sharing both of technological information and of information about dangerous persons and potential assassins.

In our statement on firearms control we made recommendations that, if adopted, would greatly curtail the risk of assassination to all who might be targets. We have recommended drastically limiting the availability of handguns through restrictive licensing. We have further recommended intensified research to develop mechanisms that would assist law enforcement officers in detecting concealed firearms and ammunition on a person. Handguns are the weapons favored by assassins (by all but one presidential assassin, for example); effective detection devices would minimize the risk of assassination in meeting halls and other enclosed gathering places.

The precautions we are urging are worthwhile whether or not this nation faces a new outbreak of political assassinations. We do not predict that such an outbreak will occur. But we feel compelled to note that some of the conditions for such an outbreak are present or may be developing. These conditions add urgency to the need to develop effective protection against assassination.

We can only hope, along with all Americans, that the conditions which have kept our society free of the scourge of conspiratorial assassination will prevail—conditions such as the ability of the American people to absorb radical challenge, to respond to the need for reform, to keep their basic democratic values intact even in periods of bewildering and buffeting social change.

IV

Whatever the future holds for the United States, it is clear that, among all public figures, Presidents, will continue to run the greatest risks of assassination. It is in the nature of their office; it is in the nature of the distorted logic by which assassins choose their targets.

The death of Pres. Kennedy poignantly demonstrated the resilience of the American people in the face of tragedy and of their institutions of government at a time of abrupt transition. With skill and grace Pres. Johnson exercised a calming influence on the nation, and the nation rallied in support of the new administration. That has been the pattern in the American past. We cannot safely assume, however, that our republic will always fare so well. An assassination of a President occurring during an edgy, critical moment in history could have disastrous consequences. Moreover, even when an assassination does not impair the strength of the nation or the continuity of its policies, the murder of a President is a tragedy of unrivaled proportions.

In the years since Pres. Kennedy's death, and as urged by the Warren Commission, the policies and procedures for guarding Presidents have been thoroughly studied and imaginatively reconsidered, and many improvements have been made. A detailed discussion here of new procedures would lessen their effectiveness. We simply state that the Secret Service has reported to this commission improvements in equipment and the various procedures of intelligence work. The Secret Service is confident that, had its new intelligence system been in effect in 1963, the activities of Lee Harvey Oswald would have brought him to the attention of the Secret Service before the fatal attack on Pres. Kennedy. As we have pointed out, more research is needed, especially in the technology of concealed weapons detection.

There can be no perfect system for guarding the President short of isolating him, confining him to the White House and limiting his communication with the American public to television broadcasts and other media. This extreme solution is neither practicable nor desirable. For political reasons and for the sake of ceremonial traditions of the office, the American people expect the President to get out and "mingle with the people." (Among the 8 Presidents who have been assassination targets, all but Garfield and Truman were engaged in either ceremonial or political activities when they were attacked.)

Still, a President can minimize the risk by carefully choosing speaking opportunities, public appearances, his means of travel to engagements, and the extent to which he gives advance notice of his movements. He can limit his public appearances to meeting places to which access is carefully controlled, especially by the use of electronic arms-detection equipment. Effective security can exist if a President permits. Moreover, during the past 20 years television has proven an accepted and effective vehicle for presidential communication with the American public, and its continued and possibly expanded use by the President is to be encouraged.

During election campaigns there are extraordinary pressures both on the incumbent President and the contenders for his office that serve to maximize their risk as targets of assassination. Rightly or wrongly, presidential candidates judge that they must be personally seen by audiences throughout the country, through such rituals as motorcades, shopping-center rallies, and whistle-stop campaigns. Whether the long grind of personal-appearance campaigning is really the most effective investment of a candidate's time is debatable, since even the most strenuous travel schedule will expose him to only a small percentage of the American people. It has been argued that the grueling pace is itself a test of the candidate. It is more difficult to argue that political rallies test the candidate's reasoned consideration of the issues, since the speeches usually are brief, superficial, and suited to the carnival atmosphere of rallies. While campaign rallies involve the public in the electoral process by bringing that process close to them, they cannot be said to involve the public deeply in the pressing, complex issues of the nation.

A more reasonable defense of personal-appearance campaigning is that it provides important "feedback" for the candidate: he can sense the public mood through audience response to his speeches, learn of their problems and feelings through the questions they raise and comments they make, and observe firsthand—as Kennedy is remembered to have done in his West Virginia Campaign—the conditions that will demand his attention if he is elected. Yet this function can be better served in the quieter atmosphere of an enclosed meeting place where, we note, the risk of assassination can be significantly reduced.

But the most promising vehicle for campaigns effective in reaching large audiences and safe to the candidates is *television*. The intimacy with which television projects events and personalities has been amply demonstrated, and it is doubtful whether heavier reliance on television appearances need sacrifice any of the intimate contact with American people which candidates now associate with personal appearances. It has also been demonstrated that the American people have come to rely heavily on television in forming their opinions of presidential candidates. In a poll conducted for the Television Information Office in Nov. 1968, 65% of the respondents said television was their best source for becoming acquainted with candidates for national office.

The fuller potentiality of television for presidential campaigning has not been explored primarily because of the high cost of television time. Yet the value of television in reaching large audiences has been recognized, and more and more campaign funds are being invested in its use. Indeed, as campaign costs continue to soar, some fear that presidential politics will eventually become a contest where only millionaires need apply.

Out of concern for the safety of Presidents and Presidential candidates, this commission recommends that the Congress enact a law that would grant free television time to presidential candidates during the final weeks preceding the national election. The amount of television time allocated to the candidates should be adequate to establish a new pattern in presidential campaigning and to reduce significantly the pressure toward personal appearances in all parts of the country.

To ensure that candidates used their time for responsible, informative presentation of themselves and their views, the free time might be allocated only in ½ hour blocks. Within his alloted time, however, a candidate would be free to choose the format best suited for his presentation.

It has long been recognized that broadcasters have a public-service commitment to the American people in exchange for their licensed use of the airwaves. To ensure an equitable sharing of that commitment, consideration would have to be given to the question of whether all networks should be required to carry each program or only one network at a time, with the burden shared in rotation. Moreover, a formula would have to be devised for allotting time in a way that would give fair expression to important minor parties.[1]   Consideration should also be given to expanding greatly federal support of public television facilities for the express purpose of having these facilities share the political education function with the commercial networks.[2]

Though this proposal is put forth out of a desire to lessen the risk of assassination to Presidents and presidential candidates, other considerations lend merit to the proposal. The superiority of television as a forum for serious consideration of modern complex issues has already been noted. Moreover, political rallies attract the curious and the party faithful. Many of the marginally motivated stay home. On the premise that it is easier to flick a dial in the living room than to drive across town to a rally, we note that television programs could widen the base of political participation in America.

V

Broader participation in American politics might be an antidote to the political violence that has been a recurring feature of American life and which has recently been on the upswing. Our concern is not simply that the future may bring to America the alien phenomenon of conspiratorial assassination. Irrational, nonpolitical killings of national leaders will also be a continuing risk as long as political violence, in rhetoric or act, is present to inspire the assassin. For while such assassins are mentally unbalanced, their beliefs are not wholly antithetical to what other Americans believe but simply distortions thereof.

Thus, assassins are not alone in believing in the efficacy of political violence. Nor are they alone in their simplistic, exaggerated view of the power of the American President. Ever since George Washington's day, we Americans have mythologized our Presidents. We have attributed to them powers beyond human limitation and far beyond the realities of our constitutional system. Through the nation's press we follow every move,

---

[1] Given television's superiority, a shift toward its greater use by presidential candidates appears inevitable. But other campaign reforms, such as the increased use of enclosed meeting places, may require strong endorsement by the major political parties if they are to be effected. It is unrealistic to expect individual candidates, acting upon their own initiative, to alter significantly the traditional pattern of campaigning.

[2] A *20th Century Fund Commission on Costs in the Electronic Era* has just issued its report, suggesting among other things that the federal government pay for television time for presidential candidates at $\frac{1}{2}$ the normal commercial rate. The commission has also recommended a formula for the allocation of such time, called "voters' time," between major and minor candidates. Though the recommendations of the 20th Century Fund commission are somewhat different from ours, we hope they will be given consideration by the President and the Congress, along with those we submit in this statement. We also note that Great Britain, with more than 20 years experience in allocating broadcast time to a number of political parties, offers proof that this knotty problem may be equitably solved.

public and private, of the President—sometimes in adulation, sometimes in malicious anticipation of some sign that the man is only human.

Political violence often arises when a group feels the government has been unresponsive to legitimate demands. This commission recognizes, as do many Americans, that the political institutions in our democracy need to be made more sensitive and responsive to the interests they are intended to represent. It is not difficult to understand the impatience and alienation of those who believe that the government has been consistently neglectful of their welfare. It is noteworthy that many are organizing new political groups to press for reforms. They are demonstrating a basic truth of American politics: groups that appreciate the complexities of American government, and that can organize to promote their ends through persuasion at the right times and places, benefit the most from policy decisions. The counter-trend— shortcutting to violence before the peaceful means of redressing grievances have been exhausted—can only be deplored. That counter-trend has been alive in this decade but not unique to it. Except for those to whom the complexities of government are workaday business, Americans have not typically been patient with the subtleties of political issues. In part this stems from the natural preference for simplicities; in part it reflects the glossing over of subtleties by politicians, journalists and the educators of our nation's children.

A significant decrease in the level of political violence in our country requires a new level of participation in the increasingly complex processes of local, state and federal government and a new level of communication between government and the people it serves. Those responsible for the institutions of government must serve both needs—by clarifying their functions and purposes, and by responding to the needs and legitimate grievances of all they are intended to represent.

Thus legislators and administrators must creatively use the political processes to ensure the prompt amelioration of wrongs. Thus legislators, administrators and private citizens must share with the President the responsibility for realistic demonstration that the society is in fact acting in behalf of all citizens.

The nation's press must respond to these needs—by clearly representing the complexities of the institutions of government, by fully and fairly reporting the issues these institutions face and by delving into the issues deserving governmental attention. By lessening its attention to the personal lives of the President and his family, with correspondingly greater attention to the working nature and limitations of the presidency, the nation's press may achieve the additional effect of discouraging a simplistic notion of the presidency that assassins are not alone in holding.

The nation's schools must also respond to these needs: by emphasizing in American history and social studies the complexities and subtleties of the democratic process; by shunning the myths by which we have traditionally made supermen of Presidents, "founding fathers" and other prominent persons; by restoring to history books a full and frank picture of violence and unrest in America's past, in confidence that children will repudiate violence and recognize its futility.

There are themes in American culture that have served us for good and ill. American folklore has always emphasized—and continues to emphasize in television heroes—direct action and individual initiative. Equally compelling within the American experience has been the emphasis placed on freedom of conscience. Many of the authentic heroes of American history have been individuals willing to suffer ostracism and to employ unconventional (and even violent) means to realize goals unpopular to a majority of citizens. While these qualities have been a source of strength and a goad to progress for our nation, it is not difficult to see that perverse relationship to the act of a demented assassin.

Perhaps a new generation of Americans, trained to these subtleties of American life, shamed by its violence as they are proud of its achievements, determined to achieve a better record for their time and sophisticated in the ways to achieve it, will guarantee a more peaceable America.

VI

These are long-range hopes, and responsible citizens must give serious attention to how we can best realize them. For the short range, this nation is not powerless to prevent the tragedy of assassination. We conclude with a reiteration of the steps that can be taken to minimize greatly the risk of assassination:

Selective expansion of the functions of the Secret Service to include protection of any federal officeholder or candidate who is deemed a temporary but serious assassination risk;

Improved protection of state and local officeholders and candidates, and strengthened ties between those holding this responsibility and the appropriate federal agencies;

Restrictive licensing of handguns to curtail greatly their availability;

Development and implementation of devices to detect concealed weapons and ammunition on persons entering public meeting places;

A significant reduction of risky public appearances by the President and by presidential candidates;

A corresponding increase in the use of public and commercial television both as a vehicle of communication by the President and as a campaign tool by presidential candidates.

INDEX